CAMBRIDGE LIBRA

Books of enduring sc

Medieval H

This series includes pioneering editions of m witnesses and contemporaries, collections of source materials such as charters and letters, and works that applied new historiographical methods to the interpretation of the European middle ages. The nineteenth century saw an upsurge of interest in medieval manuscripts, texts and artefacts, and the enthusiastic efforts of scholars and antiquaries made a large body of material available in print for the first time. Although many of the analyses have been superseded, they provide fascinating evidence of the academic practices of their time, while a considerable number of texts have still not been re-edited and are still widely consulted.

The Laws of the Earliest English Kings

Frederick Levi Attenborough (1887–1973) studied at Cambridge and was a Fellow of Emmanuel College between 1920 and 1925. He later became the Principal of University College, Leicester. In 1922 Cambridge University Press published his edition of the early Anglo-Saxon laws, with a facing-page modern English translation. A few years earlier, Felix Lieberman had published his monumental three-volume *Die Gesetze der Angelsachsen*, which is still the definitive specialist edition of the laws (as Attenborough rightly predicted), and which is also reissued in the Cambridge Library Collection. Attenborough explains that his work is for social and legal historians who do not read German, or do not require the full critical apparatus and contextual material provided by Lieberman. Attenborough's book covers the laws from Aethelbert to Aethelstan; in 1925 Cambridge published a continuation by Agnes Robertson, *The Laws of the Kings of England from Edmund to Henry I*, which is also available.

Cambridge University Press has long been a pioneer in the reissuing of out-of-print titles from its own backlist, producing digital reprints of books that are still sought after by scholars and students but could not be reprinted economically using traditional technology. The Cambridge Library Collection extends this activity to a wider range of books which are still of importance to researchers and professionals, either for the source material they contain, or as landmarks in the history of their academic discipline.

Drawing from the world-renowned collections in the Cambridge University Library and other partner libraries, and guided by the advice of experts in each subject area, Cambridge University Press is using state-of-the-art scanning machines in its own Printing House to capture the content of each book selected for inclusion. The files are processed to give a consistently clear, crisp image, and the books finished to the high quality standard for which the Press is recognised around the world. The latest print-on-demand technology ensures that the books will remain available indefinitely, and that orders for single or multiple copies can quickly be supplied.

The Cambridge Library Collection brings back to life books of enduring scholarly value (including out-of-copyright works originally issued by other publishers) across a wide range of disciplines in the humanities and social sciences and in science and technology.

The Laws of the
Earliest English Kings

EDITED AND TRANSLATED
F.L. ATTENBOROUGH

CAMBRIDGE
UNIVERSITY PRESS

University Printing House, Cambridge, CB2 8BS, United Kingdom

Cambridge University Press is part of the University of Cambridge.

It furthers the University's mission by disseminating knowledge in the pursuit of
education, learning and research at the highest international levels of excellence.

www.cambridge.org
Information on this title: www.cambridge.org/9781108084840

© in this compilation Cambridge University Press 2015

This edition first published 1922
This digitally printed version 2015

ISBN 978-1-108-08484-0 Paperback

THE LAWS

OF THE

EARLIEST ENGLISH KINGS

CAMBRIDGE UNIVERSITY PRESS

C. F. CLAY, Manager

LONDON : FETTER LANE, E.C. 4

NEW YORK : THE MACMILLAN CO.
BOMBAY ⎫
CALCUTTA ⎬ MACMILLAN AND CO., Ltd.
MADRAS ⎭
TORONTO : THE MACMILLAN CO. OF
CANADA, Ltd.
TOKYO: MARUZEN-KABUSHIKI-KAISHA

THE LAWS

OF THE

EARLIEST ENGLISH KINGS

EDITED AND TRANSLATED

BY

F. L. ATTENBOROUGH, M.A.

FELLOW OF EMMANUEL COLLEGE, CAMBRIDGE

CAMBRIDGE
AT THE UNIVERSITY PRESS
1922

PREFACE

MORE than eighty years have elapsed since an English edition of these Laws appeared, and great as were the merits of Thorpe's work, I think it will be generally agreed that a new edition is now required—not only because of the additions which have been made to the knowledge of the subject, but also because the work in question has long been out of print and is now accessible to but few readers.

A substantial advance in certain respects was made by R. Schmid's edition, *Die Gesetze der Angelsachsen*, especially the second edition which appeared in 1858. Latterly, all previous editions have been eclipsed by F. Liebermann's great work (under the same title), which will long remain the standard authority on the subject.

This book makes of course no attempt to compete with Liebermann's edition. For those who desire to make a study of the texts and their history, or to enter into a full discussion either of the Laws themselves or of the terms which are employed therein, the latter is indispensable. There are however, I am sure, many English readers interested in the early social and constitutional history of our country, who through ignorance of German are unable to use more than the text of the Laws in Liebermann's work, and many others who, though they may know German, cannot but be hampered by the very fulness of the material offered and at the same time by the conciseness with which the editor's explanations are expressed. It is primarily for such students that the present work is intended. But I would not let this opportunity pass without expressing my deep sense of the obligations laid upon me—as upon all students of our early history—by Professor Liebermann's monumental work.

I have endeavoured to keep the book within as small a compass as possible. With this object in view the Latin translation is given only when the Anglo-Saxon original is lost, though passages which may help to throw light on the meaning of the original are quoted in the notes. For the same reason the Tables of Contents and other preliminary matter found in certain manuscripts have been omitted, and so also the long Introduction to King Alfred's Laws, which is of purely literary interest and has no bearing on English Law. Variant readings are recorded as a rule only when the sense is affected. The notes are in general limited to a brief interpretation and commentary upon the text. In the rather frequent instances however when the translation or interpretation adopted differs from that of previous editors, I have aimed at indicating their views, in particular those of Liebermann, as well as my own.

In the divisions and numbering of the sections I have followed the example of previous editors; for though the system is not entirely satisfactory, any new departure would involve much inconvenience to the reader owing to the fact that the references in dictionaries are based upon it. The new sections introduced by Liebermann are in general an advantage and have nearly always been adopted.

I have collated the more important manuscripts; but the work of previous editors has been so well done, that I have scarcely been able to add anything worth mentioning. I desire however to express my cordial thanks to the Master and Librarian of Corpus Christi College for the facilities they have afforded me for copying the manuscripts in the College library, and to the Dean of Rochester and Mr F. H. Day for similar services, as well as for their kind hospitality while I was working in the Cathedral library.

I have also to express my obligations to the Master of Emmanuel, Professor H. D. Hazeltine and the Rev. Professor J. P. Whitney for giving me the benefit of their advice, and to several friends who have been kind enough to assist me in various ways. Among these I must mention Miss A.J.Robertson, whose edition of the Laws from Edmund to Canute is now approaching completion, and especially Miss N. Kershaw, who has given me valuable help in collating the manuscripts and in revising the text of the Laws. But most of all my thanks are due to Professor Chadwick. How great my obligations are to him only those who have had the privilege of working under him can form any idea. I have turned to him continually for help in the innumerable difficulties I have met with, and but for his constant and generous assistance I could hardly have completed my task. I must also thank the Syndics of the University Press for undertaking the publication of the book, and the staff for the efficient and obliging way in which the printing and corrections have been carried out.

F. L. A.

February, 1922.

CONTENTS

LIST OF ABBREVIATIONS

1. Anglo-Saxon Manuscripts. (See Liebermann, I. pp. xviii f.)

   B ......Corpus Christi College, Cambridge, 383. Cf. pp. 35, 96, 97, 113.

   Bu ...British Museum, Burney 277. Cf. p. 35.

   D ......Corpus Christi College, Cambridge, 201. Cf. p. 113.

   E ......Corpus Christi College, Cambridge, 173. Cf. p. 35.

   G ......British Museum, Cotton Nero A I. Cf. p. 113.

   H ......Textus Roffensis, Rochester Cathedral. Cf. pp. 3, 35, 97, 113.

   Ld ...W. Lambarde, Αρχαιονομια; see under *Editions*.

   Ot ...British Museum, Cotton Otho B xi. Cf. p. 113.

   So ...Canterbury Cathedral Library, B 2, n. 8. Cf. p. 113.

2. Manuscripts of the Latin version of the Laws known as Quadripartitus. (See Liebermann, *Glossar*, s.v. *Quadripartitus*, and Vol. I. p. xxxviii, LX. 17.)

   Co ...(*circa* 1310) Corpus Christi College, Cambridge, 70.

   K ......(*circa* 1310) British Museum, D II.

   Or ...(*circa* 1330) Oriel College, Oxford, 46.

   These three MSS form the 'London' group.

   Br ...'Johannis Brompton Jorevallensis chronicon' (cf. Liebermann, I. p. xix), probably 14th cent.; preserved in two 15th cent. MSS: Corpus Christi College, Cambridge, 96; British Museum, Tiberius C XIII.

   Hk ...(*circa* 1200) Holkham, no. 228, belonging to the Earl of Leicester.

   M ......(*circa* 1150) Macro, formerly belonging to Dr Cox Macro and now the property of the Gurney family at Keswick Hall, near Norwich.

   R ......(*circa* 1160) British Museum, Regius 11 B II.

   T ......(*circa* 1225) British Museum, Cotton Titus A XXVII.

3. Editions. (See Liebermann, I. pp. xlv f.)

   Ld ....W. Lambarde, Αρχαιονομια (London, 1568), republished with additions by A. Wheelock (Cambridge, 1644).

   Wilkins ......*Leges Anglo-Saxonicæ*, edited by D. Wilkins (London, 1721).

   Price ⎫
   Thorpe ⎭ ......An edition of the Laws prepared for the Commissioners on the Public Records by Richard Price, but left unfinished at his death in 1833; completed by B. Thorpe and published under the title of *Ancient Laws and Institutes of England* (London, 1840).

   Schmid.........*Die Gesetze der Angelsachsen* by R. Schmid, 1st Edition, Leipzig, 1832; 2nd Edition (revised and enlarged), 1858.

   Liebermann...*Die Gesetze der Angelsachsen* by F. Liebermann (Halle, 1903—1916).

4. Names of Kings.

    A. & G....Alfred and Guthrum.   Edm. ....Edmund.
    Abt. ...Æthelberht.   Edw. ....Edward.
    Alf. ......Alfred.   Edw. Conf....Edward the Confessor.
    As. ......Æthelstan.   H. & E. ......Hlothhere and Eadric.
    Athlr. ...Æthelred.   Henr.........Henry I.
    Can. ...Canute.   Wiht.........Wihtred.
    E. & G....Edward and Guthrum.   Wm. ....William.
    Edg. ...Edgar.

5. Legal documents not bearing the names of kings.

    Be Blaserum......*Be Blaserum and Be Morð-slihtum.*
    Be Griðe ....*Be Griðe and Be Munde.*
    Dom ....*Dom Be Hatan Isene and Wætre.*
    Duns...............Ordinance respecting the *Dunsæte.*
    Rect. ....*Rectitudines Singularum Personarum.*

6. The following also should be noted:

    B. & T. ....Bosworth and Toller, *Anglo-Saxon Dictionary.*
    Cart. Sax..........*Cartularium Saxonicum,* ed. Birch.
    C.C.C. ....Corpus Christi College, Cambridge.
    Cod. Dip. ....*Codex Diplomaticus,* ed. Kemble.
    Lond. ....The 'London' group of the Quadripartitus MSS.
    Ord. ....Ordinance of Æthelstan relating to Charities.
    Pr. ....Preamble.

THE KENTISH LAWS

THE KENTISH LAWS

Three series of Kentish laws have been preserved. The earliest are those of King Æthelberht I, who was reigning at the time when the mission from Pope Gregory the Great, under Augustine, arrived in the year 597.

To these laws Bede refers in the following passage (*Hist. Eccl.* II. 5): *Qui inter cetera bona, quae genti suae consulendo conferebat, etiam decreta illi iudiciorum, iuxta exempla Romanorum, cum consilio sapientium constituit; quae conscripta Anglorum sermone hactenus habentur, et obseruantur ab ea. In quibus primitus posuit, qualiter id emendare deberet, qui aliquid rerum uel ecclesiae, uel episcopi, uel reliquorum ordinum furto auferret; uolens scilicet tuitionem eis, quos et quorum doctrinam susceperat, praestare.*

The exact date at which the laws were issued is not certainly known[1], but it was evidently after Æthelberht's conversion. Æthelberht died on February 24th, 616 (or more probably 617).

King Earconberht, grandson of Æthelberht, is said to have issued laws, enforcing the destruction of images, and the observance of Lent, with penalties for those who refused to obey (*Hist. Eccl.* III. 8); but these laws have not been preserved.

The second series of laws, which is still extant, bears the names of Hlothhere, who reigned from 673 to 685 (or 686), and Eadric, the son of Ecgberht, Hlothhere's brother and predecessor. It is nowhere stated that these two kings reigned jointly. According to Bede (*ib.* IV. 26) Hlothhere died of wounds, received in battle against the South Saxons, whom Eadric had brought against him. Eadric succeeded to the throne and reigned a year and a half. It is uncertain, therefore, whether Eadric had been associated with his uncle for some time before the quarrel took place, or whether he merely confirmed laws previously issued by him.

The third code bears the name of Wihtred, brother of Eadric, who succeeded to the throne after a few years, during which the kingdom was ruled by *reges dubii uel externi* (*ib.* IV. 26). Among these we know the names of two, Oswine and Swefheard, the

---

[1] Liebermann, III. p. 2, gives 602-3. This is partly dependent on the date 604 for Augustine's death, for which cf. Plummer, *Baedae Opera Historica*, II. p. 81.

atter of whom was, according to Birch, *Cart. Sax.* 42, a son of Sebbe, king of Essex. The time was evidently one of great disturbance in the south east of England. The Mercian power seems to have temporarily broken down, and the kings of Essex, Wessex, Sussex and Kent were all struggling for the mastery. Wihtred succeeded in the autumn of 690 (cf. *Hist. Eccl.* v. 23), though Swefheard continued to reign along with him at least until 692, and perhaps a year or two later (cf. *Cart. Sax.* 86, if any reliance can be placed on this document). The laws appear to have been issued in the autumn of 695, probably on September 6 (cf. Liebermann, III. p. 24). Peace was made with Ine, king of Wessex, in the preceding year, according to the Saxon Chronicle (*ann.* 694); and it is worth noting that one of Wihtred's laws (28) is practically identical with one of Ine's (20)—which points to communication between the two courts.

The Kentish laws are preserved only in the Textus Roffensis (H), which was written more than four centuries after the promulgation of Wihtred's Laws, and at least five centuries after the time of Æthelberht. There is no Latin version in existence, in the Quadripartitus or elsewhere, though translations of some passages occur in the 'Laws of Henry I.'

Owing to the lateness of the MS the language of the laws has been much modernised. But this process has not been carried out consistently; the text presents a mixture of forms of various periods from the seventh to the twelfth century. Many archaic words occur, some of which are unknown elsewhere in English (e.g. *læt*), while others are found only in poetry or with specialised meanings (e.g. *dryhten,* in other prose works applied only to God, or *eorl,* in other prose works used only as a translation of the Scandinavian term *jarl*). The construction of the sentences too, especially in Æthelberht's Laws, is of a primitive character.

The Laws of Æthelberht are of special interest as being the earliest document written in the English language. Some poems indeed, such as Beowulf, may have a longer history behind them, but it is highly improbable that they were committed to writing till a much later period. No other Teutonic language possesses any original records of equal antiquity, apart from short inscriptions. The remains of Gothic literature are indeed much older, but they consist entirely of translations, while the laws of the Continental Teutonic peoples, though they begin more than a century before Æthelberht's reign, are written in Latin down to comparatively late times.

1—2

4

ÆTHELBERHT

Þis syndon þa domas, þe Æðelbirht cyning asette on Augustinus dæge.

1[1]. Godes feoh 7 ciricean XII gylde. Biscopes feoh XI gylde. Preostes feoh IX gylde. Diacones feoh VI gylde. Cleroces feoh III gylde. Ciricfriþ II gylde. Mæthl friþ[2] II gylde.

2. Gif cyning his leode to him gehateþ, 7 heom mon þær yfel gedo, II bóte 7 cyninge L scillinga.

3. Gif cyning æt mannes ham drincæþ, 7 ðær man lyswæs hwæt gedo, twibote gebete.

4. Gif frigman cyninge stele, IX gylde forgylde.

5. Gif in cyninges tune man mannan ofslea, L scill' gebete.

6. Gif man frigne mannan ofsleahþ, cyninge L scill' to drihtinbeage.

7. Gif cyninges ambihtsmið oþþe laadrincmannan[3] ofslehð, meduman leodgelde forgelde.

8. Cyninges mundbyrd L scillinga.

9. Gif frigman freum stelþ, III gebete, 7 cyning age þæt wite 7 ealle þa æhtan.

10. Gif man wið cyninges mægdenman geligeþ, L scillinga gebete.

11. Gif hio grindende þeowa sio, XXV scillinga gebete. Sio þridde XII scillingas.

---

[1] The numbers of the chapters are not found in the MS.
[2] M....friþ. H. Letters between M and f erased. Mæthl frið is found in a copy of H (Cotton Julius C II) made in 1589 [Liebermann].
[3] So Hickes. Written as three words. H.

ÆTHELBERHT

These[1]* are the decrees which King Æthelberht established in the lifetime of Augustine.

1. [Theft of] God's property and the Church's shall be compensated twelve fold; a bishop's property eleven fold; a priest's property nine fold; a deacon's property six fold; a clerk's property three fold. Breach of the peace shall be compensated doubly when it affects a church or a meeting place.

2. If the king calls his lieges[1] to him, and anyone molests them there, he shall pay double compensation, and 50 shillings to the king.

3. If the king is feasting at anyone's house, and any sort of offence is committed there, twofold compensation shall be paid.

4. If a freeman robs the king, he shall pay back a nine fold[1] amount.

5. If one man slays another on the king's premises, he shall pay[1] 50 shillings compensation[2].

6. If a man slays a free man, he shall pay 50 shillings to the king for infraction of his seignorial rights[1].

7. If [he] slays a smith in the king's service, or a messenger[1] belonging to the king, he shall pay an ordinary wergeld[2].

8. The king's *mundbyrd*[1] shall be 50 shillings.

9. If a freeman robs a freeman, he shall pay a three fold compensation, and the king shall take the fine, or[1] all [the man's] goods.

10. If a man lies with a maiden belonging to the king, he shall pay 50 shillings[1] compensation.

11. If she is a grinding slave, he shall pay 25 shillings compensation. [If she is of the] third [class], [he shall pay] 12 shillings compensation.

* The reference numbers in the translation refer to notes at the end of the book

12. Cyninges fedesl xx scillinga forgelde.

13. Gif on eorles tune man mannan ofslæhþ, xii scill' gebete.

14. Gif wið eorles birele man geligeþ, xii scill' gebete.

15. Ceorles mundbyrd vi scillingas.

16. Gif wið ceorles birelan man geligeþ, vi scillingum gebete; aet þære oþere ðeowan l scætta; aet þare þriddan xxx scætta.

17. Gif man in mannes tún ærest geirneþ, vi scillingum gebete; se þe æfter irneþ iii scillingas; siððan gehwylc scilling.

18. Gif man mannan wępnum bebyreþ, ðær ceas weorð, 7 man nænig yfel ne gedeþ, vi scillingum gebete.

19. Gif wegreaf sy gedón, vi scillingum gebete.

20. Gif man þone man ofslæhð, xx scillingum gebete.

21. Gif man mannan ofslæhð, medume leodgeld c scillinga gebete.

22. Gif man mannan ofslæhð, æt openum græfe xx scillinga forgelde, 7 in xl nihta ealne leod forgelde.

23. Gif bana of lande gewiteþ, ða magas healfne leod forgelden.

24. Gif man frigne man gebindeþ¹, xx scill' gebete.

25. Gif man ceorlæs hlafætan ofslæhð, vi scillingum gebete.

26. Gif læt ofslæhð, þone selestan lxxx scll' forgelde; gif þane oþerne ofslæhð, lx scillingum forgelde; ðane þriddan xl scilling forgelde².

¹ em. Hickes. *gebi...eð*. H.   ² em. Thorpe. *forgelden*. H.

12. 20 shillings shall be paid for killing a *fedesl*[1] belonging to the king.

13. If one man slays another on the premises of a nobleman[2], he shall pay 12 shillings[1] compensation.

14. If a man lies with a nobleman's serving maid, he shall pay 12 shillings compensation.

15. A commoner's[2] *mundbyrd*[1] shall be 6 shillings.

16. If a man lies with a commoner's serving maid, he shall pay 6 shillings compensation; [if he lies] with a slave of the second class, [he shall pay] 50 sceattas[1] [compensation]; if with one of the third class, 30 sceattas.

17. If a man is the first to make [forcible] entry into another man's premises, he shall pay 6 shillings compensation. He who comes next shall pay 3 shillings compensation; and afterwards each one shall pay a shilling.

18. If one man supplies another with weapons when a quarrel is taking place, no injury however being inflicted[1], he [the lender] shall pay 6 shillings compensation.

19. If highway robbery is perpetrated [with the aid of those weapons], [the lender] shall pay 6 shillings compensation.

20. If the man[1] is slain, [the lender of the weapons] shall pay 20 shillings compensation.

21. If one man slays another, the ordinary[1] wergeld to be paid as compensation shall be 100 shillings.

22. If one man slays another, he shall pay 20 shillings[1] before the grave is closed, and the whole of the wergeld within 40 days.

23. If a homicide departs[1] from the country[2], his relatives shall pay half the wergeld.

24. If a man lays bonds on a freeman, he shall pay 20 shillings compensation.

25. If a man slays the dependant[1] of a commoner, he shall pay [the commoner] 6 shillings[2] compensation.

26. If he slays a *læt*[1] of the best class, he shall pay 80 shillings; if he slays one of the second class, he shall pay 60 shillings; [for slaying one of] the third class, he shall pay 40 shillings.

27. Gif friman edorbrecþe gedeþ, VI scillingum gebete.

28. Gif man inne feoh genimeþ, se man III gelde gebete.

29. Gif friman edor gegangeð, IIII scillingum gebete.

30. Gif man mannan ofslea, agene scætte 7 unfacne feo gehwilce gelde.

31. Gif friman wið fries mannes wif geligeþ, his wergelde abicge, 7 oðer wif his agenum scætte begete 7 ðæm oðrum æt ham[1] gebrenge.

32. Gif man rihthamscyld[2] þurhstinð, mid weorðe forgelde.

33. Gif feaxfang geweorð, L sceatta to bote.

34. Gif banes blice weorðeþ, III scillingum gebete.

35. Gif banes bite weorð, IIII scillingum gebete.

36. Gif sio uterre hion gebrocen worðeþ, X scillingum gebete.

37. Gif butu sien, XX scillingum gebete.

38. Gif eaxle gelæmed weorþeð, XXX scill' gebete.

39. Gif oþer eare nowiht[3] gehereð, XXV scill' gebete.

40. Gif eare of weorð aslagen, XII scill' gebete.

41. Gif eare þirel weorðeþ, III scill' gebete.

42. Gif eare sceard weorðeþ, VI scill' gebete.

43. Gif eage of weorð, L scillinga gebete.

44. Gif muð oþþe eage woh weorðeþ, XII scill' gebete.

45. Gif nasu ðyrel weorð, VIIII scillingum gebete.

---

[1] em. Hickes. þam. H.
[2] *riht hamscyld.* H—Thorpe and Schmid write as two words; Liebermann as one.
[3] The original reading. Altered into *nawiht*.

27. If a freeman breaks the fence round [another man's] enclosure, he shall pay 6 shillings[1] compensation.
28. If any property be seized therein, the man shall pay a three fold compensation.
29. If a freeman makes his way into[1] a fenced enclosure, he shall pay 4 shillings compensation.
30. If one man slays another, he shall pay the wergeld with his own money and property (i.e. livestock or other goods) which whatever its nature must be free from blemish [or damage].
31. If [one] freeman lies with the wife of [another] freeman, he shall pay [the husband] his [or her][1] wergeld, and procure a second wife with his own money, and bring her to the other man's home.
32. If anyone damages[1] the enclosure[2] of a dwelling, he shall pay according to its value.
33. For seizing a man by the hair, 50 sceattas shall be paid as compensation.
34. If a bone is laid bare, 3 shillings shall be paid as compensation.
35. If a bone is damaged, 4 shillings shall be paid as compensation.
36. If the outer covering of the skull[1] is broken, 10 shillings shall be paid as compensation.
37. If both are broken, 20 shillings shall be paid as compensation.
38. If a shoulder is disabled, 30 shillings shall be paid as compensation.
39. If the hearing of either ear is destroyed, 25 shillings shall be paid as compensation.
40. If an ear is struck off, 12 shillings shall be paid as compensation.
41. If an ear is pierced, 3 shillings shall be paid as compensation.
42. If an ear is lacerated, 6 shillings shall be paid as compensation.
43. If an eye is knocked out, 50 shillings shall be paid as compensation.
44. If the mouth or an eye is disfigured, 12 shillings shall be paid as compensation.
45. If the nose is pierced, 9 shillings shall be paid as compensation.

46. Gif hit sio an hleore, III scill' gebete.

47. Gif butu ðyrele sien, VI scill' gebete.

48. Gif nasu ælcor sceard weorð, gehwylc VI scill' gebete.

49. Gif¹ ðirel weorþ, VI scill' gebete.

50. Se þe cinban forslæhð, mid XX scillingum forgelde.

51. Æt þam feower toðum fyrestum, æt gehwylcum VI scillingas;
se toþ se þanne bistandeþ IIII scill'; se ðe ðonne bi ðam
standeþ III scill'; ond² þonne siþþan gehwylc scilling.

52. Gif spræc awyrd weorþ, XII scillingas.

§1. Gif widobane gebroced weorðeþ, VI scill' gebete.

53. Se þe earm þurhstinð, VI scillingum gebete.

§1. Gif earm forbrocen weorð, VI scill' gebete.

54. Gif þuman ofaslæhð, XX scill'.

§1. Gif ðuman nægl of weorðeþ, III scill' gebete.

§2. Gif man scytefinger ofaslæhð, VIIII scill' gebete.

§3. Gif man middelfinger ofaslæhð, IIII scill' gebete.

§4. Gif man goldfinger ofaslæhð, VI scill' gebete.

§5. Gif man þone lytlan finger ofaslæhð, XI scill' gebete.

55. Æt þam neglum gehwylcum scilling.

56. Æt þam lærestan wlitewamme III scillingas ond² æt þam
maran VI scill'.

57. Gif man oþerne mid fyste in naso slæhð, III scill'.

---

¹ Liebermann suggests a word may be missing here.
² Altered to *and*.

46. If it is one cheek[1], 3 shillings shall be paid as compensation.
47. If both are pierced, 6 shillings shall be paid as compensation.
48. If the nose is lacerated otherwise [than by piercing], 6 shillings shall be paid as compensation, for each laceration.
49. If it[1] is pierced, 6 shillings shall be paid as compensation.
50. He who smashes a chin bone, shall pay for it with 20 shillings.
51. For each of the 4 front teeth, 6 shillings [shall be paid as compensation]; for each of the teeth which stand next to these, 4 shillings [shall be paid as compensation]; then for each tooth which stands next to them, 3 shillings [shall be paid as compensation]; and beyond that 1 shilling [shall be paid as compensation] for each tooth.
52. If the power of speech is injured, 12 shillings [shall be paid as compensation].

   § 1. If a collar bone is injured, 6 shillings shall be paid as compensation.

53. He who pierces an arm shall pay 6 shillings compensation.

   § 1. If an arm is broken, 6 shillings shall be paid as compensation.

54. If a thumb is struck off, 20 shillings [shall be paid as compensation].

   § 1. If a thumb nail is knocked off, 3 shillings shall be paid as compensation.

   § 2. If a man strikes off a forefinger, he shall pay 9 shillings compensation.

   § 3. If a man strikes off a middle finger, he shall pay 4 shillings compensation.

   § 4. If a man strikes off a 'ring finger,' he shall pay 6 shillings compensation.

   § 5. If a man strikes off a little finger, he shall pay 11 shillings compensation.

55. For the nails of each [of the above-mentioned fingers], 1 shilling [shall be paid as compensation].
56. For the slightest disfigurement, 3 shillings, and for a greater 6 shillings [shall be paid as compensation].
57. If one man strikes another on the nose with his fist, 3 shillings [shall be paid as compensation].

58. Gif dynt sie, scilling.

§ 1. Gif he heahre handa dyntes onfehð, scill' forgelde.

59. Gif dynt sweart sie buton wædum, xxx scætta gebete.

60. Gif hit sie binnan wædum, gehwylc xx scætta gebete.

61. Gif hrifwund weorðeþ, xii scill' gebete.

§ 1. Gif he þurhðirel weorðeþ, xx scill' gebete.

62. Gif man gegemed weorðeþ, xxx scill' gebete.

63. Gif man cearwund sie, xxx scill' gebete.

64. Gif man gekyndelice lim awyrdeþ, þrym leudgeldum hine man forgelde.

§ 1. Gif he þurhstinð, vi scill' gebete.

§ 2. Gif man inbestinð, vi scill' gebete.

65. Gif þeoh gebrocen weorðeþ, xii scillingum gebete.

§ 1. Gif he healt weorð, þær motan freond seman.

66. Gif rib forbrocen weorð, iii scill' gebete.

67. Gif man þeoh ðurhstingþ, stice gehwilce vi scillingas.

§ 1. Gyfe ofer ynce scilling, æt twam yncum twegen, ofer þry iii scll'.

68. Gif wælt wund weorðeþ, iii scillingas gebete.

69. Gif fot of weorðeþ, l scillingum forgelde[1].

70. Gif seo micle[2] ta of weorðeþ, x scll' forgelde[1].

71. Æt þam oðrum taum gehwilcum healf gelde, ealswa æt þam fingrum ys cwiden.

---

[1] em. Hickes. *forgelden.* H.
[2] Altered to *mycle.*

58. If it leaves a bruise, 1 shilling [shall be paid as compensation].

   § 1. If the blow is received with uplifted hand, a shilling shall be paid.

59. If it leaves a black bruise [showing] outside the clothes, 30 sceattas shall be paid as compensation.

60. If it [the bruise] is under the clothes, 20 sceattas shall be paid as compensation for each [bruise].

61. If the belly is wounded, 12 shillings shall be paid as compensation.

   § 1. If it be pierced through, 20 shillings shall be paid as compensation.

62. If a man receives medical treatment, 30 shillings shall be paid as compensation.

63. If a man is severely(?) wounded[1], 30 shillings shall be paid as compensation.

64. If anyone destroys the generative organ, he shall pay for it with three times the wergeld.

   § 1. If he pierces it right through, he shall pay 6 shillings compensation.

   § 2. If he pierces it partially, he shall pay 6 shillings compensation.

65. If a thigh is broken, 12 shillings shall be paid as compensation.

   § 1. If he becomes lame, the settlement of the matter may be left to friends[1].

66. If a rib is broken, 3 shillings shall be paid as compensation.

67. If a thigh is pierced right through, 6 shillings compensation shall be paid for each stab [of this kind].

   § 1. For a stab over an inch [deep][1], 1 shilling; for a stab between 2 and 3 inches [deep], 2 shillings; for a stab over 3 inches [deep], 3 shillings [shall be paid as compensation].

68. If a sinew is wounded, 3 shillings shall be paid as compensation.

69. If a foot is struck off, 50 shillings shall be paid for it.

70. If the big toe is struck off, 10 shillings shall be paid for it.

71. For each of the other toes, [a sum] equal to half that laid down for the corresponding fingers shall be paid.

72. Gif þare mycclan taan nægl of weorþeð, xxx scætta to bote.

§ 1. Æt þam oþrum gehwilcum x scættas gebete.

73. Gif friwif locbore leswæs hwæt gedeþ, xxx scll' gebete.

74. Mægþbot sy swa friges mannes.

75. Mund þare betstan widuwan eorlcundre L scillinga gebete.

§ 1. Ðare oþre xx scll', ðare þriddan xii scll', þare feorðan vi scll'.

76. Gif man widuwan unagne genimeþ, ii gelde seo mund sy.

77. Gif mon mægþ gebigeð, ceapi geceapod sy, gif hit unfacne is.

§ 1. Gif hit þonne facne is, eft[1] þær æt ham gebrenge, 7 him man his scæt agefe.

78. Gif hio cwic bearn gebyreþ, healfne scæt age, gif ceorl ær swylteþ.

79. Gif mid bearnum bugan wille, healfne scæt age.

80. Gif ceorl agan wile, swa an bearn.

81. Gif hio bearn ne gebyreþ, fæderingmagas fioh agan 7 morgengyfe.

82. Gif man mægþmon nede genimeþ: ðam agende L scillinga 7 eft æt þam agende sinne willan ætgebicge.

83. Gif hio oþrum mæn in sceat bewyddod sy, xx scillinga gebete.

84. Gif gængang geweorðeþ, xxxv scill' 7 cyninge xv scillingas.

85. Gif man mid esnes cwynan geligeþ be cwicum ceorle, ii gebete.

---

[1] em. Thorpe. *ef.* H.

72. If the nail of the big toe is knocked off, 30 sceattas shall be paid as compensation.

    §1. 10 sceattas shall be paid as compensation for the loss of each of the other toenails.

73. If a freeborn[1] woman, with long hair, misconducts herself, she[2] shall pay 30 shillings as compensation.

74. Compensation [for injury] to be paid to[1] an unmarried woman, shall be on the same scale as that paid to a freeman.

75. The compensation to be paid for violation of the *mund*[1] of a widow of the best class, [that is, of a widow] of the nobility, shall be 50 shillings.

    §1. For violation of the *mund* of a widow of the second class, 20 shillings; of the third class, 12 shillings; of the fourth class, 6 shillings.

76. If a man takes a widow who does not [of right] belong to him, double the value of the *mund* shall be paid.

77. If a man buys a maiden, the bargain shall stand, if there is no dishonesty.

    §1. If however there is dishonesty, she shall be taken back to her home, and the money shall be returned to him.

78. If she bears a living child, she shall have half the goods left by her husband, if he dies first.

79. If she wishes to depart with her children, she shall have half the goods.

80. If the husband wishes to keep [the children], she shall have a share of the goods equal to a child's.

81. If she does not bear a child, [her] father's relatives shall have her goods, and the "morning gift[1]."

82. If a man forcibly carries off a maiden, [he shall pay] 50 shillings to her owner, and afterwards buy from the owner his consent[1].

83. If she is betrothed, at a price, to another man, 20 shillings shall be paid[1] as compensation.

84. If she is brought back, 35 shillings shall be paid[1], and 15 shillings to the king.

85. If a man lies with the woman of a servant, during the lifetime of the husband, he shall pay a twofold compensation.

86. Gif esne oþerne ofslea unsynnigne, ealne weorðe forgelde.

87. Gif esnes eage 7 foot of weorðeþ aslagen, ealne weorþe hine forgelde.

88. Gif man mannes esne gebindeþ, vi scll' gebete.

89. Ðeowæs wegreaf se iii scillingas.

90. Gif þeo[1] steleþ, ii gelde gebete.

[1] w added in a different hand.

86. If one servant slays another, who has committed no offence, he shall pay his full value.

87. If the eye and[1] foot of a servant are destroyed [by blows], his full value shall be paid.

88. If a man lays bonds on another man's servant, he shall pay 6 shillings compensation.

89. The sum to be paid for[1] robbing a slave on the highway shall be 3 shillings.

90. If a slave steals, he shall pay twice the value [of the stolen goods], as compensation.

HLOTHHERE and EADRIC

þis syndon þa domas ðe Hloþhære 7 Eadric, Cantwara cyningas, asetton.

Hloþhære 7 Eadric, Cantwara cyningas, ecton þa ǽ, þa ðe heora aldoras ær geworhton, ðyssum domum þe hyr efter sægeþ.

1. Gif mannes esne eorlcundne mannan ofslæhð þane ðe sio þreom hundum scll' gylde, se agend þone banan agefe 7 do þær þrio manwyrð to.

2. Gif se bane oþbyrste, feorþe manwyrð he to gedo 7 hine gecænne mid godum æwdum þæt he þane banan begeten ne mihte.

3. Gif mannes esne frigne mannan ofslæhð þane þe sie hund scillinga gelde, se agend þone banan agefe 7 oþer manwyrð þær tó.

4. Gif bana oþbyrste, twam manwyrþum hine man forgelde 7 hine gecænne mid godum æwdum þæt he þane banan begeten ne mihte.

5. Gif frigman mannan forstele, gif he eft cuma stermelda, secge an andweardne. Gecænne hine, gif he mæge : hæbbe þare freora rim æwda manna 7 ænne mid in aþe, æghwilc man, æt þam tune þe he tohyre; gif he þæt ne mæge, gelde swa he genoh áge[1].

6. Gif ceorl acwyle be libbendum wife 7 bearne, riht is þæt hit, þæt bearn, medder folgige; 7 him mon an his fæderingmagum wilsumne berigean geselle[2], his feoh to healdenne, oþ þæt he x wintra sie.

7. Gif man oþrum mæn feoh forstele, 7 se agend hit eft ætfó, geteme to cynges sele, gif he mæge, 7 þone ætgebrenge þe him sealde; gif he þæt ne mæge, læte án, 7 fo se agend tó.

---

[1] em. Wilkins. *gono háge.* H.   [2] em. Hickes. *gefelle.* H.

HLOTHHERE AND EADRIC

These are the decrees which Hlothhere[1] and Eadric, Kings of Kent, established.

Hlothhere and Eadric, Kings of Kent, extended the laws which their predecessors had made, by the decrees which are stated below.

1. If a man's servant slays a nobleman, whose wergeld is 300 shillings[1], his owner shall surrender the homicide and pay the value of three men[2] in addition.
2. If the homicide escapes, he shall add thereto the value of a fourth man and prove by good witnesses that he has not been able to lay hands on the homicide.
3. If a man's servant slays a freeman whose wergeld is 100 shillings, his owner shall surrender the homicide and [pay] the value of another man in addition.
4. If the homicide escapes, [his owner] shall pay for him with two wergelds and prove by good witnesses that he has not been able to lay hands on the homicide.
5. If a freeman steals a man, and if he [who has been stolen] returns as informer, he shall accuse him to his face; and he [the thief] shall clear himself if he can. And every man involved in such a charge shall have a number[1] of free witnesses, and one[2] [at least] of his witnesses[3] from the village to which he himself belongs[4]. If he cannot do this[5], he must pay to the best of his ability.
6. If a man dies leaving a wife and child, it is right, that the child should accompany[1] the mother[2]; and one of his father's relatives who is willing to act, shall be given him as his guardian to take care of his property, until he is ten[3] years old.
7. If one man steals property from another, and the owner afterwards reclaims[1] it, he [who is in possession] shall bring it to the king's residence, if he can, and produce the man who sold it. him. If he cannot do that, he shall surrender it, and the owner shall take possession [of it].

8. Gif man oþerne sace tihte 7 he þane mannan mote an medle
oþþe an þinge, symble se man þam oðrum byrigean geselle
7 þam riht awyrce þe to hiom Cantwara deman gescrifen.

9. Gif he ðonne byrigan forwærne, XII scillingas agylde þam
cyninge, 7 sio seo[1] sacy swa open swa hio ær wes.

10. Gif man oþerne tihte, siþþan he him byrigan gesealdne
hæbbe, ðonne[2] ymb III niht gesecæn hiom sæmend, buton
þam ufor leofre sio þe þa tihtlan age. Siþþan sio sace ge-
semed sio; an seofan nihtum se man þam oþrum riht gedo,
gecwime an feo oððe an aþe, swa hwæder swa him leofre sio.
Gif he þonne þæt nille, gelde þonne C buton aðe, siþþan ane
neaht ofer þæt gesem bie[3].

11. Gif man mannan an oþres flette manswara hateþ oððe hine
mid bismærwordum scandlice grete, scilling agelde þam þe
þæt flet age, 7 VI scill' þam þe he þæt word to gecwæde, 7
cyninge XII scll' forgelde.

12. Gif man oþrum steop asette ðær mæn drincen, buton scylde,
an eald riht scll' agelde þam þe þæt flet age, 7 VI scll' þam
þe man þone steap aset, 7 cynge XII scll'.

13. Gif man wæpn abregde þær mæn drincen 7 ðær man nan
yfel ne deþ, scilling þan þe þæt flet age, 7 cyninge XII scll'.

14. Gif þæt flet geblodgad wyrþe, forgylde þem mæn his mundbyrd 7 cyninge L scill'.

15. Gif man cuman feormæþ III niht an his agenum hame,
cepeman oþþe oðerne þe sio ofer mearce cuman, 7 hine
þonne his mete fede, 7 he þonne ænigum mæn yfel gedo, se
man þane oðerne æt rihte gebrenge oþþe riht forewyrce.

---

[1] em. Liebermann. *sio.* Thorpe. *se.* H.
[2] em. Liebermann. 7 *ðonne.* H.
[3] em. Hickes and Edd. *hie.* H.

8. If one man brings a charge against another, and if he meets[1] the man [whom he accused], at an assembly[2] or meeting[2], the latter shall always provide the former with a surety, and render him such satisfaction as the judges of Kent shall prescribe for them[3].

9. If, however, he refuses to provide a surety, he shall pay 12 shillings to the king, and the suit[1] shall be considered as open as it was before.

10. If one man charges another, after the other has provided him with a surety, then three days later they shall attempt to find an arbitrator, unless the accuser prefers a longer delay. Within a week after the suit has been decided by arbitration, the accused shall render justice to the other and satisfy him with money, or with an oath, whichever he [the accused[1]] prefers. If, however, he is not willing to do this, then he shall pay 100 shillings, without [giving] an oath, on the day after the arbitration.

11. If one man calls another a perjurer in a third man's house, or accosts him abusively with insulting words[1], he shall pay one shilling to him who owns the house, 6 shillings to him he has accosted, and 12 shillings to the king.

12. If, where men are drinking, one man takes away the stoup of another, who has committed no offence, he shall pay, in accordance with established custom[1], a shilling to him who owns the house, 6 shillings to him whose stoup has been taken away, and 12 shillings to the king.

13. If, where men are drinking, a man draws his weapon, but no harm is done[1] there, he shall pay a shilling to him who owns the house, and 12 shillings to the king.

14. [But] if the house is stained with blood, the owner shall have his *mundbyrd* paid to him, and 50 shillings shall be paid to the king.

15. If a man entertains a stranger (a trader or anyone else who has come over the border[1]) for three days in his own home, and then supplies him with food from his own store, and [if] he [the stranger] then does harm to anyone, the man[2] shall bring the other to justice, or make amends on his behalf.

16. Gif Cantwara ænig in Lundenwic feoh gebycge, hæbbe him
þonne twegen oððe ðreo unfacne ceorlas to gewitnesse oþþe
cyninges wicgerefan.

§ 1. Gif hit man eft æt þam mæn in Cænt ætfó, þonne tæme
he to wic to cyngæs sele to þam mæn ðe him sealde, gif
he þane wite 7 æt þam teame gebrengen mæge.

§ 2. Gif he þæt ne mæge, gekyþe ðanne in wiofode mid his
gewitena anum oþþe mid cyninges wicgerefan, þæt he
þæt feoh undeornunga his cuþan ceape in wic gebohte;
and him man þanne his weorð agefe.

§ 3. Gif he þanne þæt ne mæge gecyþan mid rihtre canne,
læte þanne án, 7 se agend tofó.

16. If a man of Kent buys property[1] in London, he shall have two or three trustworthy men, or the reeve of the king's estate, as witness.

§ 1. If afterwards it is claimed[1] from the man in Kent, he shall summon as witness, to the king's residence in London[2], the man who sold it him, if he knows him and can produce him as warrant for the transaction.

§ 2. If he cannot do so, he shall declare on the altar, with one of his witnesses or with the reeve of the king's estate[1], that he bought the property openly in London, and with goods known to be his[2], and the value [of the property] shall be returned to him.

§ 3. If, however, he cannot prove that[1] by lawful declaration, he shall give it up, and the owner shall take possession of it.

WIHTRED

Ðis synd Wihtrædes domas Cantwara cyninges.

Ðam mildestan cyninge Cantwara Wihtræde rixigendum þe fiftan wintra his rices, þy niguðan gebanne, sextan dæge Rugernes, in þære stowe þy hatte Berghamstyde, ðær wæs gesamnad eadigra geþeahtendlic[1] ymcyme. Ðær wæs Birhtwald, Bretone heahbiscop, 7 se ær næmda cyning; eac þan Hrofesceastre bisceop (se ilca Gybmund wæs haten) andward wæs; 7 cwæð ælc had ciricean ðære mægðe anmodlice mid þy hersuman folcy.

Ðær ða eadigan fundon mid ealra gemedum ðas domas 7 Cantwara rihtum þeawum æcton, swa hit hyr efter segeþ 7 cwyþ:

1. Cirice an freolsdome[2] gafola;

    § 1. 7 man for cyning gebidde, 7 hine buton neadhæse heora willum weorþigen.

2. Ciricean mundbyrd sie L scll' swa cinges.

3. Unrihthæmde mæn to rihtum life mid synna hreowe tofon oþþe of ciricean gemanan[3] ascadene sien.

4. Æltheodige mæn, gif hio hiora hæmed rihtan nyllað, of lande mid hiora æhtum 7 mid synnum gewiten;

    § 1. swæse mæn in leodum ciriclicæs gemanan ungestrodyne þoligen.

5. Gif þæs geweorþe gesiþcundne mannan ofer þis gemot, þæt he unriht hæmed genime ofer cyngæs bebod 7 biscopes 7 boca dom, se þæt gebete his dryhtne C scll' an ald reht.

    § 1. Gif hit ceorlisc man sie, gebete L scll'; 7 gehwæder þæt hæmed mid hreowe forlæte.

[1] em. Thorpe. *geheahtendlic.* H.
[2] *anfreols dome.* H. Schmid, following Wilkins, writes *Ciricean freolsdome;* Liebermann, as above.
[3] em. Wilkins. *genaman.* H.

WIHTRED

These are the decrees of Wihtred[1], King of Kent.

During the sovereignty of Wihtred, the most gracious king of Kent, in the fifth year of his reign, the ninth Indiction[2], the sixth day of Rugern[3], in a place which is called Barham[4], there was assembled a deliberative council of the notables. There were present there Berhtwald, the chief bishop of Britain, and the above-mentioned king; the bishop of Rochester, who was called Gefmund; and every order of the Church of the province expressed itself in unanimity with the loyal laity [assembled there].

There the notables, with the consent of all, drew up these decrees, and added them to the legal usages of the people of Kent, as is hereafter stated and declared:

1. The Church shall enjoy[1] immunity from taxation.
    § 1. The king shall be prayed for, and they[1] shall honour him freely and without compulsion.
2. The *mundbyrd*[1] of the Church shall be 50 shillings like the king's.
3. Men living in illicit unions shall turn to a righteous life repenting of their sins, or they shall be excluded from the communion of the Church.
4. Foreigners, if they will not regularise their unions, shall depart from the land[1] with their possessions and with their sins.
    § 1. Men of our own country also shall be excluded from the communion of the Church, without being subject to forfeiture of their goods.
5. If after this meeting, a nobleman[1] presumes[2] to enter into an illicit union, despite the command of the king and the bishop, and the written law[3], he shall pay 100 shillings compensation to his lord, in accordance with established custom[4].
    § 1. If a commoner does so, he shall pay 50 shillings compensation; and [in] either [case the offender] shall desist from the union, with repentance.

6. Gif priost læfe unriht hæmed oþþe fulwihte[1] untrumes forsitte oþþe to þon druncen sie þæt he ne mæge, sio he stille his þegnungæ oþ biscopes dóm.

7. Gif bescoren man steorleas gange him an gestliðnesse, gefe him man ænes; 7 þæt ne geweorðe, buton he leafnesse habbe, þæt hine man læng feormige.

8. Gif man his mæn an wiofode freols gefe, se sie folcfry; freolsgefa age his erfe ænde wergeld 7 munde þare hina, sie ofer mearce ðær he wille.

9. Gif esne ofer dryhtnes hæse þeowweorc wyrce an sunnan æfen efter hire setlgange oþ monan æfenes setlgang, LXXX scætta[2] se dryhtne gebete.

10. Gif esne deþ his rade þæs dæges, VI se wið dryhten gebete oþþe sine hyd.

11. Gif friman þonne an ðane forbodenan timan, sio he healsfange scyldig; 7 se man se þæt arasie, he age healf þæt wite 7 ðæt weorc.

12. Gif ceorl buton wifes wisdome deoflum gelde, he sie ealra his æhtan scyldig 7 healsfange. Gif butwu deoflum geldaþ, sion hio healsfange scyldigo 7 ealra æhtan.

13. Gif þeuw deoflum geldaþ, VI scll' gebete oþþe his hyd.

14. Gif mon his heowum in fæsten flæsc gefe, frigne ge þeowne halsfange alyse.

15. Gif þeow ete his sylfes ræde, VI scll' oþþe his hyd.

16. Biscopes word 7 cyninges sie unlægne buton aþe.

---

[1] em. Thorpe. *fulwihðe.* H.   [2] *scll'.* H.

6. If a priest consents to an illicit union, or if he neglects the baptism of a sick man, or is too drunk to discharge this duty, he shall abstain from his ministrations, pending a decision from the bishop.

7. If a tonsured man, [who is] not under ecclesiastical discipline[1], wanders about looking for hospitality, once[2] [only] shall it be granted to him, and unless he has permission, he shall not be entertained further.

8. If anyone grants one of his men freedom on the altar, his freedom shall be publicly recognised[1]; [but] the emancipator shall have his heritage and his wergeld, and the guardianship of his household, wherever he [the freed man] may be, [even if it be] beyond the border.

9. If a servant, contrary to his lord's command, does servile work between sunset on Saturday evening and sunset on Sunday evening, he shall pay 80 sceattas[1] to his lord.

10. If a servant makes a journey[1] of his own [on horseback] on that day, he shall pay 6 shillings compensation to his lord or undergo the lash.

11. If a freeman works during the forbidden time, he shall forfeit his *healsfang*[1], and the man who informs against him shall have half the fine, and [the profits arising from] the labour.

12. If a husband, without his wife's knowledge, makes offerings to devils, he shall forfeit all his goods or his *healsfang*. If both [of them] make offerings to devils they shall forfeit their *healsfangs* or[1] all their goods.

13. If a slave makes offerings to devils, he shall pay 6 shillings compensation or undergo the lash.

14. If a man gives meat to his household during a fast, he shall redeem [each of them], both bond and free, by payment of his [own] *healsfang*.

15. If a slave eats of his own free will, he shall pay 6 shillings compensation or undergo the lash.

16. A bishop's or a king's word, [even] though unsupported by an oath, shall be incontrovertible.

17. Mynstres aldor hine cænne in preostes canne.

18. Preost hine clænsie sylfæs soþe, in his halgum hrægle æt-
foran wiofode ðus cweþende " Veritatem dico in Christo, non
mentior." Swylce diacon hine clænsie.

19. Cliroc feowra sum hine clænsie his heafodgemacene 7 ane
his hand on wiofode; oþre ætstanden, aþ abycgan.

20. Gest hine clænsie sylfes aþe on wiofode; swylce cyninges
ðegn[1].

21. Ceorlisc man hine feowra sum his heafodgemacene on weo-
fode; 7 ðissa ealra að sie unlegnæ.

§ 1. Ðanne is cirican canne riht:

22. Gif man biscopes esne tihte oþþe cyninges, cænne hine an
gerefan hand; oþþe hine gerefa clensie oþþe selle to swinganne.

23. Gif man gedes þeuwne esne in heora gemange tihte, his
dryhten hine his ane aþe geclænsie, gif he huslgenga sie;
gif he huslgenga nis, hæbbe him in aþe oðirne æwdan godne
oþþe gelde oþþe selle to swinganne.

24. Gif folcesmannes esne tihte ciricanmannes esne, oþþe ciricanmannes esne tihte folcesmannes esne, his dryhten hine
ane his aþe geclensige.

25. Gif man leud ofslea an þeofðe, licge buton wyrgelde.

26. Gif man frigne man æt hæbbendre handa gefo, þanne wealde
se cyning ðreora anes; oððe hine man cwelle oþþe ofer sæ
selle oþþe hine his wergelde alese.

§ 1. Se þe hine gefo 7 gegange, healfne hine age; gif hine
man cwelle, geselle heom man LXX scll'.

---

[1] em. Liebermann. *ðeng.* H.

17. The head of a monastery shall clear himself by the formula used by a priest.

18. A priest shall clear himself by his own asseveration,[standing] in his holy garments before the altar and declaring as follows "Veritatem dico in Christo, non mentior." A deacon shall clear himself in a similar way.

19. A clerk shall clear himself with [the support of] three of his own class[1], he alone[2] [having] his hand on the altar. The others shall attend for the purpose of validating the oath[3].

20. A stranger shall clear himself by his own oath, at the altar. A king's thegn [shall clear himself] in the same way.

21. A commoner may clear himself at the altar, with three of his own class; and the oath of all these [collectively] shall be incontrovertible.

   § 1. The Church has further prerogatives with regard to expurgation, [which are] as follows:

22. If a servant of a bishop or of the king is accused, he shall clear himself by the hand of the reeve. The reeve shall either exculpate him or deliver him up to be scourged.

23. If anyone brings an accusation against a bond servant of a company[1] in presence of the company, his lord shall clear him by his own oath[2] if he (the lord) is a communicant[3]. If he is not a communicant he shall get a second[4] good witness [to support him] in the oath, or pay [the fine] or deliver him up to be scourged.

24. If a layman's servant accuse the servant of an ecclesiastic, or if an ecclesiastic's servant accuse the servant of a layman, his lord shall clear him by his own oath[1].

25. If anyone slays a man in the act of thieving, no wergeld shall be paid for him.

26. If anyone catches a freeman in the act of stealing, the king shall decide which of the following three courses shall be adopted—whether he shall be put to death, or sold beyond the sea, or held to ransom for his wergeld.

   § 1. He who catches and secures him, shall have half his value. If he is put to death, 70 shillings[1] shall be paid to him.

27. Gif þeuw stele 7 hine[1] man alese, LXX scll', swa hweder swa cyning wille; gif hine man acwelle, þam agende hine[1] man healfne agelde.

28. Gif feorran cumen man oþþe fræmde buton wege gange, 7 he þonne nawðer ne hryme ne he horn ne blawe, for ðeof he bið to profianne: oþþe to sleanne oþþe to alysenne.

[1] em. Thorpe. *hi.* H.

27. If a slave steals, and is released, 70 shillings [shall be paid]—whichever the king wishes[1]. If he is put to death, half his value shall be paid to the man who has him in his power[2].

28. If a man from afar, or a stranger, quits the road, and neither shouts, nor blows a horn, he shall be assumed to be a thief, [and as such] may be either slain or put to ransom.

THE LAWS OF INE AND
OF ALFRED

THE LAWS OF INE AND OF ALFRED

The earliest laws of the kingdom of Wessex are those of Ine, who, according to Bede (*Hist. Eccl.* v. 7), reigned from 688 to 725. In the latter year he resigned the throne, and went to Rome, where he remained until his death.

The date of the laws can probably be determined within a few years. In the preamble, Ine says that he has been consulting with "my bishop Erconwald," among others. This is an uncommon name, and there can be no doubt that the person referred to is Erconwald, who became bishop of Essex (London) about 675, and whose successor, Waldhere, was already in office about 694 (cf. *ib.* IV. 11).

The date of the laws falls therefore, in all probability, between 688 and 694. It has been observed that cap. 20 of Ine's laws is practically identical with cap. 28 of Wihtred's laws, which date from 695. This may be regarded as pointing to communication between the governing authorities of the two kingdoms, such as would naturally follow the restoration of friendly relations in 694. We may further note that Ine speaks of his father Cenred as being still alive—a fact which, so far as it goes, suggests a comparatively early date in his reign.

In view of the antiquity of the laws, it is not surprising that they present many difficulties and obscurities.

It is true that the terminology in general resembles that of later times, and differs in many respects from the Kentish laws. But there are a number of terms which do not occur later, while in regard to others, we cannot be certain that they always bear the same technical meaning as in later times.

There is no record of any further legislation in Wessex for nearly two centuries after the promulgation of Ine's laws.

The next are those of Alfred the Great, who became king in 871, and died about the year 900. They are preceded by a long introduction (cap. 1–48) which contains translations of the Ten Commandments, and many other passages from the book of Exodus (cap. 20–23), followed by a brief account of Apostolic history (with quotations from the Acts of the Apostles, cap. 15), and the growth of church law, as laid down by ecclesiastical councils, both ecumenical and English (cap. 49, §§ 1–7). The concluding words (cap. 49, § 8) state that compensations for misdeeds on the part of men were ordained at many councils, and written in their records, with varying provisions.

The introduction down to this point has been omitted as having no bearing on Anglo-Saxon law. The next paragraph, however (cap. 49, § 9), is important: Alfred acknowledges his indebtedness to the laws of Ine, as well as to those of the Mercian king Offa (which are now lost), and those of Æthelberht (of Kent), the first Christian king in England.

The date of the promulgation of the laws is unknown. Liebermann (III. p. 34) favours 892–893; but the fact that Alfred describes himself as *Westseaxna cyning* perhaps points to a rather earlier date, since in the latter part of his reign he seems to have changed his title and adopted, at least in Latin documents, that of *Angul-saxonum rex* or *Anglorum Saxonum rex*, the former of which is also given to him by Asser (cf. Stevenson, *Asser's Life of King Alfred*, pp. 1, 151 f.). The title *Westseaxena cingc* appears also in Alfred's will (cf. Harmer, *English Historical Documents*, p. 15 f.); but the date of this again is unknown, though it was drawn up before 889, and the Mercian Ealdorman Æthelred, and Werferth, bishop of Worcester, are mentioned as legatees.

In all MSS the laws of Ine are added as an appendix to those of Alfred. The earliest and best of the manuscripts, C.C.C. 173 (E) —from which the following text is taken—was written, according to Liebermann, about 925. Of the others, C.C.C. 383 (B) and the Textus Roffensis (H), both of which belong to the early part of the twelfth century, may be specially mentioned[1]. In both of them the language has been modernised to a considerable extent. The first part of Ine's laws (down to cap. 23) is found also in a fragment (Bu) preserved in (Brit. Mus.) Burney 277 and dating from about 1030; while Lambarde's edition (Ld), published in 1550, used at least one MS which is now lost[2]. On the relation of the various manuscripts to one another, see Liebermann, III. p. 32.

In B each law is for the most part preceded by its proper 'Title.' In the other MSS these titles are all brought together in the form of an introductory 'Table of Contents,' prefixed to the Laws of Alfred.

In all the MSS the language of the laws of Ine has been brought into conformity with that of Alfred's time in regard to the form of words, though not to the same extent in syntax and vocabulary.

The Quadripartitus contains a Latin version of both Alfred's and Ine's laws, and a considerable portion of the former are also translated in the Instituta Cnuti.

---

[1] H*, B* indicate additions made to H or B written above the line. But where passages containing but not consisting wholly of such additions are quoted, the additions are enclosed in brackets.

[2] Readings from Ld are given, as a rule, only when they differ from those of existing MSS.

INE

[Ines cyninges asetnysse[1].]

Ic Ine, mid Godes gife, Wesseaxna kyning, mid geðeahte
7 mid lare Cenredes mines fæder 7 Heddes mines biscepes 7
Eorcenwoldes mines biscepes, [7][2] mid eallum minum ealdor-
monnum 7 þæm ieldstan witum minre ðeode 7 éac micelre
gesomnunge[3] Godes ðeowa[4], wæs smeagende be ðære hælo urra
sawla 7 be ðam staþole ures rices, þætte ryht æw 7 ryhte cyne-
domas ðurh ure folc gefæstnode 7 getrymede wæron, þætte nænig
ealdormonna ne us undergeðeodedra[5] æfter þam wære awendende
ðas ure dómas.

1. Ærest we bebeodað, þætte Godes ðeowas hiora ryhtregol
    [gyman 7[6]] on ryht healdan.
    § 1. Æfter þam we bebeodað þætte ealles folces æw 7 domas
        ðus sien gehealdene.

2. Cild binnan ðritegum nihta[7] sie gefulwad[8]; gif hit swa ne
    sie, XXX scill. gebete.
    § 1. Gif hit ðonne sie dead butan fulwihte[9], gebete he hit
        mid eallum ðam ðe he age.

3. Gif ðeowmon wyrce on Sunnandæg be his hlafordes hæse,
    sie he frioh, 7 se hlaford geselle XXX scill. to wite.
    § 1. Gif þonne se ðeowa butan his gewitnesse wyrce, þolie
        his hyde [oððe hydgyldes[10]].
    § 2. Gif ðonne se frigea ðy dæge wyrce butan his hlafordes
        hæse, ðolie his freotes [oððe LX scll'; 7 preost twy-
        scildig[10]].

4. [Be ciricsceatte[11].]
    Ciricsceattas sín agifene be scē. Martines mæssan; gif hwa
    ðæt ne gelæste, sie he scyldig LX[12] scill. 7 be XII fealdum
    agife þone ciricsceat.

---

[1] H. *Ines lage.* B. *Ines æ.* Ld.   [2] B.   [3] *somnunge.* B.
[4] *þeowena.* B.   [5] *undergeðeodendra.* B.   [6] B.   [7] *nyhtum.* Bu & H.
[8] *gefullad.* B. *gefullod.* H, Bu.   [9] *fulluhte.* B, H.   [10] B, H*.
[11] This and subsequent titles taken from B.   [12] *feortig.* B.

INE

I, Ine, by the grace of God king of Wessex, with the advice and instruction of Cenred[1], my father, of Hedde, my bishop, and of Erconwald, my bishop, and with all my *ealdormen*[2] and the chief councillors of my people, and with a great concourse of the servants of God[3] as well, have been taking counsel for the salvation of our souls and the security of our realm, in order that just law and just decrees may be established and ensured throughout our nation, so that no *ealdorman* nor subject of ours may from henceforth pervert these our decrees.

1. In the first place, we command that the servants of God heed, and duly observe, their proper 'rule.'

   § 1. After this we command that the law and decrees affecting the whole nation be observed as follows.

2. A child shall be baptised within 30 days. If this is not done, [the guardian] shall pay 30 shillings compensation.

   § 1. If, however, it dies without being baptised, he shall pay as compensation all he possesses.

3. If a slave works on Sunday by his lord's command, he shall become free, and the lord shall pay a fine of 30 shillings.

   § 1. If, however, the slave works without the cognisance of his master, he shall undergo the lash or pay the fine in lieu thereof.

   § 2. If, however, a freeman works on that day, except by his lord's command, he shall be reduced to slavery, or [pay a fine of] 60 shillings. A priest shall pay a double fine.

4. Church dues shall be rendered at Martinmas. If anyone fails to do so, he shall forfeit 60 shillings[1] and render 12 times the church dues[2] [in addition].

5. [Be ciricsocnum.]

Gif hwa sie deaðes scyldig 7 he cirican geierne[1], hæbbe his feorh 7 bete, swa him ryht wisige.

§ 1. Gif hwa his hyde forwyrce 7 cirican geierne, sie him sio swingelle forgifen.

6. [Be gefeohtum.]

Gif hwa gefeohte on cyninges huse, sie he scyldig ealles his ierfes, 7 sie on cyninges dome, hwæðer he líf age[2] þe nage.

§ 1. Gif hwa on mynster gefeohte, CXX scill. gebete.

§ 2. Gif hwa on[3] ealdormonnes huse gefeohte[4] oððe on oðres geðungenes witan[5], LX scill. gebete he 7 oþer LX geselle[6] to wite.

§ 3. Gif ðonne[7] on gafolgeldan huse oððe on gebures gefeohte, CXX[8] scill. to wite geselle 7 þam gebure[9] VI scill.

§ 4. 7 þeah hit sie on middum[10] felda gefohten, CXX scill. to wite sie agifen.

§ 5. Gif ðonne[11] on gebeorscipe hie geciden, 7 oðer hiora mid geðylde hit forbere, geselle se oðer XXX scill. to wite.

7. [Be stale.]

Gif hwa stalie, swa his wíf[12] nyte 7 his bearn, geselle LX scill. to wite.

§ 1. Gif he ðonne stalie on gewitnesse ealles his hiredes, gongen[13] hie[14] ealle on ðeowot.

§ 2. X wintre cniht mæg bion ðiefðe gewita.

8. [Be rihtes bene.]

Gif hwa him[15] ryhtes bidde beforan hwelcum scírmen oððe oþrum[16] deman 7 [him ryht][17] ábiddan[18] ne mæge, 7 him wedd sellan[19] nelle, gebete XXX[20] scill. 7 binnan VII nihton gedó hine ryhtes wierðne[21].

9. [Be þam wrecendan.]

Gif hwa wrace dó, ærðon[22] he him ryhtes bidde, þæt he him onnime agife 7 forgielde 7 gebete mid[23] XXX scill.

---

[1] geærne. Bu.   [2] hæbbe. Bu.   [3] in. B.   [4] feohte. B.
[5] witan geþungenan. H.   [6] gesylle he. B.   [7] Gif mon. Bu.
[8] xxx sol. Quad.   [9] bure. Bu.   [10] middan. B & H.   [11] ð. bið. Bu.
[12] wif (hit). H*.   [13] gan.... H.   gangen. B.   [14] hy. H.   heo. B.
[15] hine. Bu.   [16] oþrum. om. H.   [17] H.   [18] hebban. Ld.
[19] mon syllan. Ld.   [20] mid xxx. Bu.   [21] wyrðe. H, B.   weorðe. Bu.
[22] ær. H.   [23] bete. B.

5. If anyone is liable to the death penalty, and he flees to a church, his life shall be spared and he shall pay such compensation as he is directed [to pay] by legal decision.

   § 1. If anyone renders himself liable to the lash and flees to the church, he shall be immune from scourging.

6. If anyone fights in the king's house, he shall forfeit all his property, and it shall be for the king to decide whether he shall be put to death or not.

   § 1. If anyone fights in a monastery, he shall pay 120 shillings compensation[1].

   § 2. If anyone fights in the house of an *ealdorman,* or of any other distinguished councillor, he shall pay 60 shillings compensation [to the householder] and he shall pay another 60 shillings as a fine[1].

   § 3. If, however, he fights in the house of a taxpayer[1] or of a *gebur*[2], he shall pay 120 shillings[3] as a fine, and 6 shillings to the *gebur*[4].

   § 4. And even if it [the fight] takes place in the open, a fine of 120 shillings shall be paid.

   § 5. If, however, two men quarrel over their cups and one endures it patiently, the other [who has recourse to violence] shall pay a fine of 30 shillings.

7. If anyone steals[1] without the cognisance of his wife and children, he shall pay a fine of 60 shillings.

   § 1. If, however, he steals with the cognisance of all his household, they shall all go into slavery.

   § 2. A ten year old child can be [regarded as] accessory to a theft.

8. If anyone demands justice[1] in the presence of any 'shireman[2]' or of another judge and cannot obtain it, since [the accused] will not give him security, he [the accused] shall pay 30 shillings compensation[3], and within 7 days do him such justice as he is entitled to.

9. If anyone exacts redress, before he pleads for justice, he shall give up what he has taken, and pay as much again[1], and 30 shillings compensation[2].

10. [Be reaflac.]

Gif hwa binnan þam gemærum ures rices reafláć 7 niednæme dó[1], agife he ðone reaflac 7 geselle LX scill. to wite.

11. [Be landbygene.]

Gif hwa his agenne geleod[2] bebycgge[3], ðeowne oððe frigne[4],
ðeah he scyldig sie, ofer sæ[5], forgielde hine his were[6] [7 wið
Godd deoplice bete][7].

12. [Be gefangenum ðeofum.]

Gif ðeof sie gefongen, swelte he deaðe, oððe his lif be his
were man aliese.

13. [Be þam þe heore gewitnesse geleogað.]

Gif hwa beforan biscepe his gewitnesse 7 his wed aleoge,
gebete mid CXX scill.

§ 1. [(Be) hloðe.]

Ðeofas we hatað oð VII men; from VII[8] hloð oð XXXV;
siððan bið here.

14. Se ðe hloþe betygen sie, geswicne[9] se[10] hine be CXX hida
oððe swa bete[11].

15. [Be herge.]

Se ðe hereteama betygen sie, he hine be his wergilde áliese
oððe be his were geswicne[9].

§ 1. Se að sceal bion healf be huslgengum.

§ 2. Deof, siððan he bið on cyninges bende[12], nah he þa
swicne[13].

16. [Be ðeofslæge.]

Se ðe ðeof ofslihð, se[10] mot gecyðan mid aðe[14] þæt he hine
synnigne[15] ofsloge, nalles ða gegildan[16].

17. [Be forstolenum flæsce.]

Se ðe forstolen flæsc findeð 7 gedyrned[17], gif he dear, he mot
mid aðe gecyðan þæt he hit age; se ðe hit ofspyreð, he ah
ðæt meldfeoh.

---

[1] *Gif hwa reaflac 7 nydnæme binnan...rices gedo.* H.
[2] *leod.* H. *leodan.* B.   [3] *gebycge.* H.   [4] *frige.* B.
[5] *o. s. gesylle.* H.   [6] *be his were.* H & B.   [7] B.   [8] *seofon monnum.* H.
[9] *geclensie.* B.   [10] *he.* Bu.   [11] *gebete.* B.   [12] *bendum.* B.
[13] *geswicne.* B.   [14] *his aðe.* H.   [15] *scyldig.* B.   [16] *gyldan.* B.
[17] Schmid's emendation: all MSS *-neð.* *Qui furtiuam carnem inuenerit et*
celatam (occultatam). Quad.

10. If anyone within the borders of our kingdom commits an act of robbery or seizes anything with violence, he shall restore the plunder and pay a fine of 60 shillings.

11. If anyone sells one of his own countrymen[1], bond or free[2], over the sea, even though he be guilty, he shall pay for him with his wergeld[3] and make full atonement with God [for his crime].

12. If a thief is taken[1] he shall die the death, or his life shall be redeemed by the payment of his wergeld.

13. If anyone bears false witness in the presence of a bishop, or repudiates a pledge which he has given in his presence, he shall pay 120 shillings compensation.

§ 1. We use the term 'thieves' if the number of men does not exceed seven, 'band of marauders' for a number between seven and thirty-five. Anything beyond this is a 'raid.'

14. He who is accused of belonging to a band of marauders shall clear himself [of such a charge] with an oath of 120 hides[1], or pay corresponding compensation.

15. He who is accused of taking part in a raid shall redeem himself with his wergeld, or clear himself by [an oath equal in value to] his wergeld.

§ 1. An oath equal in value to half the amount shall be sufficient in the case of communicants[1].

§ 2. A thief shall not have the right of clearing himself by oath after he is in the king's power.

16. He who kills a thief shall be allowed to declare on oath that the man he slew was guilty. The associates[1] of the slain man shall not be allowed to proceed to an oath[2].

17. He who finds meat which has been stolen and hidden shall be allowed, if he dare, to declare on oath that it is his property. He who traces it shall have the reward to which an informer is entitled.

18. [Be ceorliscum ðeofum gefangenum.]
Cierlisc mon gif he óft betygen wære, gif he æt siðestan[1] sie
gefongen, slea mon hond oððe fot [of][2].

19. [Be cinges geneate.]
Cyninges geneat gif his wer bið twelfhund[3] scill., he mot
swerian for syxtig hida, gif he bið huslgengea[4].

20. [Be feorran cumenan men.]
Gif feorcund[5] mon oððe fremde butan wege geond[6] wudu
gonge 7 ne hrieme ne horn blawe, for ðeof he bið to profianne, oððe to sleanne[7] oððe to áliesanne[8].

21. [Be swa ofslagenes mannes were.]
Gif mon ðonne þæs ófslægenan weres bidde, he mot gecyþan,
þæt he hine for ðeof[9] ofsloge, nalles þæs ofslegenan gegildan[10]
ne his hlaford.

§ 1. Gif he hit ðonne dierneð, 7 weorðeð[11] ymb long yppe,
ðonne rymeð he ðam deadan to ðam aðe þæt hine moton
his mægas unsyngian[12].

22. [Be ðam þe mannes geneat stalige.]
Gif ðin geneat stalie 7 losie ðe, gif ðu hæbbe byrgean[13], mana
þone þæs angyldes; gif he næbbe, gyld ðu þæt angylde, 7 ne
sie him no ðy ðingodre[14].

23. [Be ælðeodiges mannes slæge.]
Gif mon elðeodigne ófslea, se cyning ah twædne[15] dǽl weres
þriddan dæl sunu oððe mægas.

§ 1. Gif he ðonne mægleas sie, healf kyninge, healf se gesið.

§ 2. Gif hit ðonne abbod sie oððe abbodesse, dælen on þa
ilcan wisan wið þone kyning.

§ 3. Wealh gafolgelda CXX scill., his sunu C, ðeowne[16] LX,
somhwelcne fiftegum[17]; Weales hyd twelfum[18].

---

[1] Altered to siðmestan. H.   [2] H, B, Ld.   [3] cxx scll'. H.
[4] huslgenga. H, B, Bu.   [5] feorcuman man. B.   [6] geon. B.
[7] oððe to sleanne. om. B.   [8] lesanne. Bu. lysanne. H.   [9] for ðeofðe. Bu.
[10] gyldan. B.   [11] wurð. H. wierðe. Bu.   [12] unscyldigne gedon. H.
[13] borgas. B.   [14] geðingodre. B, H.
[15] twegen dælas þæs weres. B. twegen dæl weres. H.   [16] nedþcowne. Ld.
[17] mid fiftig. H & B.   [18] mid twelfum. H & B.

18[1]. If a commoner, who has often been accused, is at last caught [in the act], his hand or foot shall be cut off.

19. A member of the king's household[1], if his wergeld is 1200 shillings, shall be allowed to swear for 60 hides, if he is a communicant.

20. If a man from afar, or a stranger, travels through a wood off the highway and neither shouts nor blows a horn, he shall be assumed to be a thief, and as such may be either slain or put to ransom.

21. If, however, anyone claims the slain man's wergeld, he [who slew him] shall be allowed to declare that he slew him, presuming him to be a thief; and neither the associates[1] of the slain man, nor his lord, shall be allowed to proceed to an oath.

§ 1. If, however, he [who slew him] conceals the fact, but long afterwards it comes to light—by such conduct he affords an opportunity to the dead man[1] to obtain an oath, by which his relatives may exculpate him.

22. If a member of your household commits a theft and escapes from you, and if you have a surety [for the thief], you shall claim the value of the stolen property from him. If the thief has no surety, you shall pay the value [of the property], but he shall not thereby become immune from punishment.

23. If anyone slays a foreigner[1], the king shall have two-thirds of his wergeld, and his son or relatives one-third.

§ 1. If he has no relatives, the king shall have one-half and the magnate[1] shall have the other.

§ 2. If, however, the person [under whose protection he has been] is an abbot or an abbess, he [or she] shall share [the wergeld] with the king in the same proportion [as the magnate does].

§ 3. [The wergeld of] a Welsh taxpayer [is] 120 shillings[1]; of his son 100 shillings[2]. [The amount to be paid for killing] a slave [is normally] 60 [shillings][3], but in some cases 50 [shillings][4]. A Welshman may compound for a scourging by the payment of 12 shillings[5].

24. Gif witeðeow Engliscmon hine forstalie, hó hine mon 7 ne
gylde his hlaforde.

§ 1. Gif hine mon ofsléa, ne gylde hine mon his mægum,
gif hie hine on XII monðum ne áliesden.

§ 2. Wealh, gif he hafað v hida, he bið syxhynde.

25. [Be cypmanna fare uppe land.]
Gif ciepemon uppe on folce ceapie, do þæt beforan gewit-
nessum[1].

§ 1. Gif ðiefefioh mon æt ciepan befo[2], 7 he hit næbbe beforan
godum weotum geceapod, gecyðe hit be wite, þæt he ne
gewita[3] ne gestala nære, oððe gielde to wite VI 7 XXX
scill.

26. [Be fundenes cildes fostre.]
To fundenes[4] cildes fostre, ðy forman geare geselle VI scill.,[5]
ðy æfterran XII[5], ðy ðriddan XXX[6],[5], siððan be his wlite.

27. [Be ðam þe dearnunge bearn stryneð.]
Se ðe dearnenga bearn gestrieneð 7 gehileð, nah se his deaðes
wer, ac his hlaford 7 se cyning.

28. [Be ðeowes mannes onfenge æt ðyfðe.]
Se [þe][7] ðeof gefehð, [he][7] ah X scill., 7 se cyning ðone ðeof;
7 þa mægas him swerian aðas unfæhða.

§ 1. Gif he ðonne oðierne 7 orige[8] weorðe, þonne bið he wites
scyldig.

§ 2. Gif he onsacan[9] wille, do he ðæt be ðam féo[10] 7 be ðam
wite.

29. [Be ðam þe his sweord alæne oðres ðeowan.]
Gif mon sweordes onlæne oðres esne, 7 he losie, gielde he
hine ðriddan dæle[11]; gif mon spere selle, healfne [dæl hine
gilde][12]; gif he horses onlæne[13], ealne he hine gylde.

---

[1] gewitnesse. H. gewitnysse. B.
[2] forstolen feoh æt ceapmen befo. H. ðeofe mon feoh æt cypmen befo. B.
[3] na gewita. H. ne wita. B.   [4] fundes. E. fundenes. H & B.
[5] 7. H.   [6] xx. H & Quad.   [7] H* & B.   [8] werige. Ld.
[9] ætsacan. B.   [10] were. H*. secundum modum pecunię et witę. Quad.
[11] Gif mon sweordes onlæne oðrum esne 7 hit losige, be ðriddan dæle he hit
gylde. B. Qui gladium prestiterit ad occidendum aliquem (homicidium), si occi-
datur homo etc. Quad.
[12] (dæl.) H.   [13] gif mon horses læne. H. gyf mon hors onlæne. B.

24. If an Englishman [living] in penal slavery absconds, he shall be hanged, and nothing shall be paid to his lord.

   § 1. If he is slain, nothing shall be paid for him to his kinsmen if they have left him unransomed for twelve months.

   § 2. The wergeld of a Welshman who holds five hides of land shall be 600 shillings[1].

25. If a trader [makes his way into] the interior of the country and [proceeds to] traffic, he shall do so before witnesses.

   § 1. If stolen property in the hands of a trader is attached, and he has not bought it in the presence of trustworthy witnesses, he shall declare with an oath equal to the penalty [involved] that he has been neither an accessory nor an accomplice [to the theft], or pay a fine of 36 shillings.

26. For the maintenance of a foundling 6 shillings shall be given in the first year, 12 shillings in the second, 30 shillings in the third, and afterwards [sums] according to his appearance[1].

27. He who begets an illegitimate child and disowns it shall not have the wergeld at its death, but its lord and[1] the king shall [have it].

28. He who captures a thief shall have 10 shillings. The thief shall be given up to the king, and his kinsmen shall swear that they will carry on no vendetta against him[1].

   § 1. If, however, the thief escapes and is lost to sight, then he[1] shall forfeit a fine.

   § 2. If he [the captor] wishes to deny his culpability, he must render an oath equivalent to the value of the stolen goods and the fine.

29. If anyone lends a sword to the servant[1] of another man, and he makes off, he [the lender] shall pay him [the owner of the servant] a third [of his value]. If he provides [the servant] with a spear, [he shall pay the owner] half [the value of the servant]. If he lends [the servant] a horse, he shall pay him [the owner] the full value [of the servant].

46 INE

30. [Be ðam þe cyrlisc¹ man feormige flyman.]
Gif mon cierliscne monnan² fliemanfeorme teo³, be his
agnum were geladige he hine; gif he ne mæge, gielde hine⁴
his agne⁵ were; ⁊ se gesiðmon [eac]⁶ swa be his were.

31. [Be þam þe man wif bycge, ⁊ seo gift wiðstande.]
Gif mon wíf gebyccge⁷, ⁊ sio gyft forð ne cume, agife þæt
feoh ⁊ forgielde ⁊ gebete þam byrgean, swa his borgbryce
sie.

32. [Be Wylisces mannes landhæfene.]
Gif Wilisc mon hæbbe hide londes, his wer bið CXX scill.;
gif he þonne healfes⁸ hæbbe, LXXX scill.; gif he nænig
hæbbe⁹, LX scillinga.

33. [Be cinincges horswale.]
Cyninges horswealh, se ðe him mæge geærendian¹⁰, ðæs
wergield bið¹¹ CC scill.

34. [Be manslihte.]
Se ðe on ðære fore wære, þæt¹² mon monnan¹³ ofsloge, ge-
triewe hine ðæs sleges ⁊ ða fore gebete¹⁴ be ðæs ofslegenan
wergielde¹⁵.

§ 1. Gif his wergield sie CC scill., gebete mid L scill., ⁊ ðy¹⁶
ilcan ryhte do man be ðam deorborenran.

35. [Be ðeofslihte.]
Se ðe ðeof slihð, he mot aðe¹⁷ gecyðan, þæt he hine fleondne¹⁸
for ðeof sloge, ⁊ þæs deadan mægas him swerian unceases¹⁹
áð. Gif he hit þonne dierne, ⁊ sie eft yppe, þonne forgielde
he hine.

§ 1. Gif mon to þam men feoh geteme, ðe his ǽr oðswaren²⁰
hæfde ⁊ eft oðswerian²¹ wille, oðswerige²² be ðam wite ⁊
be ðæs feos weorðe; gif he²³ oðswerian²¹ nylle, gebete
þone mænan að twybote.

---

¹ cyrlis. B. ² mon. H.
³ flymon feormie ⁊ hine mon teo. H. flymanfeormienne teo. B. -inge teo. Ld.
⁴ gilde (he) hine (be). H* & B. ⁵ agenan. H. agenum. B.
⁶ (eac) swa. H* & B. ⁷ bycge. H & B. ⁸ healfe. B.
⁹ næbbe nan land. B. nænig næbbe. H. ¹⁰ geærndian. H. ¹¹ is. H.
¹² þær. B. ¹³ mon. H & B. ¹⁴ oððe foregebete. B. uel emendet. Quad.
¹⁵ were. H. ¹⁶ ða. H & B. ¹⁷ mid aðe. B. ¹⁸ fleonde. H.
¹⁹ unceastes. H. ²⁰ his ætsworen. B. ²¹ ætswerian. B. ²² swerige. B.
²³ þonne. H.

30. If anyone accuses a commoner of harbouring a fugitive he shall clear himself by [an oath] equal in value to his own wergeld. If he cannot do so he shall pay for [harbouring] him [the fugitive], [a sum equal to] his own wergeld. A nobleman also shall pay according to the amount of his own wergeld.

31. If anyone buys a wife and the marriage does not take place, he [the bride's guardian] shall return the bridal price and pay [the bridegroom] as much again, and he shall compensate the trustee of the marriage according to the amount he is entitled to for infraction of his surety[1].

32. If a Welshman possesses a hide of land, his wergeld shall be 120 shillings[1]. If, however, he possesses half a hide, his wergeld shall be 80 shillings; if he possesses no land— 60 shillings.

33. The wergeld of a Welsh horseman[1] who is in the king's service and can ride on his errands shall be 200 shillings.

34. He who has been on a foray, which has resulted in[1] a man being slain, must clear himself of the homicide and pay compensation for his participation in the foray, in proportion to the wergeld of the slain man.

§ 1. If his [the slain man's] wergeld is 200 shillings, he must pay 50 shillings compensation; and in the case of a man of nobler birth the proportion [between the compensation and the wergeld] shall be the same.

35. He who kills a thief shall be allowed to declare with an oath that he whom he killed was a thief trying to escape, and the kinsmen of the dead man shall swear an oath to carry on no vendetta against him. If, however, he keeps it [the homicide] secret, and it afterwards comes to light, then he shall pay for him.

§ 1. If a man is vouched to warranty for livestock and he has previously disowned the transaction and wishes again to disown it, the oath required of him shall be equal to the amount of the fine involved and the value of the stock. If he does not wish to disown the transaction [a second time], he shall pay double compensation[1] for his false oath.

36. [Be ðeofes andfenge, 7 hine swa forlæte.]

Se ðe þeof gefehð¹ oððe him mon gefongenne agifð, 7 he hine
þonne álæte, oððe þa ðiefðe gedierne, forgielde þone þeof
[be]² his were.

§ 1. Gif he ealdormon sie, ðolie his scire, buton him kyning³
arian wille.

37. [Be ceorlisces monnes betogenesse.]

Se cirlisca mon, se ðe oft betygen wære ðiefðe, 7 þonne æt
siðestan [cyrre]⁴ synnigne [mon]⁵ gefó in ceace⁶ oððe elles
æt openre scylde, slea him mon hond⁷ óf oððe fót.

38. [Be ðam ðe rihtgesamhiwan bearn habban.]

Gif ceorl 7 his wif bearn hæbben gemæne, 7 fere se ceorl
forð, hæbbe sio modor hire bearn 7 fede⁸: agife hire mon
VI scill. to fostre, cu on sumera, oxan on wintra⁹; healden
þa mægas þone frumstol, oð ðæt hit gewintred sie.

39. [Be unalyfedum fare fram his laforde.]

Gif hwa fare unáliefed fram his hlaforde¹⁰ oððe on oðre scire
hine bestele, 7 hine mon geahsige¹¹, fare þær he ær wæs 7
geselle¹² his hlaforde¹⁰ LX scill.

40. [Be ceorles worðige.]

Ceorles worðig sceal beon wintres 7 sumeres betyned. Gif
he bið untyned¹³, 7 recð his neahgebures ceap in on his agen
geat, nah he æt þam ceape nan wuht¹⁴: adrife hine¹⁵ ut 7
ðolie [þone]¹⁶ æfwerdlan¹⁷.

41. Borges mon mót oðsacan¹⁸, gif he wát þæt he ryht deð.

42. [Be ðam þæt ceorlas habbað land gemæne 7 gærstunas.]

Gif ceorlas gærstun hæbben gemænne oððe oþer gedálland¹⁹
to tynanne, 7 hæbben sume getyned hiora dæl, sume næbben,
7 etten hiora gemænan æceras oððe gærs, gán þa þonne þe ðæt
geat agan, 7 gebeten²⁰ þam oðrum, þe hiora dǽl getynedne²¹

---

¹ fehð. H.   ² H & B.   ³ se cyning. H.   ⁴ H.   ⁵ H.
⁶ ceace. H & B. E has ceape.   ⁷ handa. B.   ⁸ 7. H*.
⁹ wintran. B.   ¹⁰ laforde. B.   ¹¹ geacsige. B. geaxie. H.
¹² gylde his. B.   ¹³ H & B. -eð. E.   ¹⁴ nan wiht. B.   ¹⁵ hit. H.
¹⁶ H & B.   ¹⁷ æfwyrlan. B. æfwyrdlan. H.   ¹⁸ ætsacan. B, H.
¹⁹ gafolland. H. alias gedalland. H*.   ²⁰ B & H. gebete. E.
²¹ betyned. H.

36. He who captures a thief or has a captured thief given into his custody, and allows him to escape, or suppresses knowledge of the theft, shall pay for the thief according to his wergeld.

§ 1. If he is an *ealdorman*[1] he shall forfeit his 'shire[2],' unless the king is willing to pardon him.

37. If a commoner has often been accused of theft and is at last proved guilty, either in the ordeal[1] or by being caught in the act of committing an offence, his hand or foot shall be struck off.

38. If a husband has a child by his wife and the husband dies, the mother shall have her child and rear it, and [every year] 6 shillings shall be given for its maintenance—a cow[1] in summer and an ox in winter; the relatives shall keep the family home[2] until the child reaches maturity.

39. If anyone moves away without permission from his lord and steals into another district[1], if he is discovered he shall return to where he was before, and give his lord 60 shillings.

40. A commoner's premises shall be fenced both winter and summer. If they are not enclosed, and a beast belonging to his neighbour strays in through the opening he himself has left, he shall have no claim on that beast, [but] he shall drive it out and suffer the damage.

41. It is permissible for one to repudiate bail [that he has given for another], if he knows he is acting justly.

42. If commoners have a common meadow or other—partible—land[1] to fence, and some have fenced their portion and some have not, [and cattle[2] get in] and eat up their common crops[3] or their grass, then those who are responsible for the opening shall go and pay compensation for the damage which has been done to the others, who have enclosed their portion.

A.   4

hæbben, þone æwerdlan¹ þe ðær gedon sie ; abidden² him³
æt þam ceape swylc ryht swylce hit kyn sie.

§ 1. Gif þonne hryðera hwelc⁴ sie þe⁵ hegas brece 7 ga in
gehwær, 7 se hit nolde gehealdan se hit age oððe ne
mæge, nime se hit on his æcere mete⁶ 7 ófslea, 7 nime
se agenfrigea his fel 7⁷ flæsc 7 ðolie þæs oðres.

43. [Be wude bærnete.]

Ðonne mon beam on wuda forbærne, 7 weorðe yppe on þone
ðe hit dyde, gielde he fulwite : geselle⁸ LX scill., forþamþe⁹
fýr bið þeof.

§ 1. Gif mon afelle¹⁰ on wuda wel monega treowa, 7 wyrð
eft¹¹ undierne, forgielde III treowu ælc mid XXX scill.;
ne ðearf he hiora má geldan¹², wære hiora swa fela swa
hiora wære ; forþon sio æsc¹³ bið melda, nalles ðeof.

44. [Be wudu andfenge.]

Gif mon þonne aceorfe an treow, þæt mæge XXX swina
undergestandan¹⁴, 7 wyrð undierne, geselle LX scill.

§ 1. Gafolhwitel sceal bion æt hiwisce VI pæninga weorð¹⁵.

45. [Be Burhbryce.]

Burgbryce mon sceal betan CXX scill. kyninges 7 biscepes,
þær his rice bið ; ealdormonnes LXXX scill. ; cyninges ðegnes
LX scill. ; gesiðcundes monnes landhæbbendes XXXV [scll']¹⁶ ;
7 bi ðon¹⁷ ansacan.

46. [Be staltihlan.]

Ðonne mon monnan¹⁸ betyhð, þæt he ceap forstele oððe
forstolenne gefeormie, þonne sceal he be LX hida onsacan¹⁹
þære þiefðe, gif he aðwyrðe²⁰ bið.

§ 1. Gif ðonne Englisc onstal²¹ ga forð, onsace²² þonne be
twyfealdum ; gif hit ðonne bið Wilisc onstal, ne bið se
að na ðy mara.

§ 2. Ælc mon mot onsacan¹⁹ frymþe²³ 7 werfæhðe, gif he
mæg²⁴ oððe dear²⁵.

---

¹ æfwyrdlan. B, H.   ² abiddon. B.   ³ heom. B & H.   ⁴·gehwilc. H.
⁵ ðæt. H.   ⁶ gemete. H & B.   ⁷ fel 7. om. H, B & Ld.   ⁸ 7 gesylle. H.
⁹ forðonðe. H.   ¹⁰ afylleð. H. afylle. B.   ¹¹ wurð þæt eft. B.
¹² he nan ma gildon. H.   ¹³ seo æx. H. seo eax. B.   ¹⁴ understandan. B.
¹⁵ syx penega wurð. B. peninga wyrð. H.   ¹⁶ H & B.   ¹⁷ bi ð(am) onsacan. B*.
¹⁸ mon. H.   ¹⁹ ætsacan. B.   ²⁰ andwyrde. B.   ²¹ Englisc mon stalað. B.
²² ætsace. B.   ²³ fyrmðe. H, B. fyrmþe 7 wær. Ld.
²⁴ mæge. B. mægg. H.   ²⁵ dearr. B & H.

They [the latter] shall demand from [the owners of] the cattle such amends as are fitting.

§ 1. If, however, any beast breaks hedges and wanders at large within, since its owner will not or cannot keep it under control, he who finds it on his cornland shall take it and kill it. The owner [of the beast] shall take its hide and flesh and suffer the loss of the remainder[1].

43. If anyone destroys a tree in a wood by fire, and it becomes known who did it, he shall pay a full fine. He shall pay 60 shillings, because fire is a thief.

§ 1. If anyone fells a large number of trees in a wood, and it afterwards becomes known, he shall pay 30 shillings for each of three trees. He need not pay for more, however many there may be, because the axe is an informer and not a thief.

44. If, however, anyone cuts down a tree that can shelter thirty swine, and it becomes known, he shall pay 60 shillings.

§ 1. The blanket paid as rent[1] from each ' household[2] ' shall be worth sixpence.

45. 120 shillings compensation shall be paid for breaking into the fortified premises[1] of the king or [those of] a bishop within his sphere of jurisdiction[2]; [for breaking into those] of an *ealdorman* 80 shillings; into those of a king's thegn 60 shillings; into those of a nobleman who holds land[3] 35 shillings. The accusation may be denied by oaths corresponding to these amounts.

46. When one man charges another with stealing cattle, or harbouring stolen cattle, he shall deny [the charge of] theft by [an oath of] 60 hides, if he is allowed to produce an oath[1].

§ 1. If an Englishman brings the accusation, then he shall deny [the charge] by an oath of double [this] value; on the other hand, if the accusation is brought by a Welshman, the [value of] the oath shall not be increased.

§ 2. Every man may clear himself from the charge of harbouring [stolen goods] or of homicide, if he can and dare do so.

4—2

47. Gif mon forstolenne[1] ceap befehð, ne mot hine mon tieman to ðeowum men.

48. [Be witeðeowum mannum.]
Gif hwelc mon bið witeðeow niwan geðeowad, 7 hine mon betyhð[2], þæt he hæbbe ǽr geðiefed[3], ær hine mon geðeowode, þonne ah se teond ane swingellan æt him: bedrife hine to swingum[4] be his ceape.

49. [Be unalefedum mæstenum andfencge.]
Gif mon on his mæstenne unaliefed swín gemete, genime þonne VI scill. weorð wed.
   § 1. Gif hie þonne þær næren[5] oftor þonne æne, geselle scill. se agenfrigea[6] 7 gecyðe, þæt hie þær oftor ne comen[7], be þæs ceapes weorðe.
   § 2. Gif hi ðær tuwa wæren, geselle twegen scill.
   § 3. Gif mon nime æfesne on swynum: æt þryfingrum [spic][8] þæt ðridde, æt twyfingrum þæt feorðe, æt þymelum þæt fifte.

50. [Be gesiðcundes mannes geðinge.]
Gif gesiðcund mon þingað wið cyning oððe wið kyninges ealdormonnan[9] for his inhiwan[10] oððe wið his hlaford for ðeowe oððe for frige, nah he þær nane witerædenne[11], se gesið, forðon[12] he him nolde ær yfles gestieran æt ham.

51. [Be þam þe gesiðcund man fyrde forsitte.]
Gif gesiðcund[13] mon landagende forsitte fierd[14], geselle CXX scill. 7 ðolie his landes; unlandagende LX scill.; cierlisc XXX scill. to fierdwite[15].

52. [Be ðyrnum geþincðe.]
Se ðe diernum geðingum[16] betygen sie, geswicne[17] hine be CXX hida þara geðingea[18] oððe CXX scill. geselle.

53. [Be forstolenes mannes forfenge.]
Gif mon forstolenne man befo æt oþrum, 7 sie sio hond oðcwolen[19], sio[20] hine sealde þam men þe hine mon ætbefeng,

---

[1] forstolene. B & Ld.   [2] betyh. B & Ld.   [3] geþeofad. B, H & Ld.
[4] swinglum. B, H & Ld.   [5] næron. B, H.   [6] agenfriga. B, H.
[7] oftor næron. H.   [8] Addition to B in 16th century.
[9] wið his ealdermon. H.   [10] innhiwum. H.   [11] witerædhdene. B & Ld.
[12] forþonðe. H.   [13] se siðcunde. B. se siþcundman. Ld.   [14] fyrde. B & H.
[15] ðrittig scill' to wite. B.   [16] geðingðum. B.   [17] geladie. H. geclænsie he. B.
[18] ðinga. B.   [19] acwolon. B. acwolen. Ld.   [20] þe. H & B.

47. If a stolen chattel is attached, a slave may not be vouched to warranty[1] for it.

48. If any man, who has recently been reduced to penal slavery, is accused of having committed theft before he was reduced to slavery, the accuser shall have the right to scourge him once; he shall compel him to submit to a scourging by [an oath equivalent to the value of] the goods [stolen from him][1].

49. If anyone finds swine intruding in his mast pasture, he may take security to the value of 6 shillings.

§ 1. If, however, they have not been there more than once, the owner [of the swine] shall pay a shilling and declare [by an oath equivalent to the value of] the pigs[1], that they have not been there before.

§ 2. If they have been there twice, he shall pay 2 shillings.

§ 3. If pannage is paid in pigs[1], every third pig shall be taken when the bacon is three fingers thick, every fourth when the bacon is two fingers thick, and every fifth when it is a thumb thick.

50. If a nobleman comes to terms with the king, or with the king's *ealdorman,* or with his lord, on behalf of his dependants, free or unfree, he, the nobleman, shall not have any portion of the fines, because he has not previously taken care at home[1] to restrain them [his men] from evil doing.

51. If a nobleman who holds land neglects military service[1], he shall pay 120 shillings and forfeit his land; a nobleman who holds no land shall pay 60 shillings; a commoner shall pay a fine of 30 shillings for neglecting military service.

52. He who is accused of making an illicit compact shall clear himself from the charge with [an oath worth] 120 hides, or pay 120 shillings.

53. If a stolen slave is attached [by the law] in the possession of another, and if the man is dead who has sold him to the man in whose possession he is attached, he shall vouch the

tieme þonne þone mon to þæs[1] deadan[2] byrgelse[3], swa oðer
fioh swa hit sie[4], 7 cyðe on þam aðe be LX[5] hida, þæt sio
deade hond hine him sealde; þonne hæfð he þæt wite
afylled mid þy aðe, [6]agife þam agendfrio þone monnan[7].

§ 1. Gif he þonne wite, hwa ðæs deadan ierfe hæbbe, tieme
þonne to þam ierfe[8] 7 bidde ða hond þe þæt ierfe hafað,
þæt he him gedó þone ceap unbeceasne[9] oþþe gecyðe,
þæt se deada[10] næfre þæt ierfe ahte.

54. [Be werfæhðe tyhlan.]

Se þe bið werfæhðe betogen 7 he onsacan[11] wille þæs sleges
mid aðe, þonne sceal bion on þære hyndenne an kyningæðe[12]
be XXX hida, swa be gesiðcundum men swa be cierliscum,
swa hwæþer swa hit sie.

§ 1. Gif hine mon gilt, þonne mot he gesellan on þara hyn-
denna gehwelcere monnan[13] 7 byrnan 7 sweord, on þæt
wergild, gif he ðyrfe.

§ 2. Witeðeowne monnan[14] Wyliscne mon sceal bedrifan be
XII hidum[15] swa ðeowne to swingum[16], Engliscne be
feower 7 XXX hida.

55. [Be eowe wyrðe.]

Ewo bið mid hire giunge[17] sceape scill. weorð oþþæt XIIII[18]
niht ofer Eastran.

56. [Be gehwylces ceapes wyrðe.]

Gif mon hwelcne ceap gebygð 7 he ðonne onfinde[19] him
hwelce[20] unhælo[21] on binnan XXX nihta, þonne weorpe þone[22]
ceap to honda[23]...oððe swerie, þæt he him nan facn on nyste,
þa he hine him sealde.

57. [Be cyrlisces mannes stale.]

Gif ceorl ceap forstilð 7 bireð into his ærne[24], 7[25] befehð
þærinne mon, þonne bið se his dǽl synnig[26] butan þam wife

---

[1] þære. H.   [2] ðæs deadan monnes. H.   [3] byrgenne. H & B.
[4] swa (hweðer swa) hit sy. H* & B.   [5] feortig. B.   [6] 7. H*.
[7] man. H & B.   [8] ðæm yrf. Ld.   [9] unbesacene. H & B.   [10] deade. B.
[11] ætsacan. B & Ld.   [12] B & H. cyningæde. E.   [13] monna. H.   [14] man. H.
[15] hyndum. B.   [16] swincum. B.   [17] geongan. H.   geonge. B.
[18] XII. E.   XIIII. H, B & Quad.   [19] afinde. B.   [20] on hwylce. H.
[21] hwylcne unhæle. B & Ld.   [22] he ðone. H.
[23] þam syllende added in B in 16th century.   [24] huse (vel ærne). H*.
[25] 7 hit. H.   hitt. B*.   [26] scyldig. H, So & Ld.

dead man's grave to warranty[1] for the slave—just as for any other property, whatever it may be—and declare in his oath—[which shall be of the value] of sixty hides—that the dead man sold the slave to him; then he shall have freed himself from the fine by the oath, and he shall give back the slave to [his] owner.

§ 1. If, however, he knows who has succeeded to the estate[1] of the dead man, he shall vouch the estate to warranty, and demand of the man who holds the estate that he shall make [his title to] the chattel[2] incontestable, or declare that the dead man never owned the property.

54. If anyone is accused of homicide and he wishes to deny the deed with an oath, there shall be in the 100 hides[1] one entitled to give a king's oath[2] of 30 hides, both in the case of the noble and the commoner—whichever he may be.

§ 1. If payment is made for the dead man, then he [the slayer] may, if need be[1], include a man[2] [i.e. a slave] and[3] a coat of mail, and[3] a sword[4], in each hundred shillings of the wergeld.

§ 2. A Welshman, who has been reduced to penal slavery, shall be compelled to submit to a scourging, as a slave, by [an oath of] 12 hides; an Englishman, by [an oath of] 34[1] hides.

55. An ewe with her lamb is worth a shilling[1], until a fortnight after Easter.

56. If anyone buys any sort of beast, and then finds any manner of blemish in it within thirty days, he shall send it back to [its former] owner...or [the former owner][1] shall swear that he knew of no blemish in it when he sold it him.

57. If a husband steals a beast and carries it into his house, and it is seized therein, he shall forfeit his share [of the household property[1]]—his wife only being exempt, since she must

anum, forðon hio sceal hire ealdore[1] hieran: gif hio dear
mid aðe gecyðan þæt hio þæs forstolenan ne onbite, nime
hire ðriddan sceat[2].

58. Oxan horn bið x[3] pæninga weorð.

59. Cuuhorn bið twegea[4] pæninga[5]; oxan tægl bið scill.[6] weorð,
cus bið fifa[7]; oxan eage bið v p[eninga][8] weorð, cus bið scill.
weorþ.

§ 1. Mon sceal simle to beregafole agifan æt anum wyrhtan.
VI wæga[9].

60. [Be hyroxan.]
Se ceorl se ðe hæfð[10] oðres geoht[11] ahyrod, gif he hæbbe ealle
on foðre to agifanne, gesceawige mon, agife ealle; gif he
næbbe, agife healf on fodre, healfe on oþrum ceape.

61. [Be ciricsceatte.]
Ciricsceat mon sceal agifan to þam healme 7 to þam heorðe,
þe se mon on bið to middum wintra.

62. [Be þam þe man to ceace fordræfe.]
Ðonne mon bið tyhtlan betygen, 7 hine mon bedrifeð to
ceace[12], nah þonne self nane wiht to gesellanne[13] beforan
ceace[12]: þonne gæð oðer mon, seleð his ceap fore, swa he
þonne geþingian mæge, on ða rædenne, þe he him ga to
honda, oð ðæt he his ceap him geinnian mæge: þonne betyhð hine mon eft oþre siðe 7 bedrifð to ceace[12]: gif hine
forð nele forstandan[14] se ðe him ær ceap foresealde, 7 he
hine þonne forfehð, þolige þonne his ceapes se, ðe he him
ær foresealde.

63. [Be gesiðcundes mannes fare.]
Gif gesiðcund mon fare, þonne mot he habban his gerefan
mid him 7 his smið 7 his cildfestran.

64. [Be ðam þe hafð xx hida.]
Se ðe hæfð xx hida, se sceal tæcnan[15] xII hida gesettes
landes, þonne he faran wille.

---

[1] hlaforde. H.   [2] gescead. H. ðæne ðriddan dæl ðære æhta. B.
[3] feowertyne. B. teon. H. tyn. Ld.   [4] v. H.   [5] p. weorð. H. wurð. B.
[6] IIII peonega wurð. B.   [7] v peninga. H. fif penega wurð. B.
[8] H & B.   [9] pundwæga. H & Ld. pundwega. Quad.   [10] hæbbe. H.
[11] oxan. B.   [12] H & B. ceape. E.   [13] syllanne. B. gesyllanne. H.
[14] gyf he hine nylle forstandan forð. B.   [15] tæcan. H & B.

obey her lord. If she dare declare, with an oath, that she has not tasted the stolen [meat], she shall retain her third of the [household] property.

58. The horn of an ox is worth 10 pence.

59. A cow's horn is worth 2 pence (5 pence, H): the tail of an ox is worth a shilling[1], a cow's tail 5 pence. The eye of an ox is worth 5 pence and a cow's is worth a shilling.

§ 1. For every labourer a man has he shall always pay six weys[1] [of barley] as 'barley-rent.'

60. If a commoner, who has hired another's yoke of oxen, is able to pay all the hire in fodder, care should be taken that he does pay it all [in this form]. If he is not able to do so, he shall pay half [the hire] in fodder, and half in other goods.

61. Church dues shall be paid from the estate[1] and the house where a man is residing at midwinter.

62. If anyone is accused, and trial by ordeal is being forced upon him, and he has nothing to pay with, in order to escape the ordeal; and if another man goes and, on whatsoever terms he may be able to arrange, gives his goods instead, on condition that he [the accused] surrenders himself into his surety's hands, until he can restore to him the goods he has pledged; and then if he is accused a second time, and trial by ordeal is forced upon him, and he who had pledged goods for him will not continue to stand for him, and the accuser arrests him—he who had given [a pledge] for him shall lose his goods.

63. If a nobleman moves his residence he may take with him his reeve, his smith, and his children's nurse[1].

64. He who has [a holding of] 20 hides shall show 12 hides of land under cultivation[1] when he means to leave.

65. [Be tyn hidum.]

Se ðe hæfð x hida[1], se sceal tæcnan[2] VI hida gesettes landes.

66. [Be ðreom hidum.]

Se ðe hæbbe þreora hida[1], tæcne[3] oþres healfes[4].

67. [Be gyrde.]

Gif mon geþingað gyrde landes oþþe mare to rædegafole 7 geereð[5], gif se hlaford him wile þæt land aræran to weorce 7 to gafole, ne þearf he him onfón, gif he him nan botl ne selð[6], 7 þolie þara[7] æcra.

68. [Be gesiðcundes mannes drafe of lande.]

Gif mon gesiðcundne monnan[8] adrife, fordrife þy botle, næs þære setene.

69. [Be sceapes gange.]

Sceap sceal gongan mid his fliese oð midne sumor; oððe gilde þæt flies mid twam pæningum[9].

70. [Be twyhindum were.]

Æt twyhyndum were mon sceal sellan to monbote XXX scill., æt VI hyndum LXXX scill., æt XII hyndum CXX scill.

§ 1. Æt X hidum to fostre X fata hunies, CCC hlafa, XII ambra Wilisc ealað, XXX hluttres, tu eald hriðeru[10] oððe X weðeras, [11]X gees, [12]XX henna, [11]X cesas, amber fulne buteran, V leaxas, XX pundwæga foðres 7 hundteontig æla.

71. [Be wertyhlan.]

Gif mon sie wertyhtlan[13] betogen 7 he hit þonne geondette beforan aðe 7 onsace ǽr, bide[14] mon mid þære witerædenne, oð ðæt se wer gegolden sie.

72. [Be wergildðeofes forefenge.]

Gif mon wergildðeof gefehð, 7 he losige ðy dæge þam monnum ðe hine gefoð, þeah hine mon gefó ymb niht, nah him mon mare æt ðonne[15] fulwite.

---

[1] *hida londes.* H.   [2] *tæcan.* H, B & Ld.   [3] *tæce.* H, B & Ld.
[4] *healfes hides gesettes.* H.   [5] *ereð.* H.   [6] *slihð.* H.   [7] *his.* H.
[8] *mann.* H.   [9] *penegum.* B & H.   [10] *twa ealda ryðeru.* B.
[11] 7. B*.   [12] 7. H*. (7 tyn gees 7 twenti henna 7 tyn cysas.) B*.
[13] *wertyhlan.* B.   [14] *abide.* B, H & Ld.   [15] *ðonon.* B.

65. He who has [a holding of] 10 hides shall show 6 hides under cultivation.

66. He who has [a holding of] 3 hides shall show one hide and a half under cultivation.

67. If a man takes a yard[1] of land or more, at a fixed rent, and ploughs it, [and] if the lord requires service as well as rent, he [the tenant] need not take the land if the lord does not give him a dwelling; but [in that case] he must forfeit the crops[2].

68. If a nobleman is evicted[1], he may be expelled from his house, but not from the cultivated land.

69. A sheep shall retain its fleece until midsummer. [If it is sheared before then], 2 pence shall be paid for the fleece[1].

70. When a wergeld of 200 shillings has to be paid, a compensation of 30 shillings shall be paid to the man's lord[1]; when a wergeld of 600 shillings has to be paid, the compensation shall be 80 shillings; when a wergeld of 1200 shillings has to be paid, the compensation shall be 120 shillings.

   § 1. 10 vats of honey, 300 loaves, 12 ambers[1] of Welsh ale, 30 ambers of clear ale, 2 full-grown cows or 10 wethers, 10 geese, 20 hens, 10 cheeses, a full amber of butter, 5 salmon, 20 pounds of fodder, and 100 eels shall be paid as food rent[2] from every 10 hides.

71. If a man is accused on a charge involving the payment of wergeld[1], and [if], when he is required to give an oath, he confesses the act, which he has previously denied, no proceedings shall be taken to secure the fine until the wergeld has been paid.

72. If a thief, who has forfeited his wergeld[1], is caught, and if he escapes the same day from his captors, yet is [re]captured before the night is passed, no more than the full fine[2] shall be exacted from them[3].

73. [Be anre nihte ðyfte.]

Gif hit bið niht eald þiefð, gebeten þa þone gylt þe hine gefengon, swa hie geþingian mægen wið cyning 7 his gerefan.

74. [Be þam þe ðeowwalh frigne man ofslea.]

Gif ðeowwealh Engliscne monnan[1] ofslihð, þonne sceal se ðe hine ah weorpan hine to honda hlaforde 7 mægum oððe LX scill. gesellan wið his feore.

§ 1. Gif he þonne þone[2] ceap nelle foregesellan[3], þonne mot hine se hlaford gefreogean; gielden siððan his mægas þone wer, gif he mægburg[4] hæbbe freo; gif he næbbe, heden his þa[5] gefan.

§ 2. Ne þearf se frige mid þam þeowan mæg gieldan[6], buton he him wille[7] fæhðe ófaceapian, ne se þeowa mid þy[8] frigean.

75. [Be forstolene ceape.]

Gif mon ceap befehþ forstolenne, 7 sio hond tiemð þonne, sio hine mon ætbefehþ, to[9] oþrum men, gif se mon hine þonne[2] onfon ne wille[10,11] 7 sægþ, þæt he him næfre þæt ne sealde, ac sealde oþer, þonne mot se gecyðan, se ðe hit tiemþ to þære[12] honda, þæt he him nan oðer ne sealde buton þæt ilce.

76. [Be godfæderes oððe godsunes slæhte.]

Gif hwa oðres godsunu slea oððe his godfæder, sie sio mægbot 7 sio manbot gelíc; weaxe sio bot be ðam were, swa ilce swa sio manbot deð þe þam hlaforde sceal.

§ 1. Gif hit þonne kyninges godsunu sie, bete be his were þam cyninge swa ilce[13] swa þære mægþe.

§ 2. Gif he þonne on þone geonbyrde þe hine slog, þonne ætfealle sio bót þæm godfæder[14], swa ilce[13] swa þæt wite þam hlaforde deð.

§ 3. Gif hit biscepsunu sie, sie be healfum þam[15].

[1] mon. H.   man. B & Ld.   [2] om. B.   [3] foresyllan. B.
[4] mægborh. B.   [5] ðonne ða. H.   [6] men gyldan. B.
[7] sylle. B.   [8] þam. H & B.   [9] ðe to. B.   [10] nylle. H & B.
[11] nylle (þæs ceapes). H*.   [12] ðara. B & Ld.   [13] same. H & B*.
[14] godfædere. B.   [15] þam seo bote. H.

73. If a night has elapsed since the theft[1], those who caught him [and allowed him to escape] shall make compensation for their offence, according to such terms as they can arrange with the king and his reeve.

74. If a Welsh slave slays an Englishman, his owner shall hand him over to the dead man's lord and kinsmen, or purchase his life for 60 shillings.

   § 1. If, however, the lord will not pay this price for him, he must liberate him; afterwards his kinsmen must pay the wergeld, if he has a free kindred; if he has not [a free kindred], then his enemies may deal with him.

   § 2. A freeman need not associate himself with a relative who is a slave, unless he wishes to ransom him[1] from a vendetta; nor need a slave associate himself with a relative who is a freeman.

75. If a stolen chattel[1] is attached, and the person in whose possession it is attached vouches it to another man, and if the man will not admit it, and says that he never sold him that, but that he sold him some other thing, he who vouched the man to warranty may declare that he [the witness] sold him none other but that same thing.

76. If anyone slays the godson[1] or the godfather of another, the sum to be paid as compensation to a man who has entered into a relationship of this kind shall be equal to the amount paid to the dead man's lord[2]. The amount of compensation shall increase according to the wergeld, just as is the case with compensation due to a man's lord.

   § 1. If, however, it is the godson of a king [who is slain], a compensation equivalent to the wergeld shall be paid to the king, as well as [the wergeld itself] to the kindred.

   § 2. If, however, he was engaged in a struggle with him who slew him, the godfather shall lose his compensation, just as [in similar circumstances] the lord loses his fine.

   § 3. In the case of the godson of a bishop, [the sum] shall be half [the amount paid for the godson of a king].

ALFRED

[Introd. 49, § 9.] Ic ða Ælfred cyning þás togædere gegaderode, 7 awritan het monege þara þe ure foregengan heoldon, ða[1]
ðe me licodon[2]; 7 manege þara þe me ne licodon ic áwearp mid
minra witena geðeahte, 7 on oðre wisan bebead to healdanne.
Forðam, ic ne dorste geðristlæcan þara minra awuht fela on
gewrit settan, forðam me was uncuð, hwæt þæs ðam lician wolde,
ðe æfter ús wæren. Ac ða ðe[3] ic gemette awðer[4] oððe on Ines
dæge, mines mæges, oððe on Offan Mercna cyninges oððe on
Æþelbryhtes[5], þe ærest fulluhte onfeng on Angelcynne, þa ðe
me ryhtoste[6] ðuhton, ic þa heron gegaderode, 7 þa oðre forlét[7].

Ic ða Ælfred Westseaxna[8] cyning eallum minum witum þas
geeowde, 7 hie ða cwædon, þæt him þæt licode eallum to[9] healdanne.

1. Æt ærestan we lærað, þæt mæst ðearf ís, þæt æghwelc mon
   his að 7 his wed wærlice healde.

   § 1. Gif hwa to hwæðrum þissa genied sie[10] on woh, oððe to
   hlafordsearwe oððe to ængum[11] unryhtum fultume, þæt
   is þonne ryhtre to áleoganne[12] þonne to gelæstanne.

   § 2. [Gif he þonne þæs weddige þe him riht sie to gelæstan-
   ne][13] 7 þæt aleoge, selle mid eaðmedum his wæpn 7 his
   æhta his freondum to gehealdanne 7 beo feowertig nihta
   on carcerne on[14] cyninges tune, ðrowige ðær swa biscep
   him scrife, 7 his mægas[15] hine feden, gif he self mete
   næbbe.

   § 3. Gif he mægas næbbe oððe þone mete næbbe, fede cyninges gerefa hine.

   § 4. Gif hine mon togenedan[16] scyle, 7 he elles nylle, gif hine
   mon gebinde, þolige[17] his wæpna 7 his ierfes.

---

[1] þara. H.   [2] lycedan. H.   [3] þa. H.   [4] aþær. H.
[5] Æþelberhtes. H.   [6] rihtest. H.   [7] forlett. H.
[8] Westseaxena cyng. H.   [9] wel to. H.
[10] to hwæðerum þisra genyd sy. H.   [11] ænigum. H.   [12] aleogenne. H.
[13] So, Ld & H.   [14] æt. H.   [15] magas. H. As frequently.
[16] togenydan. H.   [17] þolie. H.

ALFRED

Now I, King Alfred, have collected these laws, and have given orders for copies to be made of many of those which our predecessors observed and which I myself approved of. But many of those I did not approve of I have annulled, by the advice of my councillors, while [in other cases] I have ordered changes to be introduced[1]. For I have not dared to presume to set down in writing many of my own, for I cannot tell what [innovations of mine] will meet with the approval of our successors. But those which were the most just of the laws I found—whether they dated from the time of Ine my kinsman, or of Offa[2], king of the Mercians, or of Æthelberht, who was the first [king] to be baptised in England—these I have collected while rejecting the others.

I, then, Alfred, King of the West Saxons, have shewn these to all my councillors, and they have declared that it met with the approval of all, that they should be observed.

1. In the first place we enjoin you, as a matter of supreme importance, that every man shall abide carefully by his oath and his pledge.

    § 1. If anyone is wrongfully constrained to promise either of these : to betray his lord or to render aid in an unlawful undertaking, then it is better to be false [to the promise] than to perform it.

    § 2. If, however, he pledges himself to something which it is lawful to carry out and proves false to his pledge, he shall humbly give his weapons and possessions to his friends to keep, and remain 40 days in prison at a royal manor[1], and undergo there whatever [sentence] the bishop prescribes for him; and his relatives shall feed him if he himself has no food.

    § 3. If he has no relatives, and [if he] has not the [necessary] food, the king's reeve shall provide him with it.

    § 4. If he will not submit unless force is used against him, [i.e.] if he has to be bound, he shall forfeit his weapons and his property.

§ 5. Gif hine mon ófslea, licgge he orgilde[1].

§ 6. Gif he út oðfleo ær þam fierste[2], 7 hine mon gefó, sie hé feowertig nihta on carcerne, swa he ǽr sceolde.

§ 7. Gif he losige[3], sie he áfliemed 7 sie ámænsumod[4] óf eallum Cristes ciricum.

§ 8. Gif þær ðonne oþer mennisc borg sie, bete þone borg-bryce[5] swa him ryht wisie, 7 ðone wedbryce swa him his scrift scrife.

2. Gif hwa þara mynsterhama hwelcne for hwelcere scylde gesece[6], þe cyninges[7] feorm[8] to belimpe, oððe oðerne frione hiered[9] þe árwyrðe sie, age he þreora nihta fierst him to gebeorganne, buton he ðingian wille.

§ 1. Gif hine mon[10] on ðam fierste geyflige mid slege oððe mid bende oððe þurh wunde, bete[11] þara æghwelc mid ryhte ðeodscipe[12], ge mid were ge mid wite, 7 þam hiwum hundtwelftig scill. ciricfriðes to bote 7 næbbe[13] his agne forfongen[14].

3. Gif hwa cyninges borg[15] abrece, gebete þone tyht[16] swa him ryht wisie 7 þæs borges bryce mid v pundum mærra[17] pæ-ninga. Ærcebiscepes borges bryce oððe his mundbyrd gebete mid ðrim pundum. Oðres biscepes oððe ealdormonnes borges bryce oððe mundbyrd[18] gebete mid twam pundum.

4. [Be cynincges swicdome.]
Gif hwa ymb cyninges feorh sierwe[19], ðurh hine oððe ðurh wreccena[20] feormunge oððe his manna, sie he his feores scyldig 7 ealles þæs ðe he age.

§ 1. Gif he hine selfne triowan[21] wille, do þæt be cyninges wergelde.

---

[1] lecge orgylde. H.   [2] þan fyrste. H.   [3] þonne losie. H.
[4] sy he amansemod. H.   [5] borhbrice. H.
[6] hwylcne gesece for hwylcere scylde. H.   [7] þe ne c. Ld.
[8] feorme. Ld.   [9] freonne hyred. H.   [10] þonne mon. So.
[11] gebete. Ld.   [12] þeowscipe. H.   [13] hæbbe. So & H.
[14] næbbe h. a. f. omitted in Quad. & Ld.   [15] borh. H.   borh brece. So, Ld.
[16] tihtlan. H.   [17] mærsa. So. mærcna. Ld.   [18] his mundbyrd. H.
[19] syrwie. B & H.   [20] om. þurh. B.   eard added above the line in 16th cent.
[21] treowsian. B.

§ 5. If he is slain, no wergeld shall be paid for him.

§ 6. If he runs away before the term [of imprisonment is completed] and is recaptured, he shall remain in prison 40 days, as he ought to have done at first.

§ 7. If he succeeds in making his escape, he shall be banished, and excommunicated from all the churches of Christ.

§ 8. If, however, other men stand surety for him, he shall pay the compensation [due to them] for violation of bail, as the law directs him, and the compensation for breach of faith, as his confessor prescribes for him.

2. If a man flees, for any manner of offence, to any monastery which is entitled to receive the king's food rent[1], or to any other free community which is endowed[2], for the space of three days he shall have right of asylum, unless he is willing to come to terms [with his enemy][3].

§ 1. If, during that time, anyone injures him by a [mortal] blow, [by putting him in] fetters, or by wounding him, he shall pay compensation for each of these offences in the regular way, both with wergeld and fine, and he shall pay 120 shillings to the community as compensation for violation of the sanctuary of the Church, and he [himself] shall not have the payment due to him from the fugitive[1].

3. If anyone violates the king's protection[1], he shall pay compensation for the crime [to the injured person], as the law directs him, and 5 pounds of pure silver[2] pennies for violation of the king's protection; for violation of the archbishop's protection or guardianship 3 pounds must be paid as compensation; for violation of the protection or the guardianship of any other bishop or of an *ealdorman* 2 pounds must be paid as compensation.

4. If anyone plots against the life of the king, either on his own account, or by harbouring outlaws, or men belonging to [the king] himself[1], he shall forfeit his life and all he possesses.

§ 1. If he wishes to clear himself [from such a charge], he shall do it by an oath equal to the king's wergeld[1].

§ 2. Swa we éac settað be eallum hadum, ge ceorle ge eorle : se ðe ymb[1] his hlafordes fiorh sierwe[2], sie he wið ðone his feores scyldig 7 ealles ðæs ðe he age, oððe be his hlafordes were hine getriowe[3].

5. [Be ciricene friðe.]

Éac we settað æghwelcere cirican[4], ðe biscep gehalgode, ðis frið : gif hie fáhmon[5] geierne oððe geærne, þæt hine seofan nihtum nan mon út ne teo. Gif hit þonne[6] hwa dó, ðonne sie he scyldig cyninges mundbyrde[7] 7 þære cirican friðes mare, gif he ðær mare ófgefo, gif he for hungre libban mæge, buton he self út feohte.

§ 1. Gif hiwan hiora cirican maran[8] þearfe hæbben, healde hine mon on oðrum ærne[9], 7 ðæt næbbe ðon[10] ma dura þonne sio cirice[11].

§ 2. Gewite ðære cirican ealdor, þæt him mon on þam fierste mete ne selle.

§ 3. Gif he self his wæpno[12] his gefan utrǽcan wille, gehealden hi hine xxx nihta 7 hie hine his mǽgum gebodien[13].

§ 4. Eac cirican frið[14] : gif hwelc mon cirican gesece[15] for ðara gylta hwylcum, þara ðe ær geypped nǽre, 7 hine ðær on Godes naman geandette, sie hit healf forgifen.

§ 5. Se ðe stalað on Sunnanniht oððe on Gehhol[16] oððe on Eastron oððe on ðone halgan þunresdæg on[17] Gangdagas: ðara gehwelc[18] we willað sie twybote, swa on Lencten-fæsten.

6. [Be ðam ðe steleð on ciricean.]

Gif hwa on cirican hwæt geðeofige, forgylde þæt angylde, 7

---

[1] ymbe. H.   [2] syrwie. B & H.
[3] getreowie. B. getrewsie. H.   [4] æghwylcere ciricean. B.
[5] Gif gefahmon (ciricean) geyrne. B*. gif fagman hy geyrne. H.
[6] ðonon. B.   [7] mundbryces. So.   [8] mare. B & H.
[9] huse. B & Ld.   [10] þonne. H, So. & Ld.   [11] circe. H.
[12] wæpna. H. -nu So. & Ld.   [13] gebeoden. B. gebodie. H.
[14] is. B. 16th century addition.   [15] geyrne. So.   [16] Geol. B.
[17] 7 on. B & Ld. oððe. So.   [18] æghwylc. H.

§ 2. And likewise with regard to all classes, both commoners and nobles, we ordain: he who plots against the life of his lord shall forfeit his life to him, and all he possesses, or he shall clear himself by [an oath equal to] his lord's wergeld.

5. Further, we grant to every church consecrated by a bishop this right of sanctuary: if a man, attacked by enemies, reaches it either on foot or on horseback, he shall not be dragged out for seven days, if he can live despite hunger, and unless he [himself comes] out [and] fights[1]. If, however, anyone does try to drag him out, he shall forfeit the amount due for violation of the king's guardianship and the fine for violating the sanctuary of the church—and a greater amount if he seizes more than one person in such a place[2].

§ 1. If the community have so great need[1] of their church [that it cannot be used as an asylum], he [the fugitive] shall be kept in another building, and this shall not have more doors than the church.

§ 2. The chief authority of the church shall see to it, that during this time no food is given to him.

§ 3. If he himself is willing to hand over his weapons to his enemies, they shall hold him in their power for thirty days; and they shall send formal notice of his position to his kinsmen.

§ 4. The privilege of sanctuary belonging to a church includes also the following: if anyone takes refuge in a church, because of any offence which up to that time had been kept secret, and there confesses his sin in God's name, half the punishment shall be remitted him.

§ 5. We decree that he who steals on Sunday[1], or during Christmas or Easter, or on Holy Thursday, at Rogation Days[2], shall pay in each case double compensation, just as he must [if he steals] during Lent.

6. If anyone steals anything from a church, he shall pay the value of the article and the fine which is appropriate to the

ðæt wite swa to ðam angylde belimpan[1] wille, 7[2] slea mon
þa hond óf, ðe he hit mid [stæl][3] gedyde.

§ 1. Gif he ða hand lesan[4] wille, 7 him mon ðæt geðafian
wille, gelde swa to his were belimpe.

7. [Be ðam þæt man feohteð on kyninges healle.]
Gif hwa in[5] cyninges healle gefeohte, oððe his wæpn[6] gebrede,
7 hine mon gefó, sie ðæt on cyninges dome, swa deað swa
lif, swa he him forgifan wille.

§ 1. Gif he losige, 7 hine mon eft gefó, forgielde he hine self[7]
á[8] be his weregilde, 7 ðone gylt gebete, swa wer swa
wite, swa he gewyrht[9] age.

8. [Be ðam þe nunnan of mynstre ut alædeð.]
Gif hwa nunnan of mynstere ut álæde butan kyninges lefnesse[10] oððe biscepes, geselle hundtwelftig[11] scill', healf cyninge,
healf biscepe 7 þære cirican hlaforde[12], ðe ðone munuc[13] age.

§ 1. Gif hio leng libbe ðonne se ðe hie utlædde, nage hio his
ierfes owiht[14].

§ 2. Gif hio bearn gestriene, næbbe ðæt ðæs ierfes ðon mare[15]
ðe seo modor.

§ 3. Gif hire bearn mon ofslea, gielde cyninge[16] þara medren-
mæga[17] dǽl; fædrenmægum hiora dǽl mon agife.

9. [Be ðam ðæt man ofslea wif mid cilde.]
Gif mon[18] wíf mid bearne ófslea þonne þæt bearn in hire sie,
forgielde ðone wifman[19] fullan gielde, 7 þæt bearn be ðæs
fædrencnosles were healfan gelde.

§ 1. Á sie þæt wite LX scill', oð ðæt angylde árise to XXX
scill'; siððan hit to ðam árise þæt angylde, siððan sie
þæt wite CXX scill'.

§ 2. Geo[20] was goldðeofe 7 stódðeofe[21] 7 beoðeofe, 7 manig[22]

[1] gelimpan. B.
[2] æt oþrum cerre, addition to B, probably in 12th century.
[3] (stæl) dyde. H*.   [4] alysan. H.   [5] on. H & B.
[6] wæpen. H. wæpne. B.   [7] sylfne. B & H.   [8] Schmid writes selfa.
[9] gewyrhte. B.   [10] leafe. H & B.   [11] hundtwentig. B.
[12] 7 cirican hlaforde. H.   ðære cyrice hlaforde. B.
[13] þone mynecenne. So.   ða nunnan. H, B & Ld.
[14] awuht. H.   heo yrfer nawiht. B.
[15] nage...ðe mare ðe. H.   næbbe...na mare þonne. B.   [16] (þam) cyninge. H*.
[17] medramaga. B.   [18] hwa. H.   [19] heo. H.
[20] Hwilon. B & Ld.   [21] stodðeowe. B.   [22] manegu. H.

value in question, and the hand shall be struck off which committed the theft.

§ 1. If he wishes to redeem his hand, and if it is decided to give him permission to do so, he shall pay [such fine] as is appropriate to his wergeld.

7. If anyone fights or draws his weapon in the king's hall, and [if he] is arrested, it shall be for the king to decide whether he shall be put to death, or permitted to live, in case the king is willing to forgive him[1].

§ 1. If he escapes and is subsequently arrested, he shall pay for himself by his wergeld in every case; and he shall pay compensation for the offence—both wergeld[1] and fine[2]—according to the nature of the outrage he has perpetrated.

8. If anyone takes a nun from a nunnery without the permission of the king or bishop, he shall pay 120 shillings, half to the king, and half to the bishop and[1] the lord of the church, under whose charge the nun[2] is.

§ 1. If she lives longer than he who abducted her, she shall inherit nothing of his property.

§ 2. If she bears a child, it shall inherit no more of the property than its mother.

§ 3. If her child is slain, the share of the wergeld due to the mother's kindred shall be paid to the king, but the father's kindred shall be paid the share due to them.

9. If anyone slays a woman with child, while the child is in her womb, he shall pay the full wergeld for the woman, and half the wergeld for the child, [which shall be] in accordance with the wergeld of the father's kindred.

§ 1. Until the value[1] amounts to 30 shillings, the fine shall be 60 shillings in every case. When the [said] value amounts to this sum, the fine shall be 120 shillings.

§ 2. Formerly the fines to be paid by those who stole gold and horses and bees, and many other fines, were greater than

witu maran ðonne oþru ; nu sint[1] eal gelic buton man-
ðeofe : cxx scill'.

10. [Be hæmedðingum.]
Gif mon hæme mid twelfhyndes monnes wife, hundtwelftig
scill. gebete[2] ðam were ; syxhyndum men[3] hundteontig scill.
gebete ; cierliscum men feowertig[4] scill. gebete[5].

11. Gif[6] mon on cirliscre[7] fæmnan breost gefó, mid v scill. hire
gebete.
 § 1. Gif he hie oferweorpe 7 mid ne gehæme, mid x scill.
 gebete.
 § 2. Gif he mid gehæme, mid lx scill. gebete[8].
 § 3. Gif oðer mon mid hire læge[9] ǽr, sie be healfum ðæm
 ðonne sio bot[10].
 § 4. Gif hie mon teo, geladiege[11] hie be sixtegum hida[12], oððe
 ðolige[13] be healfre þære bote.
 § 5. Gif borenran[14] wifmen ðis gelimpe, weaxe[15] sio bót be
 ðam were.

12. [Be wudebernete, 7 gif man afylled bið on gemænum weorce.]
Gif mon oðres wudu bærneð oððe heaweð unaliefedne, forgielde ælc great treow mid v scill., 7 siððan æghwylc[16], sie
swa fela[17] swa hiora sie[18], mid v pænigum[19] ; 7 xxx scill.[20]
to wite.

13. Gif mon oðerne æt gemænan weorce óffelle[21] ungewealdes,
agife mon þam mægum þæt treow, 7 hi hit hæbben ær xxx
nihta of þam lande[22], oððe him fó se[23] to se ðe ðone wudu age.

14. [Be dumbra manna dædum.]
Gif mon sie dumb oððe déaf geboren, þæt he ne mæge [his][24]
synna[25] onsecggan[26] ne geandettan, bete se fæder his misdæda.

---

[1] *synd.* B & Ld.   [2] *gebete (man).* H* & B.
[3] *monnes wife.* So.   [4] *feowertigum.* B & Ld.
[5] *And þæt sy on cwycæhtum feogodum, 7 mon nænigne mon on þæt ne sylle;*
follows here in Ld instead of in cap. 18, § 1.   [6] *Eft gif.* B.
[7] *ceorliscne.* B.   [8] *hit gebete.* H.   [9] *gelæge.* H.   [10] *bote.* H.
[11] *gehladige.* B. *geladige.* H.   [12] *hidum.* B.   [13] *ðolie.* B, H.
[14] *æþelborenran.* So & Ld. *bettborenran.* H. *æðel.* 16th century addition
to B.   [15] *wexe.* B.   [16] *ælc.* H.   [17] *feola.* B.
[18] *swa monig swa þær sy.* H.   [19] *penegum.* B. *peningum.* H.
[20] *id est half pund.* 12th century addition to B.   [21] *offealle.* B, H.
[22] *lande don.* H.   [23] om. H, B, Ld & So.   [24] B, Ld.
[25] *synne.* H.   [26] *ætsacan.* B.

the rest. Now all fines, with the exception of that for stealing men, are alike—120 shillings.

10. If anyone lies with the wife of a man whose wergeld is 1200 shillings, he shall pay 120 shillings compensation to the husband; to a husband whose wergeld is 600 shillings, he shall pay 100 shillings compensation; to a commoner he shall pay 40 shillings compensation [for a similar offence].

11. If anyone seizes by the breast a young woman belonging to the commons, he shall pay her 5 shillings compensation.

§ 1. If he throws her down but does not lie with her, he shall pay [her] 10 shillings compensation.

§ 2. If he lies with her, he shall pay [her][1] 60 shillings[2] compensation.

§ 3. If another man has previously lain with her, then the compensation shall be half this [amount].

§ 4. If she is accused [of having previously lain with a man], she shall clear herself by [an oath of] 60 hides, or lose half the compensation due to her.

§ 5. If this [outrage] is done to a woman of higher birth[1], the compensation to be paid shall increase according to the wergeld.

12. If one man burns or fells the trees of another, without permission [to do so], he shall pay 5 shillings for each big tree, and 5 pence for each of the rest, however many there may be; and [he shall pay] 30 shillings as a fine[1].

13. If one man kills another unintentionally, [by allowing a tree to fall on him] while they are engaged on a common task, the tree shall be given to the [dead man's] kindred, and they shall remove it within 30 days from the locality. Otherwise, it shall be taken by him who owns the wood.

14. If anyone is born dumb or[1] deaf, so that he can neither deny nor confess his wrongdoings, his father shall pay compensation for his misdeeds.

15. [Be ðam þæt man toforan bisceope feohteð.]
Gif mon beforan ærcebiscepe[1] gefeohte oððe wæpne ge-
bregde[2], mid L scill. 7 hundteontegum gebete; gif beforan
oðrum biscepe[3] oððe ealdormen ðis gelimpe, mid hundteontegum scill. gebete.

16. [Be ðam gif man of myran folan adrifþ oððe cucealf.]
Gif mon cu oððe stodmyran[4] forstele 7 folan oððe cealf
ófadrife[5], forgelde mid scill.[6] 7 þa moder be hiora weorðe.

17. [Ðe oðrum his unmagum ætfæsteð.]
Gif hwa oðrum his unmagan oðfæste, 7 he hine on ðære
fæstinge forferie, getriowe[7] hine facnes se ðe hine fede, gif
hine hwa hwelces teo.

18. [Be nunnena andfencgum.]
Gif hwa nunnan mid hæmeðþinge[8] oððe on hire hrægl oððe
on hire breost butan hire leafe gefó, sie hit twybete[9] swa
we ær be[10] læwdum men[11] fundon.
   § 1. Gif beweddodu[12] fæmne hie forlicgge, gif hio sie cirlisc,
   mid LX scill. gebete þam byrgean[13], 7 þæt sie on cwicæhtum feogodum, 7 mon nænigne[14] mon on ðæt ne selle.
   § 2. Gif hio[15] sie syxhyndu, hundteontig scill. geselle[16] þam
   byrgean[17].
   § 3. Gif hio sie twelfhyndu, CXX scill. gebete þam[18] byrgean[17].

19. [Be þam þe heore wepna lenað to manslihte.]
Gif hwa his wæpnes oðrum onlæne[19], þæt he mon mid ófslea,
hie moton hie gesomnian gif hie willað, to þam were.
   § 1. Gif hi hie ne gesamnien[20], gielde se ðæs wæpnes onlah[21]
   þæs weres ðriddan dæl 7 þæs wites ðriddan dæl.
   § 2. Gif he hine triewan[22] wille, þæt he to ðære læne[23] facn
   ne wiste[24], þæt he mot.

---

[1] *ercebisceope.* B. *ærcebiscope.* H.   [2] *gebrede.* B & H.
[3] *bisceope.* B. *biscope.* H.   [4] *stodmære.* B.   [5] *ofadrifeð.* H.
[6] *sixtig.* B. Underlined and *feowertigum* written above it in 16th century.
feowrtigum. Ld.   [7] *getreowige.* B. *getreowsie.* H.
[8] *hæmedþinge.* B, H & So.   [9] *twybote.* H. *twibote.* B.
[10] *anfandlice be l.* H.   [11] *monnum.* H.   [12] *beweddo.* B. *beweddod.* H.
[13] *þe hit gebyrige.* H & B.   [14] *næningne.* B.   [15] *hio þonne.* So.
[16] *gebete.* H.   [17] *þe hit gebyrie.* H. *to gebyrian.* B.   [18] *ðam ðe.* B.
[19] *læne.* H & B.   [20] *ges. nellen.* H.   [21] *onlænde.* B & Ld.   [22] *triwian.* B.
[23] *to ðære fore 7 t. ð. l.* H.   [24] *nyste.* H, B & Ld.

15. If anyone fights, or draws his weapon in the presence of the archbishop, he shall pay 150 shillings compensation; if this happens in the presence of another bishop or of an *ealdorman,* he shall pay 100 shillings compensation.

16. If anyone steals a cow or a broodmare, and drives off a foal or a calf, he shall pay for the latter a shilling, and for the mothers according to their value.

17. If anyone entrusts a [child or other] helpless person[1] who is dependent on him to another, and the person accepting the charge causes the death of the person committed to him, he who nurtured him shall clear himself of criminal intention, if anyone prefers such an accusation against him.

18. If anyone lustfully seizes a nun, either by her clothes or by her breast, without her permission, he shall pay as compensation twice the sum we have fixed in the case of a woman belonging to the laity.

   § 1. If a young woman who is betrothed commits fornication, she shall pay compensation to the amount of 60 shillings to the surety[1] [of the marriage], if she is a commoner. This sum shall be [paid] in livestock, cattle[2] being the property tendered, and no slave shall be given in such a payment.

   § 2. If her wergeld is 600 shillings, she shall pay 100 shillings to the surety [of the marriage].

   § 3. If her wergeld is 1200 shillings, she shall pay 120 shillings to the surety [of the marriage].

19. If anyone lends a weapon of his to another [man], for the purpose of committing murder with it, they[1] may, if they are willing to, combine to pay the wergeld.

   § 1. If they do not combine [voluntarily], he who lent the weapon shall pay one-third of the wergeld and one-third of the fine.

   § 2. If he[1] wishes to clear himself, [by swearing] he was cognisant of no criminal intention when he made the loan, he may do so.

§ 3. Gif sweordhwita oðres monnes wæpn to feormunge onfó[1],
oððe smið monnes andweorc, hie hit gesund begen agifan,
swa hit hwæðer hiora ǽr onfenge[2], buton hiora hwæðer
ǽr þingode, þæt he hit angylde healdan ne ðorfte.

20. [Be þam þe munecan heore feoh befæstað.]
Gif mon oðres monnes munuce feoh oðfæste[3] butan[4] ðæs
munuces hlafordes[5] lefnesse[6], 7 hit him losige, þolige his
se ðe hit ǽr ahte.

21. [Be preosta gefeohte.]
Gif preost oðerne mon ófslea, weorpe mon to handa 7 eall
ðæt he him[7] hames bohte[8], 7 hine biscep onhadige, þonne
hine mon of ðam mynstre agife, buton se hlaford þone wer
forðingian wille.

22. [Be cynincges gerefan ðyfðe.]
Gif mon on folces gemote cyninges gerefan geyppe eofot[9], 7
his eft geswican wille, gestæle on ryhtran hand, gif he mæge;
gif he ne mæge, ðolie[10] his angyldes[11].

23. [Be hundes slite.]
Gif hund mon toslite oððe abite, æt forman misdæde geselle
VI scill.; gif he him mete selle, æt æfteran[12] cerre XII scill.,
æt ðriddan[13] XXX scill.
§ 1. Gif æt ðissa[14] misdæda hwelcere se hund losige, ga ðeos
bót hwæðre[15] forð.
§ 2. Gif se hund ma misdæda gewyrce, 7 he hine hæbbe, bete
be fullan were swa dolgbote swa[16] he wyrce[17].

24. [Be nytena misdædum.]
Gif neat[18] mon gewundige, weorpe ðæt neat to honda oððe
foreðingie.

25. [Be ceorles mennenes nydhemede.]
Gif mon ceorles mennen to nedhæmde geðreatað, mid V scill.
gebete þam ceorle; 7 LX scill. to wite.
§ 1. Gif ðeowmon þeowne to nedhæmde[19] genede, bete mid
his eowende[20].

---

[1] underfo. B.   [2] underfenge. B.   [3] befæste. B & Ld.
[4] buton (his) hlafordes leafe feoh befæste. H*.
[5] Underlined in B, and aldres written above, later.   [6] hleafe. B.
[7] mid him. H, B, Ld.   [8] brohte. H & B.   [9] ðeofðe. B. geeofot yppe. H.
[10] ðolige. B & H.   [11] and fo to ðam wite. H.   [12] ðam oðran. B.   [13] æt ð. cirre. H.
[14] ðisra. B.   [15] ðeah. h. B & Ld.   [16] oþþe swa hwæt he gewyrce. Ld.
[17] swa dolhbote swa he gewyrce. H & B.   [18] monnes neat. H.
[19] nydhæmede. B & H, as frequently.   [20] hyde. alias eowede in the margin. H.

§ 3. If a sword-furbisher receives a weapon or a smith receives a tool belonging to another man in order to refurbish it, in either case the article shall be returned in as good condition as that in which it has been received[1], unless it has been stipulated that there shall be no liability on the part of the said furbisher for damage done to it.

20. If property is entrusted to a monk in the service of another man without the permission of the monk's lord, and he loses it, its former owner shall bear the loss.

21. If a priest slays another man, he and all the share of the monastic property which he has bought for himself shall be given up; and the bishop shall unfrock him when he is ejected from the monastery and given up, unless the lord [of the monastery] is willing to answer for the wergeld [of the slain man][1].

22. If anyone makes an accusation [against another] at a public meeting, in the presence of the king's reeve, and afterwards wishes to withdraw it, he shall prefer the charge, if he can, against a more likely person. If he cannot he shall lose the value due to him[1].

23. If a dog tears or bites[1] a man, 6 shillings shall be paid for the first offence. If its owner continues to keep[2] it, 12 shillings shall be paid for the second offence, and 30 shillings for the third.
   § 1. If the dog disappears after committing any of these offences, this compensation must nevertheless be paid.
   § 2. If the dog commits more offences and he [its master] still keeps it, he must pay compensation for whatsoever wounds may be inflicted, according[1] to the amount of the [injured man's] full wergeld.

24. If a beast injures a man, [its owner] must hand over the beast [to the injured man], or come to terms [with him].

25. If anyone rapes the slave of a commoner, he shall pay 5 shillings to the commoner, and a fine of 60 shillings[1].
   § 1. If a slave rapes a slave, castration shall be required as compensation.

26. [Be twyhyndum men æt hloðslihte.]
Gif mon twyhyndne mon unsynnigne mid hloðe ofslea, gielde
se ðæs¹ sleges andetta sie wer 7 wite; 7 æghwelc² mon ðe
on siðe³ wære geselle xxx scill. to hloðbote.

27. [Be sixhyndum men.]
Gif hit sie syxhynde mon, ælc mon [geselle]⁴ to hloðbote
lx⁵ scill., 7 se slaga wer⁶ 7 fulwite⁷.

28. [Be twylfhendum men.]
Gif he sie twelfhynde⁸, ælc hiora hundtwelftig scill. [geselle,
7]⁹ se¹⁰ slaga wer 7 wite.

§ 1. Gif hloð ðis gedó 7 eft oðswerian¹¹ wille, tio hie¹² ealle;
7 þonne ealle forgielden þone wer gemænum¹³ hondum
7 ealle án wite, swa to ðam were belimpe¹⁴.

29. [Be ungewintredes wifmannes slæge.]
Gif mon ungewintrædne wifmon to niedhæmde geðreatige,
sie ðæt swa ðæs gewintredan monnes¹⁵ bot.

30. Gif fædrenmæga mægleas¹⁶ mon gefeohte 7 mon ófslea¹⁷, 7
þonne gif¹⁸ medrenmægas hæbbe, gielden ða¹⁹ þæs weres
ðriddan dæl, [ðriddan dæl þa gegyldan, for ðriddan dæl]²⁰
he fleo.

§ 1. Gif he medrenmægas²¹ nage²², gielden þa gegildan²³
healfne, for²⁴ healfne he fleo.

31. Gif mon swa geradne mon ofslea, gif he mægas nage, gielde
mon healfne²⁵ [were þam]²⁶ cyninge, healfne þam gegildan.

32. Gif mon folcleasunge gewyrce, 7 hio on hine geresp²⁷ weorðe,
mid nanum leohtran ðinge gebete þonne him mon aceorfe
þa tungon óf, þæt hie mon na undeorran weorðe²⁸ moste
lesan²⁹, ðonne hie mon be þam were geeahtige³⁰.

---

¹ se (ðe) þæs. H*. ² ælc. B. æghwylc þara. H. ³ ðæm syþe. H.
⁴ So. gesylle. Ld. ⁵ feowertig. B. ⁶ were. B.
⁷ fullwite. H. ⁸ Ld. adds man.
⁹ hundtwelftigum scill' geselle [h. sc. agyfe. Ld] 7 se slaga were. So, Ld.
¹⁰ ond se. H. ¹¹ ætswerian. B. ¹² teo (man). H*.
¹³ gemæne. B. ¹⁴ belimbe. B. Altered later to tobelimbe.
¹⁵ wifmonnes. So. ¹⁶ mæigleas. B. ¹⁷ on gefeohte mon of. So.
¹⁸ gif he. H. ¹⁹ hio. So. ²⁰ H. ²¹ medrenmages. H.
²² næbbe. B. ²³ gegyldan. B. gegilden. H. ²⁴ ond for. H.
²⁵ healfe. B. ²⁶ H*. ²⁷ geræf. Ld, B & H. ²⁸ wurde. B.
²⁹ alysan. H. ³⁰ geehtige. B.

26. If one of a band of marauders[1] slays an unoffending man, whose wergeld is 200 shillings, he who acknowledges the blow shall pay the wergeld and the fine; and everyone engaged in the affair shall pay[2] 30 shillings compensation for belonging to such a band.

27. If the slain man's wergeld is 600 shillings, each man shall pay 60 shillings for belonging to such a band; and the homicide [shall pay] the wergeld and the full fine[1].

28. If the wergeld of the slain man is 1200 shillings, each of them [shall pay] 120 shillings; and the homicide [shall pay] the wergeld and the fine.

§ 1. If a band of marauders acts thus and afterwards wishes[1] to deny it, they shall all be accused, and then all collectively shall pay the wergeld and one fine—whichever is appropriate to the wergeld.

29. If anyone rapes a girl who is not of age, the same compensation shall be paid to her as is paid to an adult.

30. If anyone who has no paternal relatives fights and kills a man, his maternal relatives, if he has any, shall pay one-third of the wergeld and his associates[1] shall pay one-third. In default of payment of the [remaining] third, he shall be held personally responsible[2].

§ 1. If he has no maternal relatives, his associates shall pay half [the wergeld], and in default of payment of the [other] half, he shall be held personally responsible.

31. If a man in this position is slain—if he has no relatives—half the wergeld shall be paid to the king, and half to his associates.

32. If anyone utters a public slander, and it is proved against him, he shall make amends on no lighter terms than the excision of his tongue, [with the provision that] it shall not be ransomed at a cheaper price than [its value[1]], estimated according to the [man's] wergeld.

33. [Be godborhgum.]

Gif hwa oðerne godborges oncunne 7 tion[1] wille, þæt he hwelcne ne gelæste ðara ðe he him gesealde, agife þone foreað on feower ciricum, 7 se oðer, gif he hine treowan[2] wille, in[3] XII ciricum dó he ðæt.

34. [Be cypmannum.]

Éac is ciepemonnum gereht: ða[4] men ðe hie up mid him læden[5], gebrengen[6] beforan kyninges gerefan on folcgemote, 7 gerecce[7] hu manige[8] þara sien; 7 hie nimen þa men mid[9] him þe hie mægen[10] eft to folcgemote to ryhte[11] brengan; 7 ðonne him ðearf sie ma manna[12] úp mid him to habbanne on hiora fore, gecyðe symle[13], swa óft swa him ðearf sie, in[14] gemotes gewitnesse cyninges gerefan.

35. [Be ceorlisces mannes bindelan.]

Gif mon cierliscne mon gebinde unsynnigne[15], gebete mid X scill.

§ 1. Gif hine mon beswinge, mid XX scill. gebete.

§ 2. Gif he hine on hengenne alecgge[16], mid XXX scill. gebete.

§ 3. Gif he hine on bismor to homolan bescire, mid X scill. gebete.

§ 4. Gif he hine to preoste bescire unbundenne, mid XXX scill. gebete.

§ 5. Gif he ðone beard ófascire, mid XX scill. gebete.

§ 6. Gif he hine gebinde 7 þonne to preoste bescire, mid LX[17] scill. gebete.

36. [Be speres gymeleaste.]

Eac is funden: gif mon hafað[18] spere ofer eaxle[19], 7 hine mon on asnaseð[20], gielde þone wer butan wite.

§ 1. Gif beforan eagum asnase[21], gielde þone wer; gif hine

---

[1] *teon.* B & H.　　[2] *treowian.* B, Ld.　　[3] *innan.* B. *on.* H.
[4] *þæt ða.* B.　　[5] *lædan.* B & H. Altered to *lædað.* B.
[6] *gebringe.* H. *-an.* B.　　[7] *gerecca.* B.　　[8] *monie.* B.　　[9] *up mid.* H.
[10] *magon.* H & B.　　[11] om. *to ryhte.* B.　　[12] om. *ma manna.* B.
[13] *symble.* B.　　[14] *on.* H.　　[15] *unscyldigne.* B & Ld.
[16] *gebringe.* B, H.　　[17] *feowertig* written above in 16th century. B.
[18] *hæfð.* B.　　[19] *eaxlen.* H.　　[20] *onsnæseð.* B. *on asnæseð.* H.
[21] om. B. *asnæse.* H.

33. If one man charges another respecting a solemn pledge[1] given under the sanction of God, and wishes to accuse him of neglecting to perform any [one] of the promises which he has made to him, he shall pronounce the oath [of accusation] in four churches, and the other [the defendant], if he wishes to clear himself, shall do so[2] in twelve churches.

34. Further, with regard to traders, it is decreed: they shall bring before the king's reeve, at a public meeting, the men they are taking with them up into the country, and declare how many of them there are; and they shall take with them [only] such men as they can bring to justice again, at a public meeting. And when they need to have more men with them on their journey, a similar declaration shall always be made to the king's reeve, before the assembled company, as often as need arises.

35. If anyone lays bonds on an unoffending commoner, he shall pay 10 shillings compensation.

§ 1. If anyone scourges him, he shall pay 20 shillings compensation.

§ 2. If he places him in the stocks[1], he shall pay 30 shillings compensation.

§ 3. If he cuts his hair to insult him, in such a way as to spoil his appearance, he shall pay 10 shillings compensation.

§ 4. If he cuts his hair after the fashion of a priest's[1] without binding him, he shall pay 30 shillings compensation.

§ 5. If he cuts off his beard, he shall pay 20[1] shillings compensation.

§ 6. If he lays bonds on him, and then cuts his hair after the fashion of a priest's, he shall pay 60[1] shillings compensation.

36. It is further enacted: if a man has a spear over his shoulder, and anyone is transfixed thereon, he shall pay the wergeld without the fine.

§ 1. If [the man] is transfixed before his[1] eyes, he shall pay

mon tio gewealdes on ðære dæde, getriowe[1] hine be þam
wite 7 mid ðy[2] þæt wite afelle[3],

§ 2. gif[4] se ord sie ufor[5] [þreo fingre][6] þonne hindeweard
sceaft. Gif[7] hie sien bu gelic[8], ord 7 hindeweard sceaft,
þæt sie butan pleo.

37. [Be boldgetale.]
Gif mon wille of boldgetale in oðer boldgetæl hlaford secan,
do ðæt mid ðæs[9] ealdormonnes gewitnesse, þe he ær in[10] his
scire folgode.

§ 1. Gif he hit butan his gewitnesse do, geselle se þe hine
to men feormie CXX scill. to wite : dæle he hwæðre ðæt,
healf cyninge[11] in[12] ða scire ðe he ǽr folgode, [7][13] healf
in þa ðe he oncymð[14].

§ 2. Gif he hwæt yfla[15] gedon hæbbe[16] ðær he ær wæs, bete
ðæt se ðe hine ðonne[17] to men onfo[18], 7 [sylle þam][19] cyninge CXX scill. to wite.

38. [Be ðam ðe beforan aldormen on gemote feohte.]
Gif mon beforan cyninges ealdormen on gemote gefeohte[20],
bete wer 7 wite, swa hit ryht sie, 7 beforan þam CXX scill.
ðam ealdormen to wite.

§ 1. Gif he folcgemot[21] mid wæpnes bryde árære, ðam ealdormen hundtwelftig scill. to wite[22].

§ 2. Gif[23] ðises hwæt beforan cyninges ealdormonnes gingran
gelimpe oððe cyninges preoste, XXX scill. to wite.

39. [Be cyrlisces monnes flettegefeohte.]
Gif hwa on cierlisces monnes flette gefeohte, mid syx scill.
gebete ðam ceorle.

§ 1. Gif he wæpne gebrede 7 no[24] feohte, sie be healfum ðam.

§ 2. Gif syxhyndum[25] ðissa hwæðer gelimpe, ðriefealdlice

---

[1] *getreowsie.* B.   *getrywe.* H.   [2] *mid ðam.* B.   [3] *afylle.* B, H.
[4] *7 þis beo, gif.* B.   [5] *ufon.* H*.   [6] H (cf. So, Ld).   [7] (*Ac*) *gyf.* B*.
[8] *buta gelice.* B.   [9] om. B.   [10] *on.* H.   [11] (*þam*) *cyninge.* H*.
[12] *on.* H.   [13] H*.   [14] (*þonne*) *oncymð.* H*.   [15] (*to*) *yfele.* H*, B.
[16] *hæfð.* H, B.   [17] *ðonnon.* B.   [18] *underfo.* B.   [19] So.
[20] *feohtaþ.* B.   [21] *folces gemot.* H.   [22] om. *to wite.* H.
[23] *Eft. Gyf.* B.   [24] *ne.* B, H.   [25] *syxhyndum men.* H.

the wergeld; and if he is accused of deliberate intention in the act, he shall clear himself with an oath equal to the fine, and thereby dismiss the claim for the fine,

§ 2. supposing the point to be higher than the [other] end of the shaft, by the width of three fingers[1]. If they are both on a level, the point and the [other] end of the shaft, the man with the spear shall not be regarded as responsible for causing danger[2].

37. If a man wishes [to go] from one district[1], to seek service[2] in another, he shall do it with the cognisance of the *ealdorman*, to whose jurisdiction he has previously been subject.

§ 1. If he does so without his cognisance, he who takes him into his employment shall pay a fine of 120 shillings; but he shall divide the payment, [paying] half to the king[1] in the district where the man has been residing[2], and half in that to which he has come.

§ 2. If he has committed any manner of offence in the place where he has been [residing], he who now takes him into his employment shall pay compensation for it, and a fine of 120 shillings to the king.

38. If anyone fights at a meeting in the presence of an *ealdorman* of the king, he shall pay as compensation [such] wergeld and fine as is due, but previous to this [he shall pay] a fine of 120 shillings to the *ealdorman*.

§ 1. If he disturbs the meeting by drawing his weapon, he shall pay a fine of 120 shillings to the *ealdorman*.

§ 2. If anything of this kind takes place in the presence of an official subordinate[1] to an *ealdorman* of the king, [or in the presence of] a king's priest, he shall pay a fine of 30 shillings.

39. If anyone fights in the house of a commoner, he shall pay the commoner 6 shillings[1] compensation.

§ 1. If he draws his weapon, but does not fight, the [compensation] shall be half this sum.

§ 2. If either of these [offences] occurs in the house of a man whose wergeld is 600 shillings, the compensation shall

[arise be ðære cierliscan bote, twelfhyndum men twy-
fealdlice][1] be þæs syxhyndan[2] bote.

40. [Be burhbryce.]
Cyninges burgbryce[3] við CXX scill., ærcebiscepes hundni-
gontig scill., oðres biscepes 7 ealdormonnes LX scill., twelfhyndes monnes XXX scill., syxhyndes monnes XV scill.;
ceorles edorbryce V scill.[4]

§ 1. Gif ðisses hwæt gelimpe, ðenden[5] fyrd ute sie, oððe in
lenctenfæsten, hit sie twybote.

§ 2. Gif mon in[6] lenctenne halig ryht[7] in[8] folce butan leafe
alecgge, gebete mid CXX scill.

41. [Be boclande...[9].]
Se mon se ðe bocland hæbbe, 7 him his mægas læfden[10],
þonne setton we, þæt he hit ne moste[11] sellan of his mæg-
burge, gif þær við gewrit oððe gewitnes[12], ðæt hit ðara manna
forbod[13] wære þe hit on fruman gestríndon 7 þara þe hit him
sealdon, þæt he swa ne mote; 7 þæt þonne on cyninges 7[14]
on biscopes gewitnesse gerecce beforan his mægum.

42. Eac we beodað; se mon se ðe his gefan hamsittendne[15] wite,
þæt he ne feohte, ær ðam he[16] him ryhtes bidde.

§ 1. Gif he mægnes hæbbe, þæt he his gefán beride 7 inne[17]
besitte, gehealde hine VII niht inne 7 hine[18] ón ne feohte,
gif he inne geðolian wille; 7 þonne ymb VII niht, gif he
wille on[19] hand gan 7 [his][20] wæpenu sellan, gehealde
hine XXX nihta gesundne 7 hine his mægum gebodie[21]
7 his friondum.

§ 2. Gif he ðonne cirican geierne, sie ðonne be ðære cirican
are, swa we ær bufan cwædon.

---

[1] H, B, Ld.   [2] syxhyndum. B.   [3] burh-bryce. B. burhbrice. H.
[4] ceorles eoderbryce fif scill. added to B in 16th century.
[5] ðonne. H, B.   [6] on. H, B.   [7] haligrift. Ld.   [8] on. H.
[9] A page is here missing from B, which begins again at cap. 43 with the
words dagas to eastron etc.   [10] 7 him (þonne) his yldran læfdon. H*.
[11] mot. H.   [12] gewitnesse. H.   [13] fodbod. H.   [14] ge. H.
[15] hamsittende. . H. & Ld.   [16] ðam ðe he. H. ær þon he. Ld.
[17] 7 hine inne. H.   [18] him. H.   [19] ond. H.
[20] H*.   [21] his freondum 7 his magum bebeode. H.

be increased to three times that due to a commoner; if in the house of a man whose wergeld is 1200 shillings, [it shall be increased] to twice the compensation due to a man whose wergeld is 600 shillings.

40. The fine for breaking into the fortified premises[1] of the king shall be 120 shillings; into those of an archbishop, 90 shillings; into those of another bishop or of an *ealdorman*, 60 shillings; into those of a man whose wergeld is 1200 shillings, 30 shillings; into those of a man whose wergeld is 600 shillings, 15 shillings. The fine for breaking through a commoner's fence shall be 5 shillings.

§ 1. If any of these offences occur while the army is in the field, or during the fast of Lent, the compensation [to be paid] shall be double [the above].

§ 2. If anyone, without permission, publicly disregards the laws of the Church[1] during Lent, he shall pay 120 shillings compensation.

41. We have further established, that a man who holds land by title-deed[1], which his kinsmen have left him, shall not be allowed to give it out of his kindred, if there is documentary or [other] evidence that the power to do so is forbidden him by the men who first acquired it, or by those who gave it to him. [And he who contests such an alienation] shall make a declaration to this effect in the presence of his kindred, with the king and bishop as witnesses.

42. Also we enjoin, that a man who knows his adversary to be residing at home, shall not have recourse to violence before demanding justice of him.

§ 1. If he has power enough to surround his adversary and besiege him in his house, he shall keep him therein seven days, but he shall not fight against him if he [his adversary] will consent to remain inside [his residence]. And if, after seven days, he will submit and hand over his weapons, he shall keep him unscathed for thirty days, and send formal notice of his position to his kinsmen and friends.

§ 2. If, however, he flees to a church, the privileges of the church shall be respected, as we have declared above.

§ 3. Gif he ðonne þæs mægenes ne hæbbe[1], þæt he hine
inne besitte[2], ride to þam ealdormen, [7][3] bidde hine
fultumes; gif he him fultuman ne wille[4], ride to cyninge, ær he feohte.

§ 4. Eac swelce, gif mon becume[5] on his gefán, 7 he hine ǽr
hamfæstne[6] ne wite, gif he wille his wæpen sellan, hine
mon gehealde xxx nihta 7 hine his freondum gecyðe;
gif he ne wille his wæpenu sellan[7], þonne mot he feohtan
on hine. Gif he wille on hond gan 7 his wæpenu[8] sellan,
7[9] hwa ofer ðæt on him[10] feohte, gielde swa wer swa
wunde[11] swa he[12] gewyrce, 7 wite 7 hæbbe[13] his mæg
forworht.

§ 5. Eac we cweðað, þæt mon mote mid his hlaforde feohtan
orwige[14], gif mon on ðone hlaford fiohte; swa mót se
hlaford mid þy[15] men feohtan.

§ 6. Æfter þære ilcan wisan mon mot feohtan mid his geborene[16] mæge, gif hine[17] mon on woh onfeohteð, buton
wið his hlaforde: þæt we ne liefað

§ 7. 7 mon mot feohtan órwige, gif he gemeteð oþerne æt[18]
his æwum wife, betynedum[19] durum oððe under anre
réon, oðer æt[18] his dehter æwumborenre (oððe æt[18] his
swistær [æwum][20]borenre) oððe æt[18] his medder[21] ðe
wære to æwum wife forgifen his fæder.

43. Eallum frioum monnum[22] ðas dagas sien forgifene, butan
þeowum monnum 7 esnewyrhtan: xii dagas on gehhol 7
ðone dæg þe Crist ðone deofol oferswiðde 7 scs. Gregorius
gemynddæg 7 vii dagas[23] to eastron 7 vii ofer 7 an dæg æt[24]
scē. Petres tide 7 sce. Paules 7 on hærfeste ða fullan wican[25]
ǽr scā. Marian mæssan 7 æt Eallra haligra weorðunge anne[26]
dæg; 7 iiii Wodnesdagas on iiii ymbrenwicum[25] ðeowum
monnum eallum sien[27] forgifen þam þe him leofost sie to
sellanne æghwæt ðæs ðe him ænig[28] mon for Godes noman

---

[1] mægnes næbbe. H.   [2] besitte mæge. H.   [3] H*.   [4] fultoman nelle. H.
[5] becyme. H.   [6] Altered into þam fæstne. H. [Schmid & Liebermann.]
[7] (7) gif he nelle his wæpen sellan. H*.   [8] wæpen. H.   [9] 7 gif. H.
[10] hine. H.   [11] wundwite. H.   [12] ðær he. H.
[13] 7 wite ðæt he hæbbe etc. H.   [14] Altered to on wige. H. orwite. Ld.
[15] þam. H.   [16] geborenum. H.   [17] him. H.   [18] mid. H.
[19] betynede. H.   [20] H.   [21] meder. H.   [22] freomannum. H.
[23] B begins again here.   [24] to. H.   [25] wucan. H.   [26] an. B.
[27] syn. H. sind. B.   [28] om. B.

§ 3. If, however, he has not power enough to besiege him in his house, he shall ride to the *ealdorman* and ask him for help. If he will not help him, he shall ride to the king before having recourse to violence.

§ 4. And further, if anyone chances on his enemy, not having known him to be at home, and if he will give up his weapons, he shall be detained for thirty days, and his friends shall be informed [of his position]. If he is not willing to give up his weapons, then violence may be used against him. If he is willing to surrender and hand over his weapons, and anyone after that uses violence against him[1] [the pursuer], he[2] shall pay any sum which he incurs, whether wergeld or compensation for wounds, as well as a fine, and his kinsman[3] shall forfeit his claim to protection as a result of his action[4].

§ 5. We further declare that a man may fight on behalf of his lord, if his lord is attacked, without becoming liable to vendetta[1]. Under similar conditions a lord may fight on behalf of his man.

§ 6. In the same way a man may fight on behalf of one who is related to him by blood, if he is attacked unjustly, except it be against his lord. This we do not permit.

§ 7. A man may fight, without becoming liable to vendetta[1], if he finds another [man] with his wedded wife, within closed doors or under the same blanket; or [if he finds another man] with his legitimate daughter [or sister]; or with his mother, if she has been given in lawful wedlock to his father.

43. The following days shall be granted [as holidays] to all free men, though not to slaves and hired labourers[1]: twelve days at Christmas and the day on which Christ overcame the devil[2]; the anniversary of St Gregory[3]; seven days before Easter and seven days after; one day at the festival of St Peter and St Paul[4]; and in autumn, the full week before St Mary's mass[5]; and one day at the celebration of All Saints[6]. The four Wednesdays in the four Ember weeks[7] shall be granted [as holidays] to all slaves whose chief desire is to

geselle oððe hie on ænegum hiora hwilsticcum geearnian mægen.

44. [Be heafodwunde 7 oðre liman.]
Heafodwunde to bote gif ða ban beoð butu ðyrel XXX scill. geselle him mon.

§ 1. Gif ðæt uterre[1] ban bið þyrel geselle XV scill. to bote.

45. Gif in feaxe bið wund inces lang, geselle anne scill. to bote.

§ 1. Gif[2] beforan feaxe bið wund inces lang, twegen scill. to bote.

46. Gif him mon áslea oþer eare of[3], geselle XXX scill. to bote.

§ 1. Gif se hlyst oðstande[4], þæt he ne mæge gehieran, geselle LX scill. to bote[5].

47. Gif mon men eage[6] ofáslea, geselle him mon LX scill' 7 VI scill' 7 VI pæningas[7] 7 ðriddan dǽl pæninges to bote.

§ 1. Gif hit in[8] ðam[9] heafde sie, 7 he noht geseon ne mæge mid, stande ðriddan[10] dæl þære bote inne.

48. Gif mon oðrum þæt neb ófaslea, gebete him mid LX scill'[11].

49. Gif mon oðrum ðone toð onforan heafde ófaslea, gebete[12] þæt mid VIII scill.

§ 1. Gif hit sie se[13] wongtoð, geselle[14] IIII scill. to bote.

§ 2. Monnes tux bið XV[15] scill. weorð.

50. Gif[16] monnes ceacan mon forslihð[17], þæt hie beoð forode[18], gebete mid XV scill.

§ 1. Monnes cinban, gif hit bið toclofen, geselle mon XII scill. to bote.

51. Gif monnes ðrotbolla bið þyrel, gebete[19] mid XII scill.

52. Gif monnes tunge bið of heafde oþres monnes dædum dón[20], þæt biþ gelic 7 eagan bot.

---

[1] utrre. B.   utre. H.   [2] Gif he. B.   Gif hit. Ld.
[3] ofaslea þæt oðer eare of. B.   ofasclea (þæt) oðer eare. H*.
[4] lyst ætstande. B.   [5] him to bote. B.   [6] his eage. H.
[7] peningas. H.   penegas. B.   [8] on. H.   [9] ðan. B.   [10] (se) þriddan. H*.
[11] hit mid feowertig. B.   Cap. 48 is a 16th century addition in B.
[12] gebetað. B.   [13] þe. B & H.   [14] gebete mid. om. to bote. H.
[15] syxtyne. B.   [16] Gif man mannes. B.   [17] forslea. B.
[18] beon forede. B & H.   [19] gebete ðæt. H.   [20] (ge)don. B & H*.

sell anything which has been given to them[8] in God's name, or which they are able to acquire by their labour in any portions of time at their disposal[9].

44. 30 shillings shall be given as compensation for a wound on the head, if both bones are pierced.

§ 1. If the outer bone [only] is pierced, 15 shillings shall be given as compensation.

45. If a wound an inch long is inflicted under the hair, one shilling shall be given as compensation.

§ 1. If a wound an inch long is inflicted in front of the hair, 2 shillings [shall be paid] as compensation.

46. If either ear is struck off, 30 shillings shall be given as compensation.

§ 1. If the hearing is stopped, so that he cannot hear, 60 shillings shall be given as compensation.

47. If anyone knocks out a man's eye, he shall give him 66 shillings, 6 pence and the third part of a penny as compensation[1].

§ 1. If it remains in the head, but he can see nothing with it, one-third of the compensation shall be withheld.

48. If anyone strikes off another's nose[1], he shall pay him 60 shillings compensation.

49. If anyone knocks out another's front tooth[1], he shall pay 8 shillings as compensation for it.

§ 1. If it is a back tooth[1] [that is knocked out], 4 shillings shall be given as compensation.

§ 2. A man's canine tooth[1] shall be valued at 15 shillings.

50. If anyone strikes another's jaws so violently that they are fractured, he shall pay 15 shillings compensation.

§ 1. If a man's chin-bone is broken in two, 12 shillings shall be given as compensation.

51. If a man's throat[1] is pierced, 12 shillings shall be paid as compensation.

52. If, as the result of another's actions, a man's tongue is torn from his mouth[1], the compensation [to be paid] shall be the same as that for an eye[2].

53. Gif mon bi∂ on eaxle[1] wund[2], þæt þæt li∂seaw útflowe, gebete mid xxx scill.

54. Gif se earm bi∂ forad bufan elmbogan[3], þær sculon xv scill. to bote.

55. Gif ∂a earmscancan beo∂ begen forade, sio bot bi∂ xxx scill.

56. Gif se[4] ∂uma bi∂ ófaslægen, þam sceal xxx scill. to bote.

　§ 1. Gif se nægl bi∂ ófaslegen[5], ∂am sculon v scill. to bote[6].

57. Gif se scytefinger bi∂ ófaslegen, sio bót bi∂ xv scill.; his[7] nægles bi∂ iii[8] scill.

58. Gif se midlesta[9] finger sie[10] ófaslegen, sio bot bi∂ xii scill.; 7 his nægles bot bi∂ ii scill.

59. Gif se goldfinger sie[10] ofaslegen, to þam sculon xvii scill. to bote; 7 his nægles iiii scill. to bote.

60. Gif se lytla[11] finger bi∂[12] ófaslegen, ∂am sceal to bote viiii scill., 7 an scill. his nægles, gif se[13] sie[14] ófaslegen.

61. Gif mon bi∂ on hrif wund[15], geselle him mon xxx scill. to bote.

　§ 1. Gif he ∂urhwund bi∂, æt gehwe∂erum[16] mu∂e xx scill.

62. Gif monnes ∂eoh bi∂ þyrel, geselle him mon xxx scill. to bote.

　§ 1. Gif hit forad sie, sio bot eac bi∂ xxx scill.

63. Gif se sconca bi∂ þyrel beneo∂an cneowe[17], ∂ær sculon xii scill. to bote.

　§ 1. Gif he forad sie[18] beneo∂an cneowe, geselle him[19] xxx scill. to bote.

[1] ∂a eaxle. H.　　　　　　　　　　　　　　　[2] gewunded. B.
[3] (þæm) elbogan. H*. ∂am elbogan. B.　　[4] ∂e. B.
[5] ofaslagen. B. ofaslægen. H. As frequently.
[6] seo bot bi∂ fif scill'. B.　　[7] 7 his. B.　　[8] iiii. B.　v. H.
[9] midleste. B.　　　　　[10] bi∂. H.　　　[11] lytle. B.
[12] sy. B.　　　　　　　　[13] gyf he. B.　　[14] bi∂. H.
[15] rifwund. B. Altered in 16th century to on rife gewunded.
[16] æg∂ran. B. æg∂rum. H.　　　　[17] cweowe. B.　　[18] bi∂. H.
[19] gesylle him mon. H.

53. If a man is wounded in the shoulder, so that the synovia flows out, 30 shillings shall be paid as compensation.

54. If the arm is fractured above the elbow, 15 shillings must be paid as compensation for it.

55. If both[1] bones in the arm are broken, the compensation [to be paid] shall be 30 shillings.

56. If the thumb is struck off, 30 shillings must be paid as compensation for it.

   § 1. If the nail is struck off, 5 shillings must be paid as compensation for it.

57. If the first finger[1] is struck off, the compensation [to be paid] shall be 15 shillings; for the nail of the same, 3[2] shillings [compensation shall be paid].

58. If the middle finger is struck off, the compensation [to be paid] shall be 12 shillings; for the nail of the same, 2 shillings compensation shall be paid.

59. If the third finger[1] is struck off, 17 shillings must be paid as compensation for it; and for the nail of the same, 4 shillings [must be paid] as compensation.

60. If the little finger is struck off, 9 shillings must be paid as compensation for it, and one shilling [must be paid as compensation for] the nail of the same, if it is struck off.

61. If a man is wounded in the belly, 30 shillings shall be given to him as compensation.

   § 1. If he is pierced right through, 20 shillings [shall be paid as compensation] for each orifice.

62. If a man's thigh is pierced, 30 shillings shall be given to him as compensation.

   § 1. If it is fractured, 30 shillings shall also be the compensation [to be paid].

63. If the shin is pierced below the knee, 12 shillings must be paid as compensation for it.

   § 1. If it is fractured below the knee, 30 shillings shall be given to him as compensation.

64. Gif sio micle ta bið ófaslegen, geselle him¹ xx scill. to bote.

   § 1. Gif hit sie sio æfterre ta², xv scill. to bote geselle him mon.

   § 2. Gif seo midleste ta sie ófaslegen, þær sculon³ viiii scill. to bote.

   § 3. Gif hit bið sio feorþe ta, ðær⁴ sculon vi scill. to bote.

   § 4. Gif sio lytle ta sie⁵ ófaslegen, geselle him v scill.⁶

65. Gif mon sie on þa herðan to ðam⁷ swiðe wund⁸, þæt he ne mæge bearn [gestrienan]⁹, gebete him ðæt mid lxxx scill.¹⁰

66. Gif men sie se earm mid honda mid ealle ofácorfen¹¹ beforan elmbogan¹², gebete ðæt mid lxxx scill.

   § 1. Æghwelcere wunde beforan feaxe 7 beforan sliefan 7 beneoðan cneowe sio bot bið twysceatte¹³ mare.

67. Gif sio lendenbræde¹⁴ bið forslegen, þær sceal lx scill. to bote.

   § 1. Gif hio bið onbestungen, geselle xv scill. to bote.

   § 2. Gif hio bið ðurhðyrel¹⁵, ðonne sceal ðær xxx scill. to bote.

68. Gif mon bið in¹⁶ eaxle wund¹⁷, gebete mid lxxx scill., gif se mon cwic sie.

69. Gif mon oðrum¹⁸ ða hond utan forslea, geselle him xx scill. to bote, gif hine mon gelacnian mæge.

   § 1. Gif hio¹⁹ healf onweg fleoge, þonne sceal xl²⁰ scill. to bote.

70. Gif mon oþrum rib forslea binnan gehaldre²¹ hyde, geselle x scill. to bote.

   § 1. Gif sio hyd sie tobrocen, 7 mon ban ófádo, geselle xv scill. to bote.

71. Gif monnes eage him mon ófaslea oððe his hand²² oððe his fot, ðær gæð gelic bot to eallum: vi pæningas²³ 7 vi scill. 7 lx scill. 7 ðriddan dæl pæninges²⁴.

---

¹ gesylle him mon: H & B.   ² Gif seo æftere ta sy ofaslægen. H.
³ scylan. B.   ⁴ ðar. B.   ⁵ bið. H.
⁶ gesylle him mon fif scill' to bote. B.   ⁷ to þon. H. to ðan. B.
⁸ gewundod. B & Ld.   ⁹ H. begytan. B.   ¹⁰ scillingum. H.
¹¹ ofacorven. B. -fan. Ld.   ¹² elbogan. H.   ¹³ twyggylde. B & Ld.
¹⁴ lendenbreda. B.   ¹⁵ ðurhðurl. B.   ¹⁶ on. Ld, B & H.
¹⁷ gewundad. B. -dod. Ld.   ¹⁸ on oðrum. B.   ¹⁹ he. B.
²⁰ syxtig. B. But vel feowertig written in the margin in 16th century.
²¹ gehalre. B & H.
²² Gyf mon him...ofsléa oððe his hand. B. But signs of erasure after him and oððe underlined.   ²³ penegas. B. peningas. H.   ²⁴ peniges. B & H.

64. If the big toe is struck off, 20 shillings shall be given to him as compensation.

> § 1. If it is the second toe [which is struck off], 15 shillings shall be given to him as compensation.
> § 2. If the middle toe is struck off, 9 shillings must be paid as compensation for it.
> § 3. If it is the fourth toe [which is struck off], 6 shillings must be paid as compensation for it.
> § 4. If the little toe is struck off, 5 shillings shall be given to him [as compensation].

65. If a man is so badly wounded in the testicles that he cannot beget children, 80 shillings shall be paid to him as compensation for it.

66. If a man's arm, with the hand and all below the elbow, is cut off, 80 shillings shall be paid as compensation for it.

> § 1. For every wound in front of the hair, and below the sleeve and beneath the knee, the compensation shall be doubled[1].

67. If the loin be maimed[1], 60 shillings must be paid as compensation for it.

> § 1. If it is pierced, 15 shillings shall be given as compensation.
> § 2. If it is pierced right through, then 30 shillings must be paid as compensation for it.

68. If a man is wounded in the shoulder[1], 80 shillings shall be paid as compensation, if he continues to live.

69. If a man maims another's hand outwardly[1], 20 shillings shall be given to him as compensation, if he can be cured.

> § 1. If half of it comes off, then 40 shillings must be paid as compensation.

70. If one man breaks another's rib without breaking the skin[1], 10 shillings shall be given [to him] as compensation.

> § 1. If the skin is broken and a bone is removed[1], 15 shillings shall be given [to him] as compensation.

71. If a man's eye is knocked out, or if his hand or foot is struck off, the same compensation shall follow them all—6 pennies, 66 shillings and the third part of a penny[1].

72. Gif monnes sconca[1] bi𝛿 ófaslegen wi𝛿 𝛿æt cneou[2], 𝛿ær sceal LXXX scill. to bote.

73. Gif mon o𝛿rum 𝛿a sculdru forslea, geselle him mon XX scill. to bote.

74. Gif hie[3] mon inbeslea 7 mon ban ófado, geselle mon 𝛿æs to bote mid XV scill.

75. Gif mon 𝛿a greatan sinwe[4] forslea, gif hie[5] mon gelacnian mæge, þæt hio[6] hal sie, geselle XII scill. to bote.

§ 1. Gif se mon healt sie for þære sinwe[7] wunde, 7 hine mon gelacnian ne mæge, geselle XXX scill. to bote.

76. Gif 𝛿a smalan sinwe[8] mon forslea, geselle him mon VI scill. to bote.

77. Gif mon o𝛿rum 𝛿a geweald[9] forslea uppe on þam sweoran[10] 7 forwundie[11] to þam swi𝛿e, þæt he nage þære[12] geweald, 7 hwæ𝛿re[13] lifie[14] swa gescended[15], geselle him mon C scill. to bote, buton him witan ryhtre 7 mare gereccan[16].

---

[1] sceanca. B.   scanca. H.   [2] cneow. B.   cneowe. Ld.   [3] hine. B.
[4] synewe. B.   [5] hine. B & H.   [6] he. B.   heo. H.   [7] synewe. B.
[8] synewe. B.   [9] gewald. B.   [10] sweore. B.   [11] forwundige. H.
[12] þær. B.   𝛿æra. H.   [13] 𝛿eah hwæ𝛿ere. B.   [14] lifige. B.   libbe. H.
[15] gescend. B.   gescynded. H.   [16] buton him witon mare gereccan
7 ryhtre. H.

72. If a man's shin is struck off at the knee, 80 shillings must be paid as compensation for it.

73. If anyone smashes another's shoulder[1], 20 shillings shall be given to him as compensation.

74. If anyone hacks into it [the shoulder], and a bone is removed[1], 15 shillings shall be given as compensation for it [in addition to the above].

75. If the large sinew is damaged, and if it can be treated medically so as to make it sound, 12 shillings shall be given as compensation.

   § 1. If the man becomes lame as a result of the damage to the sinew, and if he cannot be cured, 30 shillings shall be given [to him] as compensation.

76. If the small sinew [of a man] be damaged, 6 shillings shall be given to him as compensation.

77. If one man damages the tendons[1] in another's neck, and wounds him so severely that he has no control over them, but [if] nevertheless he continues to live so wounded, 100 shillings shall be given to him as compensation, unless the councillors[2] award him a juster and a greater sum.

TREATIES WITH THE DANES

TREATIES WITH THE DANES

1. Treaty of Alfred and Guthrum.

In 866 occurred the great Danish invasion which eventually put an end to all the existing English kingdoms except Wessex, and in other respects exercised a profound influence on the subsequent history of the country. The crisis of the invasion came when the Danish king Guthrum (Gythrum, Godrum) was defeated by Alfred in 878. In accordance with the terms of surrender, he submitted to be baptised, with his leading men, and to evacuate Alfred's kingdom. The following year he retired with his army to Cirencester, and thence again in 880 to East Anglia, the territories of which he distributed among his troops.

The date of the treaty here given is not exactly known. It was obviously after the occupation of East Anglia in 880, and before the death of Guthrum which, according to the Anglo-Saxon Chronicle, took place in 890. In the Anglo-Saxon Chronicle (Ann. 885 *ad fin.*) it is stated that "this year, the army of East Anglia broke truce with King Alfred"; but whether the treaty given here preceded these hostilities (as suggested by Liebermann), or followed them, can hardly be determined. In 886, according to the Chronicle, "Alfred garrisoned London, and all the English, who were not subject to the Danish yoke, submitted to him." London, it will be observed, lies outside the territories recognised in the treaty as belonging to Guthrum. On the other hand, these territories include much more than the old kingdom of East Anglia, comprising as they do the whole of Essex, Cambridgeshire and Huntingdonshire, and parts of Hertfordshire, Bedfordshire, Buckinghamshire and perhaps Northamptonshire.

Two texts of the treaty are found in B, written in the same hand (about 1125, see Introd.). The text printed below is taken from B 1, which is a longer version, and shows a more archaic form of language than B 2.

B 1 is found between the fragments *Swerian* and *Wifmannes beweddung*, B 2 after *Æthelred I* and immediately before *Edward and Guthrum*.

In the Quadripartitus the Treaty of Alfred and Guthrum follows *Ordal* and is separated from the Laws of Edward and Guthrum by a short document which is printed in Liebermann, I. p. 394 (see Liebermann, III. p. 82). On the relations of the texts, together with a lost manuscript used by Lambarde, see Liebermann, III. p. 83.

2. THE LAWS OF EDWARD AND GUTHRUM.

The preamble states that these are the ordinances decided and agreed upon, first by King Alfred and King Guthrum, and later by King Edward and King Guthrum, when peace and friendly relations were established between the English and the Danes. Since Guthrum, according to the Anglo-Saxon Chronicle, died in 890—some ten years before Alfred—he obviously cannot have made any treaty with Alfred's successor. The next Danish king we hear of in East Anglia was called Eohric, and according to the Chronicle (A) was killed in 905. Another Danish king, whose name is not given, was killed at Tempsford 16 years later (Anglo-Saxon Chronicle [A], Ann. 921). It has been supposed that this unnamed king was the Guthrum who ratified the laws with King Edward. Liebermann (III. p. 87 f.), however, holds that the preamble is not authentic, and that the laws were established after 921, when the East Anglian kingdom was destroyed. He points especially to the last chapter (12), as indicating that East Anglia was now under an *eorl* (i.e. jarl) instead of a king of its own—but to this question we shall have to refer in the notes. On the other hand, he thinks the laws date from before the death of Æthelstan, who reigned from 925(?) to 939(?), since there is no reference to that king, and more especially because East Anglia is known to have been placed under an *ealdorman* (Æthelstan 'Half-king') of West Saxon family in the course of this reign (*Hist. Ramesiensis*, cap. III). See Chadwick, *Anglo-Saxon Institutions*, p. 179 f.

The laws are found in H and B, from the former of which the following text is taken. A lost MS, in addition to B, was used by Lambarde, and a Latin version is found in the Quadripartitus.

On the relationship of the various MSS to one another, see Liebermann, III. p. 87.

It may be observed that in these two documents Scandinavian words begin to make their appearance, e.g. *eorl* (representing Scand. *jarl*), *lagu, gri∂, lysing, mark, ora, utlah.*

ALFRED and GUTHRUM

[Ælfredes laga cyninges.][1]

Ðis is ðæt friỗ[2], ỗæt Ælfred cyninc 7 Gyỗrum cyning
7 ealles Angelcynnes witan 7 eal seo ðeod ðe on Eastænglum[3]
beoỗ[4] ealle gecweden habbaỗ 7 mid aỗum gefeostnod for hy sylfe
7 for heora gingran, ge for geborene ge for ungeborene, ðe Godes
miltse reccen[5] oỗỗe ure.

1. Ærest ymb ure[6] landgemæra: up on Temese[7], 7 ðonne up
   on Ligan, 7 andlang Ligan oỗ hire æwylm, ðonne[8] on gerihte
   to Bedanforda, ðonne up on[9] Usan oỗ Wætlingastræt.

2. [Be ofslægenan mannes were.][10]
   Ðæt is ðonne, gif[11] man ofslægen[12] weorỗe, ealle we lætaỗ
   efen dyrne Engliscne 7 Deniscne, to[13] VIII healfmearcum
   asodenes goldes, buton ðam ceorle ðe on gafollande sit 7
   heora liesengum[14], ða syndan eac efen dyre: ægỗer to CC
   scill.

3. [Be ðegnum ðe betogene synd.][15]
   7 gif man cyninges ðegn beteo manslihtes, gif he[16] hine
   ladian dyrre, do he ðæt mid XII cininges ðegnum[17]; gif mon[18]
   ðone man[19] betyhỗ, ðe biỗ læssa maga ðone se cyninges ðegn,
   ladige he hine mid XI his gelicena 7 mid anum cyninges
   ðægne—7[20] swa ægehwilcre spræce ðe mare sy ðone[21] IIII
   mancussas—; 7 gyf he ne dyrre[22], gylde hit ỗrygylde[23], swa
   hit man gewyrỗe.

[1] B 2.　　[2] fryþe þ. Æ. cyning 7 Gyỗrun. Ld.　　[3] Eastenglum. B 2, Ld.
[4] 7 gesworen habbaỗ *, ge for hy sylfe ge for heora ofspryng† are the remaining
words of B 2.
　　　　* 7 mid aþum gefæstnod, 16th century addition to B 2.
　　　　† Altered to gingran in 16th century.
[5] recce. MSS.　　[6] heora. B 2.　　[7] andlang Témese. B 2.　　[8] ðanon. B 2.
[9] þanon upon. B 2.　ðon. Ld.　　[10] Ld.　　[11] 7 ‡ hi cwædon, gyf. B 2.
　　　　‡ þæt is ðonne, added in 16th century.
[12] ofslag. Ld.　　[13] þæt is to. B 2.
[14] lysyngon, B 2, which stops here, but þa syndon eac efen dyre: ægþer twa
hund scyll added in 16th century.　　[15] Ld.　　[16] 7 he. B 2.
[17] þegnas B 2.　　[18] ma. B 1. mon. B 2.　　[19] ðegn. Ld. thainus. Quad.
[20] The remaining words of the cap. are not found in B 2.
[21] ðonne. Ld.　　[22] dyrne. Ld.　　[23] gyld hit ỗrygyld. Ld.

ALFRED AND GUTHRUM

[The Laws of King Alfred.]

These are the terms of peace which King Alfred and King Guthrum, and the councillors of all the English nation, and all the people[1] who dwell in East Anglia[2], have all agreed upon and confirmed with oaths, on their own behalf and for their subjects[3], both living and unborn, who are anxious for God's favour and ours.

1. First as to the boundaries between us. [They shall run] up the Thames, and then up the Lea, and along the Lea to its source, then in a straight line to Bedford, and then up the Ouse to Watling Street.

2. Secondly, if a man is slain, whether he is an Englishman or a Dane, all of us shall place the same value on his life—namely 8 half-marks[1] of pure gold, with the exception of commoners who occupy tributary land, and freedmen of the Danes. These also shall be valued at the same amount—[namely] 200 shillings—in either case.

3. If anyone accuses a king's thegn of homicide, if he dares to clear himself, he shall do so with [the oaths of] twelve king's thegns. If anyone accuses a man who belongs to a lower order than that of king's thegn, he shall clear himself with [the oaths of] eleven of his equals and one king's thegn[1]. And this law shall apply to every suit which involves an amount greater than 4 mancuses[2]. And if he [the accused] dare not [attempt to clear himself], he shall pay [as compensation] three times the amount at which the stolen property is valued.

7—2

4. [Be getymum.][1]

7 ðæt ælc man wite his getyman be mannum 7 be horsum
7 be oxum.

5[2]. 7 ealle we cwædon on ðam[3] dæge ðe mon ða aðas swor, þæt
ne ðeowe ne freo ne moton in ðone here faran butan leafe,
ne heora nan ðe ma to us. Gif ðonne gebyrige, þæt for neode
heora hwylc[4] wið ure bige habban wille oððe we wið heora
mid yrfe 7 mid æhtum, ðæt is to ðafianne on ða wisan, þæt
man gislas sylle friðe to wedde[5] 7 to swutulunge, þæt man
wite, ðæt man clæne[6] bæc[7] hæbbe.

---

[1] Ld. This cap. is omitted in B 2.

[2] Cap. 5 in B 2 reads as follows: *7 ealle hig gecwædon ða man þa aðas swor,
þæt naðor ne we on ðone hère faran buton leafe, ne heora nan ða ma to us, buton
man trywan 7 betwynan gyslas sylle, friðe to wedde 7 to swutelunge, þæt man mid
rihte fare, gyf þæt geneodige, þæt ure ænig to oðrum fæce mid yrfe and mid æhtum.*

[3] *ða.* MSS. *ðæm.* Ld.   [4] *hwylce.* Ld.   [5] *to wedde* 7, omitted in Ld.

[6] *clæn.* Ld.   [7] *alias flæsc,* in the margin of Ld.

4. Every man shall have knowledge of his warrantor when he buys slaves, or horses, or oxen.

5. And we all declared, on the day when the oaths were sworn, that neither slaves nor freemen should be allowed to pass over to the Danish host[1] without permission, any more than that any of them [should come over] to us. If, however, it happens that any of them, in order to satisfy their wants, wish to trade with us, or we [for the same reason wish to trade] with them, in cattle and in goods, it shall be allowed on condition that hostages are given as security for peaceful behaviour, and as evidence by which it may be known that no treachery is intended[2].

EDWARD and GUTHRUM

Ðis syndon þa domas ðe Ælfred cyncg 7 Guðrum
cyncg gecuron[1].

And[2] þis is seo gerædnis eac, þe Ælfred cyng 7 Guðrum[3]
cyng 7 eft Eadward cyng (7 Guðrum cyng) gecuran 7 gecwædon,
þa þa Engle 7 Dene to friþe 7 to freondscipe fullice fengon;
7 þa witan eac, þe syððan wæron, oft 7 unseldan þæt seolfe[4]
geniwodon 7 mid gode geiehtan[5].

§ 1. Ðæt is ærest[6], þæt hig gecwædon, þæt hí ænne God lufian
woldon 7 ælcne hæþendom georne aworpen.

§ 2. 7 hig[7] gesetton woruldlice stéora eac, for ðam þingum þe
hig wistan, þæt hig elles ne mihton manegum gesteoran, ne
fela manna nolde to godcundre bote elles gebugan, swa hy[8]
sceolden[9]; 7 þa woruldbote hig gesetton[10] gemæne Criste
7 cynge, swa hwár swa man nolde godcunde bote gebugan
mid rihte to bisceopa dihte.

1. 7 þæt is þonon ærest, þæt hig gecwædon, þæt cyricgrið binnan
wagum 7 cyninges handgrið stande efne unwemme[11].

2. 7 gif hwá Cristendom wyrde oððe[12] hæþendom weorþige
wordes oððe weorces, gylde swa wer[13] swa wite swa lahslitte[14],
be þam þe syo dæd[15] sy.

3. 7 gyf gehadod man gestalie oððe gefehte oððe forswerige
oððe forlicge, gebete þæt be þam þe seo dæd[15] sy, swa be
were swa be wite swa be lahslitte[14], 7 for Gode[16] huru bete,
swa canon tǽce, 7 þæs borh finde oððe carcern[17] gebuge.

§ 1. 7 gif mæssepreost folc miswyssige æt freolse oððe æt

---

[1] *Eft his* 7 *Guðrumes* 7 *Eadwardes.* B.   [2] Ld begins *Ðis is* etc.
[3] *Gyþrum.* B.   [4] *sealf.* Ld.
[5] *gehihtan.* H.   *gehuhtan,* B altered to *gehyhtan* in 16th century [Lieber-
mann]. *adauxerunt.* Quad.   [6] B. *Ðis ærest.* H.   [7] *hi.* B, as frequently.
[8] *he.* B, Ld.   [9] *sceolde.* H. *deberent.* Quad.
[10] *settan.* B. *setton g. Crist* 7 *cyning s. hwær.* Ld.
[11] *unwemne.* B, Ld.   [12] *oððon.* B & Ld.
[13] *gyld swa were.* Ld.   [14] *lahslite.* B, Ld.   [15] *dæde.* H. *dæd.* B.
[16] *for God.* Ld.   [17] *carcer.* B. *on carcerne.* Ld.

EDWARD AND GUTHRUM

These are the decrees which King Alfred
and King Guthrum enacted.

This also is the legislation which King Alfred and King
Guthrum, and afterwards King Edward and King Guthrum,
enacted and agreed upon, when the English and the Danes
unreservedly entered into relations of peace and friendship. The
councillors[1] also who have been [in office] since then, frequently
and often have re-enacted the same, and added improvements
thereto.

§ 1. In the first place they declared they would love one God,
and zealously renounce all heathen practices.

§ 2. And they also fixed secular penalties because they knew
that otherwise there would be many people whom they
would not be able to control, and that otherwise many men
would not be willing to submit as they ought to do, to
the amends required by the church. And they fixed secular
amends which should be divided between Christ and the
king, wheresoever people would not legally submit to the
amends required by the church and determined by the
bishops.

1. Next after this, they declared that sanctuary within the
walls of a church, and the protection granted by the king
in person, shall remain equally inviolate.

2. If anyone offends against the Christian religion, or honours
heathen practices by word or deed, he shall pay either wergeld
or fine or *lahslit*[1], according to the nature of the offence.

3. And if a man in orders steals or fights, or commits perjury
or adultery, he shall pay either wergeld or fine or *lahslit*,
according to the nature of the offence; and in any case
shall he make compensation to God as the canon directs;
and he shall find surety for the compensation or go to prison.

§ 1. If a mass priest misdirects the people with regard to a

fæstene, gylde xxx scill' mid Englum 7 mid Denum
þreo healfmarc[1].

§ 2. Gif preost[2] to rihtandagan crisman ne fecce, oððe ful-
luhtes forwyrne þam þe þæs þearf sy, gylde[3] wíte mid
Englum 7 mid Denum lahslit[4], þæt is twelf oran.

4. [Be siblegerum.][5]

7 æt syblegerum þa witan geræddan, þæt cyng ah þone
uferan[6] 7 bisceop þone[7] nyþeran, butan hit man gebete for
Gode[8] 7 for worulde, be þam þe seo dæd[9] sy, swa bisceop
getæce.

§ 1. Gif[10] twegen gebroðra oððe[11] twegen genyhe magas[12]
wið an wif forlicgan, beten swyþe[13] georne, swa swa man
geþafige, swa be wíte swa be lahslitte, be þam þe seo
dæd[9] sy.

§ 2. Gif[14] gehadod man hine forwyrce mid deaþscylde, ge-
wilde hine man 7 healde to bisceopes dome.

5. 7 gif deaþscyldig man scriftspræce gyrne, ne him man næfre
ne wyrne.

§ 1. 7 ealle Godes gerihto forðige[15] man georne be Godes
mildse 7 be þam wítan þe witan toledan[16].

6. Gif[17] hwa teoþunge forhealde, gylde lahslit mid Denum,
wíte mid Englum.

§ 1. Gif hwa Rómfeoh forhealde, gylde lahslit mid Denum,
wíte mid Englum.

§ 2. Gif hwa leohtgesceot[18] ne gelæste, gylde lahslit mid
Denum, wíte mid Englum.

§ 3. Gif hwa sulhælmyssan ne sylle, gylde lahslit mid
Denum, wíte mid Englum.

§ 4. Gif hwá ænigra godcundra gerihto forwyrne[19], gylde
lahslit mid Denum, wíte mid Englum.

---

1 *healf mare.* H. *healfmarc.* B, Ld.   2 *mæssepreost.* Ld.
3 *gild.* Ld.   4 *lahslite.* Ld.   5 Ld.   6 *yferan.* B.
7 *ðæne.* B. *ðære.* Ld.   8 *God.* Ld.   9 *dæde.* H. *dæd.* B.
10 *7 gyf.* B.   11 *oððon.* B, Ld.   12 *genydmagas.* B.
13 *betan swiþe.* Ld.   14 *7 gyf.* B.
15 *gerihte fyrðrie.* B. *rihte fyrþrie mon.* Ld.   16 *to lædon.* Ld.
17 *7 gyf.* B.   18 *hleohtgesceot.* B.   19 *gerihta forwyrna.* B.

festival or a fast, he shall pay 30 shillings in an English district, and 3 half-marks[1] in a Danish district.

§ 2. If a priest does not fetch the chrism on the appointed day[1], or withholds baptism from any one who is in need of it, he shall pay a fine in an English district, and *lahslit*—that is 12 ores[2]—in a Danish district.

4. And in the case of incestuous unions, the councillors[1] have decided that the king shall take possession of the male offender, and the bishop the female offender, unless they make compensation before God and the world as the bishop shall prescribe, in accordance with the gravity of the offence.

§ 1. If two brothers or two near relatives lie with one woman, they shall pay as compensation and with all promptness whatever sum may be approved—whether as fine or *lahslit*—according to the gravity of the offence.

§ 2. If a man in orders places his life in jeopardy by committing a capital crime, he shall be arrested, and his case shall be reserved for the bishop's decision.

5. If a man condemned to death desires confession, it shall never be refused him.

§ 1. And all ecclesiastical dues shall be promptly rendered, on pain of forfeiting God's mercy and incurring the fines which the councillors[1] have imposed.

6. If anyone withholds tithe, he shall pay *lahslit* in a Danish district, and a fine in an English district.

§ 1. If anyone withholds Peter's Pence, he shall pay *lahslit* in a Danish district, and a fine in an English district.

§ 2. If anyone neglects to pay 'light-dues[1]' [to the church], he shall pay *lahslit* in a Danish district, and a fine in an English district.

§ 3. If anyone does not pay 'plough alms[1],' he shall pay *lahslit* in a Danish district, and a fine in an English district.

§ 4. If anyone refuses [to render] any church dues, he shall pay *lahslit* in a Danish district, and a fine in an English district.

§ 5. 7 gif he wigie 7 man gewundie[1], beo his weres[2] scyldig.

§.6. Gif he man to deaþe gefylle, beo he þonne útlah[3], 7 his hente mid hearme ælc þara þe riht wille.

§ 7. 7 gif he gewyrce, þæt hine man afylle, þurh þæt [he ongean][4] Godes ryht oððe þæs cynges geonbyrde, gif man þæt gesoðige, licge ǽgylde[5].

7. [Be freolsdæges weorcum.][6]
Sunnandæges cypinge gif hwa agynne, þolie þæs ceapes 7 twelf orena[7] mid Denum 7 xxx scll' mid Englum.

§ 1. Gif frigman[8] freolsdæge wyrce, þolie his freotes oððe gylde wíte, lahslite. Ðeowman þolie his hyde oððe hydgyldes.

§ 2. Gif hlaford his þeowan freolsdæge nyde to weorce, gylde lahslitte [se hlaford][9] inne on 'Deone[10] lage 7 wíte mid Englum.

8. [Be fæstenum.][11]
Gif frigman rihtfæsten abrece, gylde wíte oððe lahslite. Gif hit þeowman gedó, ðolie his hyde oððe hydgyldes.

9. [Be ordele 7 aþum.][12]
Ordel 7 aðas syndan[13] tocwedene freolsdagum 7 rihtfæsten-dagum; 7 se ðe þæt abrece, gylde lahslit mid Denum, wíte[14] mid Englum.

§ 1. Gif man wealdan mage, ne dyde man næfre on Sunnan-dæges freolse ænigne forwyrhtne, ac wylde 7 healde, þæt se freolsdæg agan sy.

10. Gif limlæweo[15] lama, þe forworht wære, weorþe forlæten, 7 he æfter þam ðreo niht[16] alibbe, siððan man mot hylpan be bisceopes leafe, se ðe wylle beorgan sare 7 saule.

---

[1] gewundia. B. [2] feorhes. Ld. uita. Quad. [3] uthlah. B.
[4] B. hine man gean. H. [5] he orgylde. Ld. [6] Ld.
[7] ore. B, Ld. [8] friman. B. freoman. Ld.
[9] B, Ld. dominus. Quad. [10] Dæge. B. Dæna. Ld. [11] Ld.
[12] Ld. [13] syndon. B, Ld. [14] 7 wite. B. [15] limlæpeo. Ld, B.
[16] nihte. Ld.

§ 5. And if he fights and wounds anyone[1], he shall forfeit his wergeld.

§ 6. If he strikes a man[1] dead, he shall then be outlawed, and he shall be pursued with hostility[2] by all those who wish to promote law and order.

§ 7. If he so acts as to bring about his own death by setting himself against the laws of God and the king, no compensation shall be paid for him, if this can be proved.

7. If anyone proceeds to bargain on a Sunday, he shall forfeit the goods, and 12 ores[1] [in addition] in a Danish district, and 30 shillings in an English district.

§ 1. If a freeman works during a church festival, he shall be reduced to slavery, or pay a fine or *lahslit*. A slave shall undergo the lash or pay the fine in lieu thereof.

§ 2. If a slave is compelled to work by his lord during a church festival, he [the lord] shall pay *lahslit* within the Danelagh[1], and a fine in an English district.

8. If a freeman breaks a legally ordained fast, he shall pay a fine or *lahslit*. If a slave does so, he shall undergo the lash or pay the fine in lieu thereof.

9. Trial by ordeal[1] and [the rendering of] oaths are forbidden during festivals, and days of legally ordained fasting. He who breaks this [decree] shall pay *lahslit* in a Danish district, and a fine in an English district.

§ 1. If it can be so contrived, no capital offender shall ever be put to death during the feast of Sunday, but he shall be arrested and kept in custody until the festival is over.

10. If a criminal who has been mutilated and maimed is abandoned, and three days later he is still alive, after this time [has elapsed] he who wishes to have regard to his wounds and his soul may help him with the permission of the bishop.

11. [Be wicum, wiglerum, mansworum etc.]¹

Gif wiccan oðð wigleras, mansworan oððe morðwyrhtan oððe
fule, afylede, æbere horcwenan ahwar on lande wurðan
agytene, ðonne fyse² hi man of earde 7 clænsie þa ðeode,
oððe³ on earde forfare hy mid ealle, buton hig geswican 7
þe deoppor gebetan.

12. [Be gehadedum 7 ælþeodigum.]⁴

Gif man gehadodne oððe ælðeodigne þurh enig ðing forræde
æt féo oððe æt feore, þonne sceal him cyng beon—oððan
eorl ðær on lande—7 bisceop ðere þeode for mæg 7 for
mundboran, buton he elles⁵ oðerne hæbbe; 7 bete . man
georne be ðam þe⁶ seo dæd⁷ sy Criste⁸ 7 cyninge, swa hit
gebyrige; oððe þa dæde wrece swiðe deope þe cyning sy on
ðeode.

¹ Ld.   ² fyrsie. Ld.   ³ oððon. B, Ld.   ⁴ Ld.
⁵ helles. B.   ⁶ ðeo. B.   ⁷ dæde. H. dæd. B, Ld.
⁸ Ld. Xpe. B, H.

11. If wizards or sorcerers[1], perjurers or they who secretly compass death[2], or vile, polluted, notorious prostitutes be met with anywhere in the country, they shall be driven from the land and the nation shall be purified; otherwise they shall be utterly destroyed in the land—unless they cease from their wickedness and make amends to the utmost of their ability.

12. If any attempt is made to deprive in any wise a man in orders, or a stranger, of either his goods or his life, the king—or the earl of the province[1] [in which such a deed is done]—and the bishop of the diocese shall act as his kinsmen and protectors, unless he has some other. And such compensation as is due shall be promptly paid to Christ and the king according to the nature of the offence; or the king within whose dominions the deed is done shall avenge it to the uttermost.

THE LAWS OF EDWARD THE
ELDER AND OF ÆTHELSTAN

THE LAWS OF EDWARD THE ELDER
AND OF ÆTHELSTAN

Two series of laws which were issued by Edward the Elder (900?–925?) are extant. One of them, the Concilium Exoniense (II Edward), appears to be later than the other (I Edward); cf. II Edw., cap. 1, where there is a reference to earlier laws. From cap. 5, § 2 Liebermann infers that at the date of the promulgation of the later laws the Northumbrian, as well as the East Anglian territories, were already subject to the king, and consequently that these laws must belong to the last years of the reign—the chronology of which is unfortunately far from certain. Cap. 5, § 2, however, seems to me to point to a different conclusion (see the notes).

It will be observed that the laws of Edward are of a more coherent and logical form than those of earlier kings. They did not supersede the latter. According to Liebermann, III. p. 93, the expression *domboc*, which occurs several times, denotes the laws of Ine and Alfred collectively.

The manuscript authorities are the same as those for the laws of Edward and Guthrum (see Liebermann, III. p. 92).

THE LAWS OF ÆTHELSTAN.

Six series of laws issued by Æthelstan (925?–939?) have been preserved, in addition to a short ordinance respecting charities, which in earlier editions, including Schmid's, was prefixed to the second series. The dates at which these various series were promulgated cannot be accurately determined, but references from one series to another render it clear that II preceded III–VI; V preceded III, IV and VI; and IV preceded VI (cf. Liebermann, III. pp. 100, 108, 115). I preceded III and may have been composed as an introduction to II (cf. Liebermann, III. p. 96 f.).

I is of exclusively ecclesiastical import, dealing with the payment of tithes and other church dues, and judging from the preamble, it seems to proceed from the king and bishops only.

The preamble to II is lost, but from the last chapter, as well as from references in other laws, it is clear that this series was promulgated at a council held at Grately, near Andover. It is concerned mainly with the administration of justice. Chapters 13 to 18, however, are of a different character from the rest, and make use of a different introductory formula. They were evidently intended for the use of boroughs, and it is very probable that originally they were promulgated separately, and only incorporated into II at a subsequent date, whether under Æthelstan himself or at some later period. III largely repeats what is found in II, V, and probably I, but its form is that of a letter to the king from the archbishop, thegns, and people of Kent. IV, like II, is mainly concerned with the administration of justice. It was promulgated at a council held at a place called *Thunresfeld*, perhaps Thundersfield near Reigate. V is of a similar character, and was promulgated at a meeting of the council held at Exeter. VI is an ordinance drawn up by the bishops and reeves who held jurisdiction in London. It is concerned chiefly with the gilds belonging to the borough.

The Ordinance on Charities gives directions for the maintenance of poor men, and for the release of penal slaves. There is nothing definite to fix its date, but Liebermann suggests it may have been issued as a supplement to I.

The original (Anglo-Saxon) text of III is entirely lost, and the document is only known from a Latin version in the Quadripartitus. The same is true in the case of IV, except for a fragment of the original, which is contained in H. As regards the other laws, V and VI are preserved in H, as well as in the Quadripartitus. V is also preserved in Lambarde's edition from a lost manuscript. I is contained in D (C.C.C. 201) and G (Brit. Mus. Cotton Nero, A 1), as well as in the Quadripartitus, while another [lost] text was used by Lambarde. II is preserved in H and B; in Ot (Brit. Mus. Cotton Otho, B XI); in Lambarde's edition, which is derived partly from B and partly from a lost manuscript; in (So) Somner's 17th century paper manuscript (Canterbury Cathedral Library, B 2, n. 8); and in the Quadripartitus.

The Ordinance on Charities is preserved only in Lambarde's edition and in the Quadripartitus. The Anglo-Saxon text contains a very large number of late and incorrect forms (see the notes).

On the relationship of the various manuscripts, see Liebermann, III. pp. 96, 98 ff., 107 f., 110, 112, 114.

A.   8

I EDWARD

Eadwerdes gerædnesse[1].

[Be dome 7 spræce.][2]

Eadwerd cyning byt ðam gerefum eallum, ðæt ge deman swa rihte domas swa ge rihtoste cunnon, 7 hit on ðære dombec stande. Ne wandiað[3] for nanum ðingum folcriht to geregceanne; 7 ðæt gehwilc spræce[4] habbe andagan, hwænne heo gelæst sy, þæt ge ðonne gereccan.

1. [Be ceapunge.][5]

   7 ic wille, ðæt gehwilc man hæbbe his geteaman; 7 nan man ne ceapige butan porte, ac hæbbe þæs portgerefan gewitnesse oððe oþera ungeligenra manna[6], ðe man gelyfan mæge.

   § 1. 7 gif hwa butan porte ceapige, ðonne[7] sy he cyninges oferhyrnesse scyldig; 7 gange se team þeah forð, oð þæt man wite, hwær he oðstande.

   § 2. Eac we cwædon: se ðe tyman scolde, þæt he hæfde ungeligene gewitnesse ðæs ðæt he hit on riht tymde, oððe þone að funde, ðe se gelyfan mihte[8] ðe onsprece.

   § 3. Swa we cwædon be þære agnunge ðæt ylce, þæt he gelædde ungeligene gewitnesse ðæs, oððe ðone aþ funde, gif he mæhte, ungecorenne, ðe se onspeca on gehealden wære.

   § 4. Gif he ðonne[7] ne mehte, ðonne[7] namede him man VI men on ðam ylcan [geburscipe][9], þe he on hamfæst wære, 7 begete þara[10] syxa ænne æt anum hryðere, oððe æt þam orfe þe ðæs weorð sy; 7 syððan wexe be ðæs ceapes æhte, gif þær ma to scyle.

---

[1] gerænesse. H. om. B. [2] Ld. [3] wandieþ. B. wandigeþ. Ld.
[4] spræc. B. [5] Ld. [6] man. B. manna. Ld.
[7] ðone. B. [8] mæge. B. [9] B. geburhscipe. H, Quad.
[10] æt ðæra. Ld.

I EDWARD

Edward's Ordinances.

King Edward commands all [his] reeves: that ye pronounce such legal decisions as ye know to be most just and in accordance with the written laws[1]. Ye shall not for any cause fail to interpret the public law[2]; and at the same time it shall be your duty to provide that every case shall have a date fixed for its decision[3].

1. And my will is that every man shall have a warrantor [to his transactions] and that no one shall buy [and sell] except in a market town; but he shall have the witness of the 'portreeve[1]' or of other men of credit, who can be trusted.

    § 1. And if anyone buys outside a market town, he shall forfeit the sum due for insubordination to the king[1]; but the production of warrantors shall nevertheless be continued, until the point is known at which they can no longer be found[2].

    § 2. Further, we have declared that he who has to vouch [another man] to warranty, shall have trustworthy witness that he is doing so in accordance with the law; or he shall produce an oath[1] which he who brings the accusation may place confidence in.

    § 3. We have similarly declared, that in cases where a man wishes to substantiate his plea of ownership, he shall produce trustworthy witness to this effect, or he shall produce such an oath—an unselected oath[1] if he can— as the plaintiff shall be bound to accept.

    § 4. If, however, he cannot do so, then six men from the same locality[1] in which he is resident shall be nominated to him, and he shall choose one of these six for each cow or for livestock of an equivalent value[2]. Afterwards, if more witnesses are necessary, the number shall be increased in proportion to the value of the property [in dispute].

§ 5. Eac we cwædon; gif enig yfelra manna[1] wære ðe wolde oðres yrfe to borge settan for wiðertihtlan, ðæt he gecyþe ðonne mid aðe, ðæt he hit for nanum facne ne dyde, ac mid [folcrihte][2] butan brede 7 bigswice[3]; 7 se dyde þonne swa ðer he dorste, ðe hit man ætfenge[4]: swa he hit agnode, swa he hit tymde.

2. [Be ðone ðe oþrum rihtes wyrnþ.][5]
Eac we cwædon, hwæs se wyrðe wære þe oðrum ryhtes wyrnde aðor oððe on boclande oððe on folclande; 7 ðæt he him geandágode of þam folclande[6], hwonne he him riht worhte beforan ðam gerefan.

§ 1. Gif he ðonne nan riht næfde ne on boclande ne on folclande, þæt se wære þe rihtes wyrnde[7] scyldig xxx scll' wið þone cyning, 7 æt oðrum cyrre eac swa, æt ðriddan cyrre cyninges oferhyrnesse, ðæt is cxx scll', buton he ær geswice.

3. [Be mansworenum.][8]
Eac we cwædon be þam mannum ðe mánsworan wæran, gif ðæt geswutelod wære, oððe him að burste[9] oððe ofercyðed wære, þæt hy siððan aðwyrðe næran, ac ordales wyrðe.

---

[1] gif hwa gemearra manna. B.   [2] B. fulryhte. H.
[3] biswicè. B. beswice. Ld.   [4] ætfence. B.   [5] Ld.
[6] 7 ðæt he...folclande omitted in B.   [7] wyrde. B. wyrd. Ld.
[8] Ld.   [9] oþburste. Ld.

§ 5. We have further declared, that if there is any evil man who by way of a countercharge[1] wishes to place another's livestock under distraint, he shall swear an oath[2] that he does it for no wicked end, but in accordance with public law and without fraud and guile; and in that case he in whose possession the stock has been attached, shall adopt whichever he dares to [of the following two courses]: either he shall substantiate his title to it, or he shall vouch it to warranty.

2. Further, we have declared what [penalty] he is liable to, who withholds from another his rights either in 'bookland[1]' or 'folkland.' And with regard to the 'folkland' [we have declared] that he [the plaintiff] shall appoint a day when he [the defendant] shall do him justice in the presence of the reeve[2].

§ 1. If, however, he [the plaintiff] does not obtain his rights either in 'bookland' or 'folkland,' he [the defendant] who withholds the rights shall forfeit a fine of 30 shillings to the king, and 30 shillings also on the second occasion, and on the third occasion the fine for insubordination to the king, that is 120 shillings, unless he has already desisted [from his wrong-doing].

3. We have further declared, with regard to men who have been accused of perjury: if the charge has been proved, or if the oath on their behalf has collapsed[1], or has been overborne by more strongly supported testimony, never again shall they have the privilege of clearing themselves by oaths, but only by the ordeal[2].

II EDWARD (AT EXETER)

[Be fryþe.]¹

Eadweard cyning myngode his wytan, þa² hy æt Exanceastre³
wæron, þæt hy smeadon ealle, hu heora friÞ betere beon mæhte,
þonne⁴ hit ær Þam wæs; forÞam him þuhte, þæt hit mæctor
gelæst wære, þonne hit scolde, þæt he ær beboden hæfde.

§ 1. He agsode hy þa, hwa to Þære bote cyrran wolde 7 on Þære
geferræddenne beon Þe he wære, 7 þæt lufian Þæt he lufode,
7 Þæt ascunian Þæt he ascunode, ægÞer ge on sæ ge on lande.

§ 2. Ðæt is Þonne, Þæt nan man oÞrum ryhtes ne wyrne.

§ 3. Gif hit hwa dó, bete⁵ swa hit beforan awriten is: æt forman
cyrre xxx scll. 7 æt oÞran cyrre ealswa 7 æt þriddan⁶ mid
cxx scll. Þam cyninge.

2. [Be gerefan Þe mid riht ne amanige.]⁷
7 gif hit se gerefa ne amanige mid rihte on Þara manna
gewitnesse, Þe him to gewitnesse getealde syndon, þonne
bete mine oferhyrnesse mid cxx scll'.

3. [Be þyfÞe betogenum.]⁸
Gif hwa ÞifÞe betógen sy, þonne niman hine on borh Þa þe
hine hlaforde⁹ befæston, þæt he hine þæs getrywsige; oÞÞe
oþere frynd, gif he hæbbe, don þæt sylfe.

§ 1. Gif he nyte, hwa hine on borh nime, þonne niman þa
Þe hit togebyreÞ on his æhtan inborh.

§ 2. Gif he naÞor næbbe ne æhta ne oÞerne borh, Þonne
healde hine man to dome.

¹ Ld.　　　　² Eadweard cyning mid his witan, Þu etc. B.
³ Exceastre. B.　　　⁴ Þone. B.　　　⁵ gebete. Ld.
⁶ þriddan cyrre. Ld. terciam uicem. Quad.　　⁷ Ld.　　⁸ Ld.
⁹ ær hlaforde. B.

II EDWARD (AT EXETER)

King Edward exhorted all his councillors, when they were at Exeter, to consider how the public peace for which they were responsible could be kept better than it had been[1], because it seemed to him that his previous orders[2] had not been carried out so well as they ought to have been.

§ 1. He asked which of them would devote themselves to this [work of] reformation and which of them would cooperate with him in his efforts, favouring what he favoured and discountenancing what he discountenanced, both by land and sea.

§ 2. Now his concern is that no man shall withhold from another his rights.

§ 3. If anyone does so he shall pay such compensation as has been already prescribed[1]—on the first occasion 30 shillings, on the second the same amount, and on the third 120 shillings to the king.

2. And if the reeve does not exact it [the fine] in accordance with the law, and in the presence of men who have been assigned to him as witnesses[1], he shall pay 120 shillings compensation for insubordination to me.

3. If anyone is accused of theft, those who have found him a lord[1] shall stand surety for him, that he shall clear himself from the accusation; or if he has any other friends, they may perform the same office.

§ 1. If he knows no one who will stand surety for him, those concerned may take security from his property[1].

§ 2. If he has neither property nor any other [means of providing] security, then he shall be kept for trial[1].

4. [Be ðon ðe heora agen secan willon[1].][2]
Eac ic wylle, þæt ælc man hæbbe symle[3] þa men gearowe
on his lande, ðe lǽdan ða men ðe heora ágen secan willen[4],
7 hy for nanum medsceattum ne werian, ne fúl náwar friðian
ne feormian willes ne gewealdes.

5. [Be ðon ðe ful friþiaþ.][5]
Gif hwa ðis oferhebbe 7 his að 7 his wæd[6] brece, ðe eal ðeod
geseald hæfð, bete swa dómboc tæce.

§ 1. Gif he ðonne nelle, ðolige ure ealra freonscipes[7] 7 ealles
ðæs ðe he age.

§ 2. Gif hine hwa feormige syððan, bete swa seo domboc
sæcge, 7 se scyle ðe flyman feormige, gif hit sy herinne ;
gif hit sy east inne, gif hit sy norð inne, bete be ðam
þe þa friðgewritu[8] sæcgan.

6. [Be ðon ðe his freot forwyrce.][9]
Gif hwa þurh stæltihtlan freot forwyrce 7 his hand on hand
sylle, 7 hine his magas forlætan, 7 he nyte, hwa him forebete[10], ðonne sy he ðæs ðeowweorces wyrðe, ðe ðærto gebyrige ; 7 oðfealle[11] se wer ðam magum.

7. [Be ðone ðe oþres mannes man underfehþ butan leafe.][12]
Ne underfó nan man oðres mannes man butan þæs leafe ðe
he ær fyligde 7 ær[13] he sy[14] laðleas wið ælce hand. Gif hit
hwa dó, bete mine oferhyrnesse.

8. [Be gemote andagum.][15]
Ic wille, þæt ælc gerefa hæbbe gemot á ymbe feower wucan ;
7 gedon ðæt ælc man sy folcrihtes wyrðe, 7 ðæt ælc spræc
hæbbe ende 7 andagan, hwænne hit forðcume. Gif hit hwa
oferhebbe[16], bete swa we ær cwædon.

---

[1] *nyllon.* Ld. *willon.* Quad.   [2] Ld.   [3] *symble.* B.
[4] *willan.* B.   [5] Ld.   [6] *hæbbe* 7 *his wedde.* Ld.
[7] *freondscipes.* Ld. *freodscipes.* B.   [8] B. *friðgehwritu.* H.   [9] Ld.
[10] *forbete.* Ld.   [11] *offealle.* Ld.   [12] Ld.   [13] *hær.* H.
[14] *syl.* H. *sy.* B.   [15] Ld.   [16] *oferhæbbe.* Ld.

4. It is my will also that everyone shall have always ready on his estate men who will guide others wishing to follow up their own [cattle][1]; and they [who guide] shall not for any bribes whatsoever hinder them; nor shall they anywhere shield crime, nor willingly and deliberately harbour [a criminal].

5. If anyone neglects this and breaks his oath and his pledge[1], [an oath and pledge] which the whole nation has given, he shall pay such compensation as the written laws[2] declare.

   § 1. If, however, he is not willing to do so, he shall forfeit the friendship of all of us, and all that he possesses.

   § 2. If anyone subsequently harbours him, he shall pay such compensation as the written laws declare of him who harbours a fugitive[1], if the offence is committed in our own kingdom[2]. If the offence is committed in the eastern or northern kingdoms[3], compensation shall be paid in accordance with the provisions of the treaties[4].

6. If any man, through [being found guilty of] an accusation of stealing, forfeits his freedom and gives up his person to his lord, and his kinsmen forsake him, and he knows no one who will make legal amends for him, he shall do such servile labour as may be required[1], and his kinsmen shall have no right to his wergeld [if he is slain].

7. No man shall take into his service one who has been in the service of another without the permission of the latter, and until he is free of all charges from any other quarter. If any man does so, he shall pay as compensation the amount due for insubordination to me[1].

8. It is my will that every reeve shall hold a meeting every four weeks[1]; and they shall see to it that every man obtains the benefit of the public law, and that every suit shall have a day assigned to it on which it shall be heard and decided. And if anyone neglects [to do] this he shall pay such compensation as we have already ordained.

I ÆTHELSTAN

Æðelstanes gerædnes[1].

Ic Æþelstan cyng[2], mid geþehte Wulfhelmes [mines][3] arcebiscopes[4] 7 eac minra oþerra biscopa, cyþe[5] þam gerefan to gehwylcere[6] byrig 7 eow bidde on Godes naman 7 on ealra[7] his haligra 7 eac be minum freondscipe beode, þæt ge ærest of minum agenum góde agyfan þa teoþunga, ægþer ge on cwicum ceape ge on þæs geares eorðwæstmum, swa man rihtast mæge oððe gemetan oððe getellan oððe awegan; 7 þa biscopas þonne þæt ylce don on heora agenum gode, 7 mine ealdormen 7 mine gerefan þæt sylfe.

1. Ic wille, þæt [mine] biscopas[8] 7 þa gerefan hit beodan[9] eallum þam[10] þe him hyran scylan, 7 þæt hit to þam rihtan andagan gelæst sy [7 ðæs sie to ðæm dæg ðær beheafdunges seint Iohannes þæs fulhteres][11].

2. Utan geþencan, hu[12] Iacob cwæð se heahfæder[13]: "Decimas et hostias pacificas offeram tibi"; 7 hu Moyses cwæð on Godes lage: "Decimas et primitias non tardabis offerre Domino."

3.[14] Us is to geðencanne[15], hu ondryslic hit on bocum gecweden is: "Gyf we þa teoþunga Gode gelæstan nellaþ, þæt he us benimeð[16], þara nigon dæla, þonne we læst wenað, 7 eac we habbað, þa synna to eacan."

1 Æðelstanes cinyncges gerædnes. D.
2 cyningc. D. cyning. Ld. 3 Ld. 4 hehbisceopes. Ld.
5 bebeode eallum minum gereafum ðurh ealle mine rice on þæs Drihtænes nama 7 ealra halgena 7 for mine lufu, þæt hi ærost mines agenes æhtes ðam teoþe gesyllaþ, ge ðæs libbēdes yrfes ge ðæs gearlices westmes; 7 ðæt ilce gedo eac ða bisceopas heora gehwylcra 7 eac mine ealdormanna 7 gereafa. Ld. 6 hwilcere. D.
7 eallum. D. 8 mine bisceopes. Ld. 9 ðæs demaþ. Ld.
10 ðe hio gehyrsumian gebyraþ, 7 þæt ilce to ðam tide fulfremaþ ðe we hio settaþ, 7 ðæs sie etc. Ld. 11 Ld. 12 we, hwæt. Ld.
13 to ðam Drihten cwæþ "Ic ðe wille gesyllan mine teoþan 7 mine siblac." And Drihten seolfe on ðam godspel cwæþ; "Eallum ðæm hæbbendum mon sceal agyfan, 7 hi genyhtsumiaþ."
14 We moton eac ðæs ðencan, ðe egeslic on ðissum bocum is gewriten: "Gif we ure teoðan gesyllan nyllaþ, us ða nygon dælas biþ ætbrædene, 7 se teoþa an us biþ to laf." Ld. 15 ðencanne. D. 16 benimað. D.

I ÆTHELSTAN

Æthelstan's Ordinance.

I, King Æthelstan, with the advice of my Archbishop, Wulfhelm[1], and my other bishops also, inform the reeve in every borough[2], and pray you in the name of God and of all His saints, and command you also by my friendship, that in the first place ye render tithes of my own property, both in livestock and in the yearly fruits of the earth, measuring, counting and weighing [them] in accordance with the strictest accuracy. And the bishops shall do the same with their own property, and my *ealdormen* and my reeves likewise.

1. And I desire my bishops and the reeves to give this order to all those whose duty it is to obey them, and that it [the payment] be rendered on the legally appointed day; and that shall be the day on which Saint John the Baptist was beheaded[1].

2. Let us remember how Jacob the Patriarch declared "*Decimas et hostias pacificas offeram tibi*[1]," and how Moses declared in God's Law "*Decimas et primitias non tardabis offerre Domino*[2]."

3. It behoves us to remember how terrible is the declaration stated in books[1]; "If we are not willing to render tithes to God, he will deprive us of the nine [remaining] parts, when we least expect it, and moreover we shall have sinned also."

4.[1] 7 ic wille eac, þæt mine gerefan gedon, þæt man agyfe þa
ciricsceattas 7 þa sawlsceattas to þam stowum þe hit mid
rihte togebyrige 7 sulhælmessan on geare, on þa gerad þæt
þa his brucan æt þam haligan stowan, þe heora cyrcan begán
willað 7 to Gode 7 to me geearnian willað. Se ðe þonne
nelle, þolige þære are oððe eft to rihte gecyrre.

§ 1. [Se godcunde lare us gemynaþ, þæt we ða heofonlica
ðinga mid ðam eorþlicum 7 ða ecelic mid ðam hwil-
wendlicum geearniaþ.][2]

5. Nu ge gehyrað, cwæð se cyng, hwæs[3] ic Gode ann, 7 hwæt
ge gelæstan sceolan[4] be minre oferhyrnysse. 7 gedoð eac,
þæt ge me unnon[5] mines agenes, þe ge me mid rihte
gestrynan magan. Nelle ic, þæt ge me mid unrihte ahwar
oht[6] gestrynan; ac ic wille eowres agenes geunnan eow
rihtlice, on þa gerad þe ge me unnan[7] mines; 7 beorgað
ægþer ge eow ge ðam þe ge myngian scylan[8] wið Godes
yrre 7 wið mine oferyrnesse[9].

---

[1] Cap. 4 omitted in Ld.   [2] Ld. Omitted in G, D.
[3] hwæt Drihtene us bebeod, 7 hwæt us fulfremian gebyraþ. Gedó þæt ge georniaþ ðara ðinga ðe ge me rihtlic begytan mæg. Ic nylle, þæt ge me hwæt mid woh
begytaþ. Gif ic eow ealla eowra ðinga geunne, on ða gerade ðe ge me mine georniaþ,
warniaþ eow 7 hio ðe eowe tobelimpaþ ðæs Drihtenes eorres 7 mines. Ld.
[4] sculon. D.   [5] geunnon. D.   [6] aht. D.
[7] geunnan. D.   [8] sculon. D.   [9] oferhirnesse. D.

4. And I further desire that my reeves see to it that church dues and payments for the souls of the dead[1] are rendered at the places to which they are legally due, and that 'plough alms[2]' [are rendered] yearly—on the understanding that all these payments shall be used at the holy places by those who are willing to attend to their churches, and wish to gain the favour of God and me. He who is not willing [to attend to his church] shall either forfeit his benefice or revert to a proper discharge of his duties.

§ 1. For the divine teaching instructs us that we gain the things of heaven by those of the earth, and the eternal by the temporal.

5. Now ye hear, saith the king, what I grant to God, and what ye must perform on pain of forfeiting the fine for insubordination to me[1]. And ye shall see to it also that ye grant me that which is my own, and which ye may legally acquire for me. I do not wish that ye should anywhere acquire anything for me wrongfully, but I will rightfully grant you that which is yours, on the condition that ye grant me what is mine. And ye must guard against the anger of God and insubordination to me, both yourselves and those whom it is your duty to admonish.

ORDINANCE RELATING TO CHARITIES

Ic Æþelstane cyning, eallum minum gerefum binnon mine rice gecyþe, mid geþeahte Wulfhelmes mines ærcebisceopes 7 ealra mina oþra bisceopa 7 Godes ðeowa, for mina sinna forgyfenesse, þæt ic wille, þæt ge fedaþ ealle wæga án earm Engliscmon, gif ge him habbaþ, oþþe oþerne gefindaþ.

1. Fram twam minra feorma agyfe mon hine elce monaþ ane ambra meles 7 án sconc spices oþþe án rám weorþe IIII peningas 7 scrud for twelf monþa ælc gear. 7 þæt ge alysaþ an witeðeowne. 7 ðæs ealle sie gedón for Drihtenesse mildheortnesse 7 mine lufu under þæs bisceopes gewitnesse on ðæs rice it sie.

2. 7 gif se gereafa ðis oferheald, gebete xxx scill., 7 sie þæt feoh gedæled ðæm ðearfum ðe on ða tun synd, ðe ðis ungefremed wunie, on ðæs bisceopes gewitnesse.

II ÆTHELSTAN

Æþelstanes gerædnesse[1].

1. [Be ðeofum.][2]
Ærest[3] þæt mon ne sparige nænne þeof þe æt hæbbendre honda[4] gefongen sy, ofer XII winter[5] 7 ofer eahta peningas.

§ 1. 7 gif hit hwa do, forgylde ðone þeof be his were—7 ne beo[6] þam þeofe no ðe geþingodre—oþþe hine be þam geladie[7].

§ 2. Gif he hine þonne[8] werian wille oððe oðfleo[9], ðonne[8] ne sparige hine mon[10].

§ 3. Gif mon ðeof on carcerne[11] gebringe, ðæt he beo XL nihta on carcerne[12], 7 hine mon ðonne[13] lyse út mid

[1] gerænesse. H.　[2] B.　[3] An ærest. Ot. On ærest. So.
[4] hand. B & Ld.　[5] winterne. B, Ld, and originally H [Schmid].
[6] sie. So.　[7] ladige. So.　[8] ðænne. B.
[9] fleo. B. fleon. Ld, So.
[10] B & Ld add ær ðam oþer. So, ær ðam oder æfter.
[11] cwearterne. B. cwearcerne. Ld.　[12] þær inne. B.　[13] ðænne. B.

ORDINANCE RELATING TO CHARITIES

I, King Æthelstan, with the advice of Wulfhelm[1], my arch-bishop, and of all my other bishops and ecclesiastics[2], for the forgiveness of my sins[3], make known to all my reeves within my kingdom, that it is my wish that you shall always provide a destitute Englishman with food, if you have such an one [in your district], or if you find one [elsewhere].

1. From two of my rents[1] he shall be supplied with an amber[2] of meal, a shank of bacon or a ram worth four pence[3] every month, and clothes for twelve months annually. [And I desire you] to make free annually one man who has been reduced to penal slavery. And all this shall be done for the lovingkindness of God, and for the love you bear me, with the cognisance of the bishop in whose diocese the gift is made.

2. And if the reeve neglects [to do] this, he shall pay 30 shillings compensation, and the money shall be divided, with the cognisance of the bishop, among the poor who are on the estate where [this] remains unfulfilled.

II ÆTHELSTAN

Æthelstan's Ordinances.

1. First, no thief shall be spared, who is seized in the act, if he is over twelve years old and [if the value of the stolen goods is] more than 8 pence.

§ 1. And if anyone does spare such a thief, he shall either pay for him to the amount of his[1] wergeld—though in that case the thief shall not be any the less liable to punishment—or clear himself [of the accusation] by an oath of equivalent value.

§ 2. If, however, he [the thief] tries to defend himself, or if he takes to flight, he shall not be spared[1].

§ 3[1]. If a thief is put in prison, he shall remain there forty days, and then he may be released on payment of

CXX scll'; 7 ga sio mægþ[1] him on borh, ðæt he æfre
geswice.

§ 4. 7 gif he ofer ðæt stalige, forgildon[2] hy hine be his were
oþþe hine eft ðær inne gebringan[3].

§ 5. 7 gif hine hwa forstonde[4], forgilde hine be his were, swa
þam cyninge swa ðam ðe hit mid ryhte togebyrige; 7 ælc
man ðara ðe þær midstande gesylle ðam cyninge CXX
scll' to wite.

2. [Be lafordleasum mannum.][5]
Ond we cwædon be þam hlafordleasan mannum, ðe mon[6] nán
ryht ætbegytan ne mæg, þæt mon beode[7] ðære mægþe[8], ðæt
hi hine to folcryhte gehamette 7 him hlaford finden[9] on
folcgemote.

§ 1. 7 gif hi hine ðonne begytan nyllen[10] oððe ne mægen[11]
to þam andagan[12], ðonne beo he syþþan flyma, 7 hine
lecge for ðeof[13] se þe him tocume.

§ 2. 7 se ðe hine ofer ðæt feormige, forgylde hine be his
were oþþe he[14] hine be ðam ladige.

3. Be ryhtes wærnunge.
Se[15] hlaford se[16] ryhtes wyrne ond for his yfelan mon[17] licge:
7 mon ðone[18] cing foresece[19], forgilde þæt ceapgild[20] 7 gesylle
þam[21] cynge CXX scll'. 7 se ðe ðone cyng sece[22] ær he him[23]
ryhtes bidde swa oft swa him togebyrie, gilde ðæt ilce wite
þe[24] se oþer sceolde, gif he him ryhtes wyrnde[25].

§ 1. [Be ðam hlaford þe his þeowan æt þyfðum gewita sie.][26]
7 se hlaford[27] þe his ðeowan æt þyfþe gewita sy, 7 hit
him on open wurðe, ðolige ðæs þeowan 7 beo his weres

[1] mægþe. Ld.   [2] ðonn forgyldan. B.   þonne forgylden. So.
[3] eft ingebringen. B.   [4] foran forstande. So.   [5] B.
[6] ðe nan man. B.   [7] bude. B, So.   [8] þær mæg. So.
[9] fundon. B. finde. So. hlaforde funden. Ld.   [10] nellon. B.
[11] magon. B.   [12] andagum. So.   [13] ðeofe. Ld.   [14] om. B, So.
[15] And se. B, So.   [16] ðe. B.   [17] men. So.   [18] þonne. So.
[19] forsece. B, So.   [20] ceapegylde. Ld.   [21] þonne. So. þæne. B.
[22] Altered to gesece. H. sece. B, So.   [23] hine. B.   [24] þæt. B.
[25] forwyrnd. So.   [26] So.   [27] hlaforde. Ld.

120 shillings, but his relatives shall stand as surety that he shall cease for ever after [from thieving].

§ 4. If he steals after that, they [his kinsmen] shall pay for him to the amount of his wergeld or put him back there[1].

§ 5. If anyone defends him, he shall pay for him to the amount of his[1] wergeld, either to the king or to him[2] to whom it is legally due, and everyone who renders him assistance shall pay a fine of 120 shillings to the king.

2. With regard to lordless men from whom no [legal] satisfaction can be obtained, we have declared that their relatives shall be commanded to settle them in a fixed residence where they will become amenable to public law[1], and find them a lord at a public meeting.

§ 1. If, however, on the appointed day they [the relatives of such a man] will not or cannot, he shall be henceforth an outlaw, and he who encounters him may assume him to be a thief and kill him.

§ 2. And he who harbours him after he has been declared an outlaw, shall pay for him to the amount of his[1] wergeld, or clear himself with an oath of equivalent value.

3. If a lord refuses justice[1], by taking the part of one of his men who has done wrong, and application is made to the king [about the matter, the lord] shall pay the value of the goods [in dispute] and give 120 shillings to the king. He who applies to the king before he pleads as often as is required[2] for justice [at home], shall pay the same fine as the other would have had [to pay] if he had refused him [the plaintiff] justice.

§ 1. And if a lord is accessory to a theft by one of his slaves, and it afterwards becomes known, he shall on the first occasion suffer the loss of his slave and forfeit his[1]

scyldig æt frumcyrre; gif he hit oftor dó, beo he ealles
scyldig þæs[1] he age.

§ 2. 7 eac swilce cynges hordera[2] oððe ure gerefena hwylc[3]
ðara ðeofa gewita wære ðe staledon, beo he be ðam ilcan.

4. Be hlafordsearwum[4].

Ond we cwædon be hlafordsearwe[5], ðæt he beo[6] his feores
scyldig, gif he his[7] ætsacan[8] ne mihte oþþe eft on þam þrimfealdum[9] ordale ful wære.

5. [Be cyricbryce.][10]

7 we cwædon be ciricbryce : gif he ful wære on ðam þry-
fealdan[11] ordale, bete be þam þe sio dómboc secge.

6. Be wiccecræftum.

Ond we cwædon be þam wiccecræftum 7 be liblacum 7 be
morðdædum, gif mon þær acweald[12] wære, 7 he his ætsacan[8] *
ne mihte[13], þæt he beo his feores scyldig.

§ 1. Gif he[14] þonne ætsacan[8] wille 7 on ðam þrimfealdum[15]
ordale fúl weorðe, þæt he beo CXX nihta on carcerne ; 7
nimen[16] þa magas hine siððan ut 7 gesyllan þam cynge
CXX scll' 7 forgildon[17] ðone wer[18] his[19] magum 7 gongon
him[20] on borh, ðæt he æfre swylces geswice.

§ 2. Be blæserum.

Ða[21] blysieras[22] ond þa ðe ðeof wrecen[23], beon þæs ilcan[24]
ryhtes wyrðe[25].

§ 3. 7 se þe ðeof wrecan wille 7 nanne mon ne gewundige,
gesylle þam cyninge CXX scll' to wite for ðan æhlype[26].

7. [Be anfealdum ordale.][27]

7 we cwædon be ðam anfealdum ordale æt þam monnum þe
oft betihtlede[28] wæron : 7 hy fule wurdon[29] 7 hy niten, hwa

---

[1] ðæs ðe. B.   þe. So.   [2] hordere. B.   [3] hwylc. B.   hwelc. So.
[4] hlafordsearwe. So.   [5] hlafordsearwan. B.   [6] wære. B, So, Ld.
[7] hit. B.   [8] oðsacan. So.   [9] ðryfealdan. B.   [10] B, Ld.
[11] þreofealdum. So.   [12] mon acwealde. Ld.   [13] mæge. Ld.   mæg. So.
[14] he hit. Ld.   he his þonne oðsacan. So.   [15] ðryfealdum. Ld. þreofealdum. So.
[16] niman. Ld, So.   [17] forgylden. Ld, So.   [18] were. So.
[19] ðæs mannes. Ld, So.   [20] hi. Ld.   -gen hi. B.   -gan him. So.
[21] And þa. Ld, So.   [22] al[ias] "beligeras," quod sonat: accusatores
falsos in the margin of Ld.   [23] -can. Ld, So.   [24] ylca. Ld, So.
[25] wyrð. So.   om. ryhtes. B, So.   [26] Altered to æthlype. H.
om. to wite. B, So.   [27] Ld, So.   [28] ðe ðeofþe getyhtlod. Ld. oft getyhlod. So.
[29] wyrden. Ld.   wyrðen. So.   * B comes to an end here.

wergeld. If he repeats the offence he shall forfeit all
he possesses.

§ 2. And in like manner also, any of the royal treasurers[1] or
[any] of our reeves who have been accessories of thieves,
who have been guilty of stealing, shall suffer the same
[penalty].

4. And we have declared with regard to one who is accused of
plotting against his lord, that he shall forfeit his life if he
cannot deny it, or [if he does deny it and] is afterwards
found guilty in the threefold ordeal[1].

5. And we have declared with regard to breaking into a
church—if he [who is accused of doing so] is found guilty
in the threefold ordeal[1], he shall pay such compensation for
it as the written law declares[2].

6. And we have declared with regard to witchcrafts and sorceries
and deadly spells[1], if death is occasioned thereby, and [the
accused] cannot deny it [the charge], that he shall forfeit
his life.

§ 1. If, however, he wishes to deny it, and is found guilty
in the threefold ordeal[1], he shall remain in prison for
120 days; and afterwards the relatives may take him
out and give 120 shillings to the king and pay the
wergeld [of the dead man] to his relatives, and stand as
surety for the offender that he shall cease from such
practices for ever.

§ 2. Incendiaries, and those who avenge a thief[1], shall be
subject to the same law.

§ 3. And he who seeks to avenge a thief, but does not
wound anyone, shall pay a fine of 120 shillings to the
king for [making such an] assault.

7. And we have declared, with regard to the simple ordeal[1] for
men who have often been accused of theft, and have been
found guilty [thereby], and do not know anyone who will

hy on borh nime, gebringe man hy[1] on carcerne 7 man hy[2]
do[3] út, swa hit her beforan cweden[4] is.

8. Be landleasum mannum.

    Ond we cwædon, gif hwylc londleas mon folgode on oþre[5]
scire 7 eft his mægas gesece[6], þæt he hine[7] on þa gerad[8]
feormige, ðæt he hine to folcryhte læde[9], gif he þær gylt
gewyrce, oþþe forebete.

9. Be yrfes ætfenge[10].

    Se[11] ðe yrfe befó, nemne[12] him mon v men his neahgebura[13],
7 begite ðara v : I, ðæt him midswerige, þæt he hit on folc-
ryht him toteo; 7 se þe hit him geagnian[14] wille, nemne
him mon x men, 7 begite þara twegen 7 sylle þone að, þæt
hit on his æhte geboren wære, buton þam rimaðe; 7 stonde
þes cyreoþ ofer xx penega[15].

10. Be hwearfe[16].

    7 nan[17] mon ne hwyrfe nanes yrfes buton ðæs gerefan gewit-
nesse oððe þæs mæssepreostes oððe þæs londhlafordes oþþe
þæs horderes oððe oþres ungelygnes monnes. Gif hit hwa
dó, gesylle[18] xxx scll' to wite, 7 fó se londhlaford[19] to þam
hwearfe[20].

§ 1. Be wore[21] gewitnesse.

    Gif mon þonne afinde[22], þæt heora ænig on wore[23] ge-
witnesse wære[24], þæt næfre his gewitnes eft noht[25] ne
forstonde; 7 eac gesylle xxx scll' to wite.

11. [Be ðon ðe scyldgunge bæde æt ofslegenum.][26]

    Ond we cwædon: se ðe[27] scyldunga bæde æt ofslagenum
þeofe, ðæt he eode ðreora sum to, twegen on fæderanmaga[28]
7 þridda on medren, 7 þone aþ syllen[29], ðæt hy on heora
mæge nane þyfðe nysten[30], ðæt he his feores wyrðe nære for

---

[1] *hine.* Ld, So.   [2] *hine man.* Ld, So.   [3] *don.* H. *do.* Ld, So.
[4] *gecweden.* Ld, Ot.   [5] *oþer.* Ld.   [6] *sece.* Ld, Ot.
[7] *he ðe hine.* Ld.   [8] *gerade.* Ld, So.   [9] Altered to *gelæde.* H.
[10] *Be ðonne ðe yrf befehþe.* Ld. *Be þam þe yrfe befó.* Ot.   [11] *And se.* Ld, Ot.
[12] *namne.* Ld.   [13] *nehbura.* Ld.   [14] *agnian.* Ld, Ot.   [15] *peningas.* Ot.
[16] *Be yrfa gehwyrfe.* Ld.   [17] *Ðæt nan.* Ld.   [18] *gylde.* Ld. *gilde.* Ot.
[19] *landhlaforde.* Ld.   [20] *gehwyrfe.* Ld.   [21] Altered to *wohre.* H.
[22] *onfinde.* Ld, Ot.   [23] *fore.* Ld.   [24] *sy.* Ld. *sie.* So.
[25] *nawht.* Ld. *nauht.* Ot.   [26] Ld. *æt ofs. þeof.* Ot.   [27] *be ðon ðe.* Ld.
[28] *twegen fæderamagas.* Ld. *t. fæderanmagas.* Ot.   [29] *sealde.* Ld, So.
[30] Altered to *nyston.* H. *nysten.* Ld, Ot.

stand as surety for them, they shall be put in prison and they shall be liberated [only] on the conditions stated above.

8. And we have declared if any landless man who has been serving in another shire[1], returns to his relatives, he who entertains him shall do so [only] on the condition that if he commits any offence there, he [who entertains him] shall bring him to justice, or pay compensation on his behalf.

9. He who attaches livestock shall have five men nominated to him from among his neighbours, and he shall select one of the five to swear with him that he is attaching the live-stock in accordance with public law. And he who wishes to maintain his claim [to the livestock] shall have ten men nominated to him, and he shall select two of them without calling for the testimony of the whole number[1], and swear an oath that the livestock was born in his possession. Recourse shall be had to this selected oath[2] when the stock exceeds the value of 20 pence[3].

10. And no one shall exchange any cattle unless he has as witness the reeve or the mass-priest, or the landowner, or the treasurer[1], or some other trustworthy man. If anyone does so, he shall pay a fine of 30 shillings[2], and the land-owner shall take what has been exchanged.

  § 1. But if it is found that any one of them has borne false witness, never again shall his witness be valid; and moreover he shall pay a fine of 30 shillings.

11. And we have declared that he who demands redress for a slain thief shall go with three[1] others, two [of the three] belonging to the father's kindred and one to the mother's, and they shall give an oath that they know of no theft committed by their kinsman, for perpetrating which he deserved to be

ðon[1] gilte; 7 hy gán siððan XII sume[2] 7 gescyldigen[3] hine, swa hit ær gecweden wæs; 7 gif ðæs deadan mægas ðider cuman noldon[4] to ðam andagan, gilde ælc ðe hit ær sprece[5] CXX scll'.

12. [Be ðon ðe mon ne ceapige butan porte.][6]
Ond we cwædon, þæt[7] mon nænne ceap[8] ne geceapige[9] buton porte ofer XX penega[10]; ac ceapige ðær binnon on þæs port-gerefan gewitnesse oððe on oþres unlygnes[11] monnes, oððe eft on þara gerefena gewitnesse on folcgemote[12].

13. [Be burga gebettunge.][13]
Ond we cweðaþ[14], ðæt ælc burh sy gebet XIIII niht ofer gongdagas.

§ 1. Oþer: þæt ælc ceaping[15] sy binnon port.

14. Be myneterum.
Ðridda: þæt[16] an mynet sy ofer eall[17] ðæs cynges onweald[18]: 7 nan mon ne mynetige buton on port[19].

§ 1. 7 gif se mynetere fúl wurðe, slea mon of þa hond, ðe he ðæt fúl mid worhte, 7 sette up on[20] ða mynetsmiððan; 7 gif hit þonne tyhtle sy, 7 he hine ladian wille, ðonne ga he to þam hatum isene, 7 ladige þa hond, mid ðe[21] mon tyhð, ðæt he þæt facen mid worhte; 7 gif he on[22] þam ordale ful wurðe, dó mon þæt ilce, swa hit ær[23] beforan cwæð.

§ 2. On Cantwarabyrig VII myneteras: IIII þæs cynges 7 II þæs biscopes I ðæs abbodes; to Hrofeceastre [III][24]: II cynges[25] 7 I þæs biscopes to Lundenbyrig VIII; to Wintaceastre VI; to Læwe II; to Hæstingaceastre I; oþer to Cisseceastre; to Hamtune II: to Wærham II; [to Dorcaceastre I][26]; to Execeastre[27] II; to Sceaftes-byrig[28] II; elles to þam oðrum burgum I.

---

[1] Altered to ðam. H. ðæm gylt. Ld.   [2] twelfa sum. Ld.   [3] gescylden. Ld.
[4] nyllen. Ld. nellan. Ot.   [5] spræc. So. spræce. Ld.   [6] Ld.
[7] be ðon þæt. Ld.   [8] ceape. Ld.   [9] ceapige. Ld, So.   [10] peninga. Ld, Ot.
[11] ungeligenes. Ld, So.   [12] folcmote. Ld.   [13] Ld. Be burhbot. So.
[14] cwædon. Ld, Ot.   [15] ylc ceapunge. Ld.   [16] we cwædon þæt. Ld.
[17] ealle. Ld, So.   [18] anwealde. Ld.   [19] butan port. Ld, Ot.
[20] ufan on. Ld, So.   [21] ðæm. Ld.   [22] ðonne on. Ld, Ot.
[23] her. Ld, Ot.   [24] Ld, Ot.   [25] twegen þæs cynges. Ld, Ot.
[26] So. in Dorchecestre unus. Quad.   [27] Eaxanceastre. Ld.
[28] Sceaftesbyrg. Ot.

put to death. The homicide shall go with twelve others
and charge the dead man with guilt in the manner already
ordained[2]. And if the kinsmen of the dead man will not
come thither at the appointed day, each of those who have
demanded redress shall pay 120 shillings.

12. And we have declared that no one shall buy goods[1] worth
more than 20 pence, outside a town; but he shall buy
within the town, in the presence of the port-reeve or some
other trustworthy man, or again, in the presence of the
reeves at a public meeting.

13. And we declare[1] that every fortress shall be repaired by a
fortnight after Rogation days[2].

§ 1. Secondly: that all trading shall be carried on in a town.

14. Thirdly: [we declare] that there shall be one coinage throughout the king's realm, and no man shall mint money except
in a town[1].

§ 1. And if a moneyer is found guilty [of issuing base or
light coins] the hand shall be cut off with which he
committed the crime, and fastened up on the mint.
But if he is accused and he wishes to clear himself,
then shall he go to the hot iron [ordeal][1] and redeem
the hand with which he is accused of having committed
the crime. And if he is proved guilty the same punishment shall be inflicted as we have already declared.

§ 2. In Canterbury there shall be seven moneyers: four for
the king, two for the archbishop, one for the abbot[1]. In
Rochester, two for the king and one for the bishop. In
London eight; in Winchester six; in Lewes two; in
Hastings one; another in Chichester; two in Southamp-
ton; two in Wareham; [one in Dorchester]; two in
Exeter; two at Shaftesbury, and one in [each of] the
other boroughs[2].

15. [Be scyldwyrhtum.]¹
Feorðe : þæt² nan scyldwyrhta ne lecge nan scepes fel³ on
scyld ; 7 gif he hit dó, gilde xxx scll'.

16. Fifte : ðæt ælc mon hæbbe æt þære⁴ syhl ɪɪ [wel]⁵ gehorsede
men.

17. [Be ðæm ðe æt þeofe medsceatte nimaþ.]⁶
Syxte : Gif hwa æt þeofe medsceat nime 7 oþres ryht⁷ afylle,
beo⁸ he his weres scyldig.

18. [Be horsum.]⁹
Seofoðe : þæt nan mon ne sylle nan hors ofer sǽ, buton he
hit gifan wille.

19. [Be ðeowman ðe ful wurþe æt ordale.]¹⁰
Ond we cwædon be þeowan men¹¹, gif he fúl wurþe¹² æt
þam ordale, þæt mon gulde¹³ þæt ceapgild¹⁴ 7 swinge hine
man ðriwa oððe þæt oþer gild¹⁵ sealde¹⁶ : 7 sy þæt wite be
healfum wurðe¹⁷ æt þam ðeowum¹⁸.

20. [Be ðon ðe gemot forsitte.]¹⁹
Gif hwa gemot forsitte þriwà, gilde ðæs cynges oferhyrnesse ;
7 hit beo²⁰ seofon nihtum ær geboden, ær ðæt gemot sy.

§ 1. Gif he þonne ryht²¹ wyrcan nylle²² ne þa oferhyrnesse
syllan, þonne ridan²³ þa yldestan men to, ealle þe to þære
byrig hiron, 7 nimon eall²⁴ ðæt he age 7 setton hine on
borh.

§ 2. Gif hwa þonne nylle ridan²⁵ mid his geferan²⁶, gilde
cynges oferhyrnesse.

§ 3. Ond beode mon on þam gemote²⁷, ðæt mon eal friþige,
þæt se cyng friþian wille ; 7 forgá þyfðe²⁸ be his feore
7 be eallum þam þe he age.

§ 4. 7 se þe be [ðissum]²⁹ geswican nylle, ðonne ridon³⁰ þa
yldestan men to, ealle þe to þære.byrig hyron, 7 nimon

---

¹ Ld.   ² we cwædon þæt. Ld.   ³ sceapes felle. Ld.   ⁴ ðær. Ld.
⁵ Ld.   ⁶ Ld.   ⁷ rihte. Ld.   ⁸ be. Ld.   ⁹ Ld.   ¹⁰ Ld.
¹¹ ðeowmen. Ld.   ¹² wyrþe. Ld, Ot.   ¹³ gylde. Ld.   ¹⁴ ceapgylde. Ld.
¹⁵ gylde. Ld.   ¹⁶ sylle. Ld. sealde. Ot.   ¹⁷ healfan wyrþe. Ld.
¹⁸ ðeowan. Ld.   ¹⁹ Ld.   ²⁰ sy. Ld. sie. Ot.
²¹ rihte. Ld.   ²² nelle. Ot.   ²³ riden. Ld, Ot.
²⁴ ealle ða yldestan men, ðe to ðær byrig hyren, 7 nimen ealle. Ld.
²⁵ nelle toridan. Ld. ge::dan. Ot.   ²⁶ geferum. Ld, Ot.   ²⁷ gemot. Ld.
²⁸ ðyfþa. Ld, Ot.   ²⁹ Ld. witum. H. þysum. Ot.
³⁰ riden. Ld, as frequently.

15. Fourthly: [we declare] that no shield-maker shall cover a shield with sheepskin. If he does he shall pay 30 shillings.

16. Fifthly: [we declare] that every man shall provide two well-mounted men[1] for every plough in his possession.

17. Sixthly: [we declare] if anyone takes bribes from a thief and [by so doing] frustrates the just claims of another, he shall forfeit his wergeld.

18. Seventhly: [we declare] that no man shall send any horse across the sea unless he wishes to make a present of it.

19. And we have declared with regard to a slave who has been found guilty in the ordeal[1], that [his master] shall pay the amount involved, and either inflict three scourgings on him or pay a second sum equal to the amount involved. And the fine for theft by a slave shall be half the amount [paid by a freeman for a similar offence].

20. And if anyone fails to attend an assembly three times, he shall pay the fine due to the king for insubordination[1]. And the meeting of the assembly shall be announced seven days before it is held.

§ 1. If, however, he will not comply with the law, and pay the fine for insubordination, then all the chief men who belong to the borough shall ride [to his house] and take all that he owns, and place him under surety.

§ 2. If anyone refuses to ride [on such a mission] with his companions, he shall pay the fine for insubordination to the king[1].

§ 3. And it shall be proclaimed in the assembly, that men shall respect everything which the king wishes to be respected, and refrain from theft on pain of death and [the loss of] all they possess.

§ 4. Again, if any even then will not desist, all the chief men who belong to the borough shall ride and take all he possesses, and the king shall receive half, and

eall ðæt he age—7 fó se cyng to healfum, to healfum ða
men ðe on þære rade beon[1]—7 setton hine on borh.

§ 5. Gif he nite[2], hwa hine aborgie, hæfton hine.

§ 6. Gif he nylle hit geþafian, leton[3] hine licgan, buton he
oþwinde[4].

§ 7. Gif hwa hine wrecan[5] wille oððe [heora ænigne][6] fǽlæce,
þonne beo[7] he fah wið ðone cyng 7 wið ealle his freond.

§ 8. Gif he ætwinde[8], 7 hine hwa feormige, sy he his weres
scyldig, buton he hine ladian durre be þæs flyman were,
þæt he hine flyman[9] nyste.

21. [Be ðæm ðe for ordale ðingiaþ.][10]
Gif hwa þingie for ordal, ðingie on ðam ceapgilde þæt he
mæge, 7 noht[11] on ðam wite, buton hit se gifan wille þe hit
togebyrige.

22. [Be ðon ðe oþres mannes man underfehþ.][12]
7 ne underfó nan mon oþres monnes mon, buton his[13] leafe
þe he ær folgode.

§ 1. Gif hit hwa dó, agife þone[14] mon 7 bete [ðæs] cynges[15]
oferhyrnesse.

§ 2. 7 non mon ne tæce[16] his getihtledan mon from him, ær
he hæbbe ryht geworht[17].

23. [Be ðon ðe ordales weddigaþ.][18]
Gif hwa ordales weddige, ðonne cume he þrim nihtum ær to
þam mæssepreoste þe hit halgian scyle, ond fede hine sylfne
mid hlafe 7 mid wætre 7 sealte 7 wyrtum, ær he togan scyle,
7 gestonde him mæssan[19] þæra þreora daga ælcne[20], 7 offrige[21]
to 7 gá to husle ðy dæge þe he to ðam ordale gan scyle, 7
swerige ðonne þone að þæt he sy mid folcryhte unscyldig
ðære tihtlan, ær he[22] to þam ordale gá.

§ 1. 7 gif hit sy wæter, ðæt he gedufe oþre healfe[23] elne

---

[1] *rad syn.* Ld.　*rade sien.* Ot.　　[2] *nyt.* Ld.　　[3] *lætan.* Ld.
[4] Altered to *ætwinde.* H.　　　　[5] *Gif hine ðonne hwa awrecan.* Ld.
[6] Ld, Ot.　*hine.* H.　　　[7] *sy.* Ld.　　[8] *ðonne oþwinde.* Ld.
[9] *flymene.* Ld.　　　[10] Ld.　　[11] *nawiht.* Ld.　　　[12] Ld.
[13] *ðæs.* Ld, Ot.　　[14] *he ðone.* Ld.　　　[15] *ðæs cynges.* Ld, Ot.
[16] *getæce.* Ld.　　[17] *geworhte.* Ld.　　[18] Ld.　　[19] *his mæssan.* Ld.
[20] *ylce.* Ld.　　　[21] *geoffrige.* Ld, Ot.　　　　[22] *ðe he.* Ld.
[23] *ðreo healf elne.* Ld.

the men who ride to apprehend him the other half, and they shall place him under surety.

§ 5. And if he knows no one who will act as surety for him, they shall arrest him.

§ 6. And if he is not willing to consent thereto, they shall put him to death, unless he escapes.

§ 7. And if anyone tries to avenge him, or institutes a vendetta against any of them [who slew him], then he shall incur the hostility of the king and all his friends.

§ 8. If he escapes and anyone harbours him, he [who does so] shall forfeit his[1] wergeld unless he dares to clear himself by [declaring on an oath equal to] the fugitive's wergeld, that he did not know he was a fugitive.

21. If anyone compounds for an ordeal, he shall make what terms he can for the amount involved, but on no account shall he compound for the fine[1], unless he to whom it is due is willing to consent[2].

22. And no one shall receive a man who is subject to another, without the permission of him whom he has been serving.

§ 1. If anyone does so, he shall give up the man and pay as compensation the sum due to the king for insubordination[1].

§ 2. And no one shall send away one of his men, if he has been accused, before the man has complied with the demands of the law.

23. If anyone engages to undergo an ordeal, he shall come three days before to the mass-priest who is to consecrate it[1], and he shall feed himself on bread and water and salt and herbs before he proceeds thither[2], and he shall attend mass on each of the three days. And on the day he has to go to the ordeal, he shall make an offering and attend communion; and then before he goes to the ordeal, he shall swear an oath that according to the public law he is innocent of the accusation.

§ 1. And if the ordeal is by water he shall sink to a depth

on þam rape; gif hit sy ysenordal[1], beon ðreo niht[2], ær
mon þa hond undó[3].

§ 2. 7 ofga ælc mon his tihtlan mid foreaðe[4], swa we ær
cwædon; 7 beo þæra ælc fæstende on ægþera[5] hond se[6]
ðær mid sy, on[7] Godes bebode 7 ðæs ærcebiscopes[8]; 7
ne beo ðær on naþre healf[9] na ma monna þonne XII.
Gif se getihtloda mon ðonne maran werude beo[10] þonne
twelfa sum, þonne beo þæt ordal forod[11], buton hy him
from gan willon[12].

24. [Be ðæm ðe yrfe bycgaþ.][13]
Ond se þe yrfe bycge on gewitnesse 7 hit eft tymon[14] scyle,
þonne onfó se his þe he hit ǽr ætbohte, beo he swa[15] freoh
swa ðeow, swa hweðer he sy.

§ 1. 7 ðæt nan cyping ne sy Sunnondagum; gif hit ðonne
hwa dó, þolige ðæs ceapes 7 gesylle[16] XXX scll' to wite.

25. Gif minra gerefena hwylc[17] þonne þis don nylle 7 læs ymbe[18]
beo þonne we gecwæden habbað, þonne gylde he mine oferhyrnesse 7 ic finde oþerne ðe wile.

§ 1. Ond se biscop amonige þa oferhyrnesse æt þam gerefan,
þe hit on his folgoþe sy.

§ 2. Se ðe of ðissa gerædnesse gá, gilde æt frumcirre V pund,
æt oþrum cirre his wer, æt þriddan cirre ðolige ealles[19]
þæs he age 7 ure ealra freondscipes.

26. [Be mansworum.][20]
Ond se ðe manað[21] swerige, 7 hit him on open wurþe[22], ðæt
he næfre eft aðwyrþe ne sy, ne binnon nanum gehalgodum
lictune ne licge, þeah he forðfore[23], buton he hæbbe ðæs

---

[1] sy isen. Ld.   [2] syn ðreo nihte. Ld.   [3] ondo. Ld, Ot.
[4] tyhtan mid foreaþ. Ld.   [5] ægþere. Ld.   [6] ðe. Ld, Ot.   [7] be. Ld.
[8] bisceopes. Ld.   [9] Altered to healfe. nawþre healfa. Ld.
[10] weorod sy. Ld. weorode sie. Ot.   [11] sy ðæt ordale forode. Ld.
[12] wille. Ld. willen. Ot.   [13] Ld.   [14] mon teaman. Ld.
[15] sy swa. Ld.   [16] ceapgyld 7 sylle. Ld.   [17] gehwylce ðis. Ld.
[18] oþþe læsse ymb sy. Ld.   [19] ealle. Ld.   [20] Ld.   [21] mænne aþ. Ld.
[22] weorþe. Ld.   [23] gefære. Ld.

of one-and-a-half ells on the rope[1]. If the ordeal is by [hot] iron three days shall elapse before the hand is unwrapped.

§ 2. And every man shall precede his accusation with an oath, as we have already declared[1], and everyone who is present in both parties shall fast according to the command of God and the archbishop. And there shall not be more than twelve on either side. If, however, the accused man is one of a party greater than twelve, the ordeal shall be invalidated, unless they[2] will leave him.

24. And if anyone buys cattle in the presence of a witness, and afterwards has to vouch it to warranty, then he from whom he has bought it shall receive it back again[1], whether he be a slave[2] or a freeman—whichever he may be.

§ 1. And no trading shall take place on Sundays; and if anyone does so he shall lose the goods and pay a fine of 30 shillings.

25.[1] If any of my reeves is not willing to carry out this [our ordinance], or shows less regard for it than we have declared [he must], then he shall pay the fine due to me for insubordination, and I will find another [reeve] who will be willing.

§ 1. And the fine for insubordination shall be exacted from the reeve by the bishop, within whose diocese the offence is perpetrated.

§ 2. He who violates these ordinances shall, on the first occasion, pay 5 pounds[1]; on the second occasion, his wergeld; and on the third he shall lose all that he has, and the friendship of us all.

26. And if anyone swears a false oath and it becomes manifest he has done so, he shall never again have the right to swear an oath; and he shall not be buried in any consecrated burial ground when he dies, unless he has the testimony of the

biscopes gewitnesse, ðe he on his scriftscire[1] sy, þæt he hit swa gebet[2] hæbbe, swa him his scrift scrife.

§ 1. 7 his scrift hit gecyþe þam biscope[3] binnon xxx nihta, hweþer he to þære bote cirran wolde[4]. Gif he swa ne dó, bete be þam þe se biscop[5] him[6] forgifan wille.

[Ealle ðis wæs gesetted on ðam miclan synoþ æt Greatanleage; on þam wæs se ærcebisceop Wulfhelme mid eallum þæm æþelum mannum 7 wiotan, ðe Æþelstan cyning mihte[7] gegadrian.][8]

III ÆTHELSTAN

Decretum episcoporum et aliorum sapientum de Kantia[9] de pace observanda.

Karissime! Episcopi tui de Kantia[9] et omnes Cantescyræ Thaini[10], Comites et Villani tibi, domino karissimo[11] suo, gratias agunt, quod nobis de pace nostra præcipere voluisti, et de commodo nostro quærere[12] et consulere, quia magnum inde nobis est opus, divitibus et pauperibus[13].

1. Et hoc incepimus quanta diligentia[14] potuimus, auxilio sapientum eorum[15] quos ad nos misisti.

§ 1. Unde, karissime Domine, primum est de decima nostra, ad quod multum[16] cupidi sumus et voluntarii, et tibi suppliciter[17] gratias reddimus[18] admonitionis tue.

2. Secundum est de pace nostra, quam omnis populus teneri desiderat, sicut apud Greateleyam sapientes tui posuerunt, et sicut etiam nunc dictum est in concilio apud Favresham[19].

[1] *scire.* Ld.   [2] *gebete.* Ld.   [3] *þær bisceop.* Ld.
[4] *bote wille.* Ld.   [5] *bete swa se bisceop.* Ld.   [6] *hine.* Ld.
[7] om. Ld; supplied from Quadr. (*congregare potuit*).   [8] Ld.
[9] *Cantia.* T.   *Kent.* M.   [10] *de Kent et omnis Kentescire t(h)ayni.* Br, M.
[11] *dilectissimo.* Br.   [12] *perquirere.* Br, M.   [13] *egenis.* Br, M.
[14] *quantum diligentius.* Lond.   [15] *consilio horum sapientium.* Br, M.
[16] *quod valde.* Br, M, etc.; *quam v-.* T.   [17] *supplices.* M.
[18] *agimus.* Br, M.   [19] *Fefresham.* Br, M.

bishop, in whose diocese he is, that he has made such amends as his confessor has prescribed to him.

§ 1. And his confessor shall make known to the bishop within thirty days whether he has been willing to make amends. If he [the confessor] does not do so, he shall pay such compensation as the bishop is willing to allow him [to pay].

All this was established at the great assembly at Grately[1], at which Archbishop Wulfhelm[2] was present, with all the nobles and councillors whom King Æthelstan had assembled.

III ÆTHELSTAN

The decree of the bishops[1] and other councillors in Kent, concerning measures for the preservation of the public peace.

Most beloved! your bishops in Kent, and all the thegns[2] of that county, nobles and commoners, give thanks to you their most beloved lord, because you have been willing to advise us concerning the peace of our land; and to enquire into, and provide for our welfare; for we, both rich and poor, have great need thereof.

1. And this we have undertaken, with all the zeal of which we were capable, and with the help of the councillors whom you have sent to us.

§ 1. The first [of the provisions] most beloved lord! relates to our tithes[1], for the [payment of] which we are very eager and desirous; and we humbly return thanks to you for your injunction.

2. The second relates to the measures enacted by your councillors at Grately[1], and now also proclaimed in the Council at Faversham[2], for the peace of our land, for the preservation of which the whole people is much concerned.

3. Tertium est, quod gratiant omnes misericorditer te[1], karissimum[2] dominum suum, super[3] dono quod forisfactis hominibus concessisti; hoc est, quod pardonatur omnibus forisfactura de quocumque furto,quod ante concilium de Favresham[4] factum fuit, eo tenore ut[5] semper deinceps ab omni malo quiescant, et omne latrocinium suum[6] confiteantur et emendent hinc ad Augustum.

4. Quartum, ne aliquis recipiat alterius hominem sine licentia eius[7] cui ante[8] folgavit nec intra mercam nec extra;

   § 1. et etiam ne dominus libero homini hlafordsoknam[9] interdicat, si eum recte custodierit.

5. Quintum, qui ex hoc discedat, sit dignus eorum quæ in scripto pacis dicuntur[10], quod apud Greateleiam institutum est.

6. Sextum, si aliquis homo sit adeo dives vel tantæ parentelæ ut[11] castigari non possit vel idem[12] cessare nolit, ut facias[13] qualiter abstrahatur in aliam aliquam partem regni tui, sicut dictum est in occiduis partibus, sit alterutrum quod sit, sic[14] comitum sic[14] villanorum.

7. Septimum, ut omnis homo teneat homines suos in fideiussione sua contra omne furtum.

   § 1. Si tunc sit aliquis qui tot homines habeat, quod non sufficiat omnes custodire, præponat sibi singulis villis præpositum unum, [talem prepositum][15] qui credibilis ei sit, et qui concredat hominibus.

   § 2. [Et si præpositus alicui eorum hominum concredere non audeat, inveniat XII plegios cognationis suæ, qui ei stent in fideiussione sua.][16]

   § 3. Et si [dominus vel][16] præpositus vel aliquis homo hoc infringat vel abhinc exeat, sit dignus eorum quæ apud Greateleiam dicta sunt, nisi regi [magis][16] placeat alia iustitia.

---

[1] om. Br, M.   [2] h'mu. Hk, M.   [3] de. Br.   [4] Fefresham. Br, M.
[5] quo. Br, M.   [6] om. Br, M.   [7] ipsius. Br, M.   [8] prius. Br, M.
[9] hlasocnam. Br, M.   [10] habentur. Br, M.   [11] cur. M, Hk, Br, etc.
[12] illud. Br.   [13] efficias. Br, M.   [14] sit. Or, T.   [15] K.
[16] Br, M.

3. Thirdly, all humbly[1] thank you, their most beloved lord, for the favour you have granted to criminals; namely that all criminals shall be pardoned[2] for any crime whatsoever, which was committed before the Council of Faversham, on the condition that henceforth and forever they abstain from all evil doing, and between now and August confess their crimes and make amends for everything of which they have been guilty.

4. Fourthly, no one shall receive a man who has been in the service of another, without the permission of him he has been serving[1], whether within our borders or beyond them.

   § 1. And a lord also shall not prohibit a free man from seeking for himself a [new] lord[1], if he has conducted himself[2] rightly.

5. Fifthly, he who neglects this shall be liable to those [punishments] which are stated in the statute relating to the public peace[1], which was drawn up at Grately.

6. Sixthly, if any man is so rich[1], or belongs to so powerful a kindred that he cannot be punished, and moreover is not willing to desist [from his wrongdoing], you shall cause him to be removed to another part of your kingdom, as was declared in the west[2]—whatever his station in life, whether he be noble or commoner.

7. Seventhly, every man shall stand surety for his own men against every [charge of] crime[1].

   § 1. If, however, there is anyone who has so many men, that he is not able to control them, he shall place each estate in charge of a reeve, whom he can trust, and who will trust the men.

   § 2. And if there is any of those men whom the reeve dare not trust, he shall find twelve supporters from among his kindred, who will stand as security for him.

   § 3. And if a lord or a reeve or any man breaks this decree or departs from it, he shall suffer the penalties declared at Grately, unless the king prefers to inflict a different penalty.

A.   10

8. Octavum, quod omnibus placuit de opere scutorum sicut dixisti.

Precamur, Domine, misericordiam tuam, si in hoc scripto alterutrum sit[1], vel nimis vel minus, ut hoc emendari[2] iubeas secundum[3] velle tuum. Et nos devote parati sumus ad omnia quæ nobis præcipere velis, quæ unquam aliquatenus implere valeamus.

IV ÆTHELSTAN

Decretum sapientum Angliæ.

1. [Ubi hæc judicia fuerunt instituta.][4]

   Hæc sunt iudicia quæ sapientes Exoniæ consilio Æþelstani regis instituerunt et item[5] apud Fefresham[6] et tertia vice apud Ðunresfelde, ubi totum[7] hoc definitum[8] simul et confirmatum est.

2. [De judiciis observandis, quæ apud Greateleiam edita fuerunt.]

   Et hoc inprimis est, ut observentur omnia iudicia, quæ apud Greateleiam posita fuerunt, præter mercatum civitatis et diei Dominicæ.

3. [De divitibus vel generosis a furto vel latronum firmatione non desistentibus.]

   Et si quis adeo dives sit vel tantæ cognationis, ut a furto vel defensione latronum vel firmatione revocari non possit, educatur de patria ista[9] cum uxore et pueris et omnibus rebus suis ad eam partem regni huius, quam rex velit[10], sit quicumque sit, sic[11] comitum, sic[11] villanorum, eo tenore quo numquam in patriam redeat[12]. Et si umquam[13] in patria ista obviet alicui[14], sit tamquam in manus habens[15] fur inventus.

   § 1. Et qui eum firmabit vel suorum aliquem mittet ad eum, pecuniæ suæ reus sit in omnibus quæ habebit.

---

[1] *sit in hoc, sit alterutrum.* Br, M, Hk, T.   [2] *emendare.* Br, M.   [3] *iuxta.* Br, M.
[4] The titles are taken from Brompton.   [5] *iterum* (where no MS authority is stated the variant is common to MSS other than those of the London group).
[6] *Favr-.* Lond.   [7] om. M, Hk, Br.   [8] *diff-.* Lond.   [9] om. *de patria ista.* M, Hk, Br.   [10] *voluerit.*   [11] *sit.*   [12] *revertatur.*
[13] *numquam.* Lond.   [14] *Et deinceps numquam obviet alicui in patria ista.*
[15] *fur inter manus habens.* R, T, M, Hk.

8. Eighthly, we have all agreed that shields shall be made in accordance with your declarations[1].

And we beseech your clemency, lord! if this document contains either too much, or too little, to command alterations to be made according to your wishes. And we are zealously prepared to carry out everything you are willing to order us, in so far as it lies within our power to do so.

IV ÆTHELSTAN

1. These are the ordinances which the councillors established at Exeter[1] by the advice of King Æthelstan, and again at Faversham[2], and on a third occasion at Thundersfield(?)[3] where all these provisions were drawn up, and ratified.

2. And first of all; all the decrees shall be observed, which were established at Grately except those which relate to trading in a town[1] and trading on Sunday[2].

3. And if anyone is so rich or belongs to so powerful a kindred[1], that he cannot be restrained from crime or from protecting and harbouring criminals, he shall be led out of his native district with his wife and children, and all his goods[2], to any part of the kingdom which the king chooses, be he noble or commoner, whoever he may be—with the provision that he shall never return to his native district. And henceforth, let him never be encountered[3] by anyone in that district; otherwise he shall be treated as a thief caught in the act[4].

§ 1. And if anyone harbours him, or sends to him any of his[1] men, he shall be liable to the confiscation of all his property.

10—2

§ 2. Hoc autem igitur est quia iuramenta et vadia, quæ regi et sapientibus suis data fuerunt, semper infracta[1] sunt et minus observata quam pro Deo[2] et seculo conveniat.

4. [De illo qui alterius hominem recepit.]
Et qui alterius hominem suscipiet[3] intra mercam vel extra, quem pro malo suo dimittat et castigare non possit, reddat regi centum viginti solidos, et redeat intus unde exivit, et rectum faciat ei cui servivit antea[4].

5. [Ne dominus libero homini ius prohibeat.]
Et item, ne dominus libero homini hlafordsocnam prohibeat, qui ei per omnia rectum fecerit.

6. [De fure capto, qui personam vel locum pacis adierit.]
Et sit fur qui furatus est postquam concilium fuit apud Ðunresfeld vel furetur[5], nullo modo vita dignus habeatur[6]; non per socnam, non per pecuniam, si per verum reveletur in eo; sit liber, sit servus, sic[7] comitum, sic[7] villanorum, sit domina, sit pedissequa, sit quicumque sit, sic[8] handhab-benda, sic[8] non handhabbenda; si pro certo sciatur—id est si verbum non dixerit[9] ut andsaca[10] sit—vel in ordalio reus sit[11], vel per aliud aliquid [culpabilis][12] innotescat.

§ 1. Si regem vel archiepiscopum requirat vel sanctam Dei ecclesiam, habeat novem noctes de termino; et quærat quicquid quærat, non habeat vitam diutius, de quo vere palam erit[13], nisi capi non possit.

§ 2[14]. Si episcopum vel comitem vel abbatem vel alderman-num vel thainum requirat, habeat terminum tres noctes; et quærat quicquid[15] quærat, non habeat vitam diucius, si capiatur.

§ 3. Si autem fugiat[16] prosequatur[17] eum omnis homo super vitam suam qui velit quod rex, et occidat eum cui obviabit. Qui ei pepercerit vel eundem firmaverit[18], indignus sit omnium quæ habebit et vitæ suæ, sicut

---

[1] R, T, M, Hk. *superinfracta.* Lond.   [2] *quam Deo.* Lond.   [3] *recipiet.*
[4] *servierat.* R, T, M, Hk.   [5] *furabitur.*   [6] *sit.*   [7] *sit.* T, M, Hk.
[8] *sit.* T.   [9] *direxerit.* R, T, M, Hk.   [10] *ādsaca.* Lond. See note *ad loc.*
[11] *appareat.*   [12] *om.* Lond.   [13] *fuerit.* R, T, M, Hk.   [14] In K (fol-lowed by Price and Schmid) § 3 comes before § 2.   [15] *quod.* Or, R, T, M, Hk.
[16] *aufugiat.*   [17] *persequatur.* R, T, M, Hk.   [18] *firmabit.* R, T, M, Hk.

§ 2. And the reason for this is that the oaths and pledges which were given to the king and his councillors have been continuously violated[1], or observed[2] less strictly than is acceptable to God and to the secular authority.

4. If anyone shall receive a man who has been in the service of another[1], within or beyond the border[2], whom the latter has dismissed for his wrongdoing, and whom he has not been able to punish, he shall pay 120 shillings to the king[3]; and the fugitive shall return to the place from which he came and render satisfaction to him in whose service he has been.

5. And further, a freeman who has acted rightly in all respects to his lord, shall not be prevented from seeking a [new] lord[1].

6. And if there is a thief who has committed theft since the Council was held at Thundersfield, and is still engaged in thieving, he shall in no way be judged worthy of life, neither by claiming the right of protection[1] nor by making monetary payment, if the charge is truly substantiated against him[2]— whether it is a freeman or a slave, a noble or commoner, or, if it is a woman, whether she is a mistress or a maid— whosoever it may be, whether taken in the act or not taken in the act, if it is known for a certainty—that is, if he shall not make a statement of denial[3]—or if the charge is proved in the ordeal[4], or if his guilt becomes known in any other way.

§ 1. And if he seeks the king, or the archbishop, or a holy church of God, he shall have respite for nine days; but let him seek [whomsoever or] whatsoever he may, unless he cannot be captured, he shall not be allowed to live longer, if the truth becomes known about him.

§ 2. And if he seeks a bishop[1] or a nobleman, an abbot or an *ealdorman* or a thegn, he shall have a respite for three days. But let him seek whatever he may, he shall not be spared longer, if he is caught.

§ 3. If however he takes to flight, he shall be pursued to his death by all men who are willing to carry out the king's wishes[1], and whoever shall meet him shall kill him. And he who spares or harbours him shall forfeit his life and all that he has as if he were a thief himself, unless he

fur, nisi se possit allegiare quod nec furtum cum eo
sciret nec facnum[1], pro quo vitæ suæ[2] reus esset.

§ 4. Si libera mulier sit, præcipitetur de clivo vel submer-
gatur.

§ 5. Si servus homo sit, eant sexaginta et[3] viginti servi et
lapident eum. Et si colpus alicui fallat ter, verberetur
et ipse ter.

§ 6. Tunc[4] quando furatus servus mortuus fuerit[5], reddat
unusquisque servorum illorum tres denarios domino suo.

§ 7. Si serva ancilla sit et ipsa furetur alicubi præterquam
domino suo et[6] dominæ suæ, adeant sexaginta et viginti
ancillæ et afferant singulæ tria ligna et comburant eam
unam ancillam, et conferant totidem denarios, quot servi
deberent, aut verberentur, sicut de servis dictum est.

7. [De infringentibus ista statuta et eorum pœna.]
Et si quis præpositus hoc non fecerit[7] nec inde curam habu-
erit[8], det regi centum viginti solidos, si per verum recitetur
super eum, et etiam indecentia perferat, sicut dictum est[9].
Et si thainus sit qui hoc faciat vel aliquis alius, sit hoc idem.

Fragment of IV Æthelstan.

6. § 1. 7 we gecwædon æt Đunresfelda on þæm gemote, gif
hwilc þeof oððe reafere gesohte þone cing oþþe hwylce
cyrican 7 ðone biscop, þæt he hæbbe nigon nihta fyrst.

§ 2. 7 gif he ealderman oððe abbud oþþe ðegen sece, hæbbe
ðeora nihta fyrst.

§ 3. 7 gif hine hwa lecge binnan ðæm fyrste, þonne gebete
he ðæs mundbyrde ðe he ær sohte, oþþe he hine twelfa
sum ladige, þæt he þa socne nyste.

§ 4. 7 sece swylce socne swylce he sece, þæt he ne sy his
feores wyrðe, butan swa feola nihta swa we her beufan
cwædon.

§ 5. 7 se ðe hine ofer þæt feormige sy ðæs ilcan wyrðe þæs
ðe se ðeof, butan he hine ladian mæge, ðæt he him nan
facn ne nane ðyfþe on nyste.

---

[1] facinus. K, T, Or. factum. M, Hk.   [2] mortis.
[3] om. sexaginta et. R, T, M, Br.   [4] Et.   [5] erit mortuus. R, T, M, Hk.
[6] vel.   [7] hoc disperdat.   [8] adhibeat.   [9] diximus.

can prove that he was not aware of any theft or crime for which his [the fugitive's] life was forfeit.

§ 4. In the case of a free woman, she shall be thrown from a cliff or drowned.

§ 5. In the case of a male slave, sixty and twenty[1] slaves shall go and stone him. And if any of them fails three times to hit him, he shall himself be scourged three times.

§ 6. When a slave guilty of theft has been put to death, each of those slaves shall give three pennies to his lord[1].

§ 7. In the case of a female slave who commits an act of theft anywhere except against her master or mistress, sixty and twenty female slaves shall go and bring three logs each and burn that one slave; and they shall pay as many pennies as male slaves would have to pay[1], or suffer scourging as has been stated above[2] with reference to male slaves.

7. And if any reeve will neither carry out nor show sufficient regard for this [ordinance], he shall give 120 shillings to the king[1] if the accusation against him is substantiated, and suffer also such disgrace as has been ordained[2]. And if it is a thegn or anyone else who acts thus, the same punishment shall be inflicted.

Fragment of IV Æthelstan.

6. § 1. And we declared in the Council at Thundersfield, that if any thief or robber fled to the king, or to any church and to the bishop, he should have a respite of nine days.

§ 2. If he flees to an *ealdorman*, or an abbot or a thegn, he shall have a respite of three days.

§ 3. If anyone slays him within that period of respite, he shall pay as compensation the *mundbyrd* of him to whom the thief has fled or clear himself [by asseverating] with the support of eleven others that he was not aware that the privilege of sanctuary had been obtained.

§ 4. But let him seek what sanctuary he may, his life shall be spared only for as many days as we have declared above.

§ 5. And he who harbours him longer shall be liable to the same treatment as the thief, unless he can clear himself, [by proving] that he was unaware of any crime or theft committed by him.

V ÆTHELSTAN

Æðelstan[1] cyng cyþ, þæt ic hæbbe geahsod, þæt ure frið is wyrs[2] gehealden ðonne me lyste[3], oþþe hit æt Greatanlea gecweden wære; 7 mina[4] witan secgað, þæt ic hit to lange forboren hæbbe.

§ 1. Nu hæbbe ic funden[5] mid ðæm witum, þe mid me wæron æt Eaxanceastre to middanwintre, ðæt þa ealle beon[6] gearwe mid him[7] silfum 7 mid wife 7 mid ærfe[8] 7 mid eallum þingum to farenne ðider ic wille[9]—buton[10] hy ofer þis geswican willan—on þa gerad þæt hy[11] næfre eft on eard[12] ne cuman[13].

§ 2. 7 gif heo man æfre eft on earde gemete[14], ðæt hy sýn swa scyldige, swa se ðe æt hæbbendre[15] handa gefongen[16] sy.

§ 3. 7 se þe hy feormige oþþe hyra manna ænigne, oððe ænigne man [him][16] tosænde, sy he scyldig his sylfes 7 ealles þæs þe he age; ðæt is ðonne forþon[17] ðe ða aþus 7 þa wedd 7 þa borgas synt[18] ealle oferhafene 7 abrocene, ðe þær gesealde[19] wæron. 7 we nytan[20] nanum oðrum þingum to getruwianne, butan hit ðis sy.

1. [Be ðon (þe) oþres monnes[10] man underfehþ.]

7 se ðe oþres monnes man underfó, ðe he for his yfele him from[10] dó, 7 him [gesteoran][21] ne maege his yfeles, gylde hine ðæm þe he ær folgode, 7 gesylle þam cynge cxx scll.

§ 1. Gif se hlaford þonne wille ðone man mid woh fordon, berecce hine þonne, gif he mage, on folcgemote; 7 gif he laþleas[22] beo[23], sece swylcne[24] hlaford on þa gewitnesse swylcne he wille[25]; forðy þe ic an[26], ðæt ælc ðara þe laþleas[22] beo, folgie swilcum hlaforde swylcum he wille[27].

---

[1] Ic, Æðelstan, Ld, from which all the variant readings are taken.
[2] Altered to wyrse. H. [3] lyst. [4] mine. [5] Altered to gefunden.
[6] syn. [7] hire. [8] yrfe. [9] ðider ðider ic ðonne wille.
[10] o altered to a. H. [11] on ða gerade ðe heo. [12] eorda. [13] cumen.
[14] on ðæm eorda gemitte. [15] hebbendra. [16] om. H. [17] forðæm.
[18] syn. [19] ðæs geseald. [20] nyten. [21] getruwian. H.
[22] Ld. ladleas. H. [23] sy. [24] hwylcne. [25] þonne wille.
[26] forþon ic wille. [27] ðonne wille.

V ÆTHELSTAN

I, King Æthelstan, declare that I have learned that the public peace has not been kept to the extent, either of my wishes, or of the provisions laid down at Grately. And my councillors say that I have suffered this too long.

§ 1. Now I have decided with the councillors who have been[1] with me at Exeter at midwinter, that all [disturbers of the peace][2] shall be ready to go themselves, with their wives, with their property[3], and with everything [they possess], whithersoever I wish, unless henceforth they are willing to cease [from wrongdoing]—with the further provision that they never afterwards return to their native district.

§ 2. And if anyone ever meets them afterwards in their native district[1], they shall be liable to the same punishment as one who is taken in the act of thieving[2].

§ 3. And he who harbours them, or any of their men, or sends any man to them, shall forfeit his life and all he possesses[1]. The cause [which has led us to issue this decree] is, that all the oaths, pledges, and sureties which were given there[2], have beèn disregarded and violated, and we know of no other course which we can follow with confidence, unless it be this.

1. And he who takes into his service one who has been in the service of another, whom the latter has dismissed[1] because of his evil conduct, and because he has not been able to restrain him from evil doing, shall pay compensation for him, to the man in whose service he has been, and give 120 shillings to the king[2].

§ 1. If, however, the lord wrongfully intends to ruin the man, he [the man] shall clear himself, if he can, in a public meeting. If he proves himself free from crime, he may seek, with the witness of those present, any lord he wishes; for I give permission to everyone who is free from crime to serve any lord he may wish.

§ 2. 7 swylc gerefa swylc ðis foregemeleasie 7 ymbe beon
nylle, gesylle ðam cinge his oferhyrnesse, gif hit¹ man
him ongerecce mid soþe, [7 he hine ungereccan ne
mæge]².

§ 3. 7 swylc gerefa swylc medsceat³ nime 7 oþres ryht ðurh
þæt alecge, gylde þæs cinges oferhyrnesse 7 wege eac
ða ungerisnu, swa swa we gecweden habbað.

§ 4. 7 gif hit sy ðegen ðe hit dó, sy þæt ilce.

§ 5. 7 nemne man on¹ ælces gerefan manunge swa fela
manna swa man wite, þæt ungelygne syn, þæt hy¹ beon
to gewitnesse gehwylcere spræce. 7 sien heora aþas
ungelygenra manna be þæs feos wyrðe butan cyre.

2. [Be ðon ðe yrfe bespyrige.]
7 se þe bespirige yrfe innan⁴ oþres land, aspirige hit ut se
[þe]⁵ þæt lond⁶ age, gif he mæge. Gif he ne mæge, stande þæt
spor for þone foraþ, gif he ðærinne hwæne⁷ teo.

3. 7 man singe ælc⁸ Frigdæge æt ælcum mynstre ealle þa
Godes þeowan⁹ an fiftig [sealmas]¹⁰ for þone cyng 7 for ealle
þe willaþ¹¹ ðæt he wile 7 for þa oþre, swa hy¹² geearnian.

§ 1. [And ylce man ðe wille mot gebeten ylce gestale wiþ
ðone teonde butan ylcum wite oþ gong-dagas; 7 beo
syþþan swa hit ær wæs.]

---

¹ om. Ld.   ² Ld. *et se non possit reicere.* Quadr. Not in H.
³ *midsceattas.*   ⁴ *in on.*   ⁵ Ld. Not in H.   ⁶ *o* altered to *a.* H.
⁷ *hwone.*   ⁸ *ylce.*   ⁹ *ðeowas.*   ¹⁰ Ld. Not in H.
¹¹ *ða ðe willen.*   ¹² *swa hi swa.*

§ 2. And any reeve who neglects this, and pays no heed to it, shall pay [the fine] for insubordination to the king[1], if he is justly accused and cannot clear himself.

§ 3. And any reeve who takes bribes, and frustrates thereby the just claims of another, shall pay the fine for insubordination to the king, and suffer also such disgrace as we have ordained[1].

§ 4. And if it is a thegn who acts thus, the same punishment shall be inflicted[1].

§ 5. And in every reeve's district, as many men as are known to be honest shall be nominated to be witnesses in all suits[1]. And the number of honest men required to give oaths [in each case] shall be in proportion to the value of the [disputed] goods, and they shall be ' unselected[2].'

2. If any one traces cattle to another man's estate, he who owns the estate shall, if he can, follow the trail, until it passes beyond his boundary[1]. If he cannot do so, the trail shall serve for the oath of accusation[2], if he [the plaintiff] charges anyone on the estate.

3. And in every monastery, all the servants of God[1] shall sing every Friday fifty psalms[2] for the king, and for all who are minded to carry out his wishes[3]. And [they shall sing psalms] for these others according to their merits[4].

§ 1. And every man who so wishes may pay to his accuser compensation for every theft, without any manner of fine[1], until Rogation days[2]. But after that it [the fine] shall be [paid], as it has been in the past.

VI ÆTHELSTAN

Iudicia Civitatis Lundoniæ.

Ðis io seo gerǽdnes þe þa biscopas 7 þa gerefan þe to Lundenbyrig hyrað gecweden habbað, 7 mid weddum gefæstnod on urum friðgegyldum, ægðer ge eorlisce ge ceorlisce, to ecan þam domum þe æt Gréatanléa 7 æt Exanceastre gesette wæron, 7 æt þunresfelda.

Ðæt is þonne ærest :

§ 1. Þæt man ne sparige nánan þe[ofe][1] ofer XII pæningas 7 ofer XII wintre mánn þone þe wé on folcriht geáxian, þæt [he][2] ful sý 7 to nánán andsæce ne mæge ; þæt wé hine ofslean 7 niman eall þæt he áge; 7 niman ærest þæt ceapgyld of ðam yrfe, 7 dæle man syððan þone ofereácan on III[3] : ænne dǽl þam wife, gif heo clæne sy 7 þæs fácnes gewita nære, 7 þæt oðer on II ; to healfum fó se cyng, to healfum se ferscipe. Gif hit bocland sy oððe bisceopa land[4], þonne ah se landhlaford þone[5] healfan dǽl wið þone geferscipe[6] gemæne.

§ 2. 7 se þe ðeof dearnunga feormige 7 ðæs facnes 7 ðæs fúles gewita sy, do him man þæt ilce.

§ 3. 7 se ðe mid þeofe stánde 7 midfeohte, lecge hine man mid þam þeofe.

§ 4. 7 se ðe þyfðe oft ǽr forworht wære openlice 7 to órdale gá 7 þar fúl weorðe, þæt hine man slea, buton þa magas oððe se hlaford hine útniman willan be his were 7 be fullan ceapgilde 7 eac hine on borh gehabban syððan, þæt he ælces yfeles geswice. Gif he eft ofer þæt stalie, agifan þa mágas þonne hine swa gewyld swa hine[7] ær

---

[1] þe. H. ofe added later.   [2] em. Thorpe.   om. H.
[3] Thorpe, Schmid, etc. emend to II.
[4] Quadr. adds id est terra testamentalis vel episcopalis.
[5] þonne. H. em. Thorpe.
[6] gerefscipe. H. em. Thorpe. cum societate communis. Quadr.
[7] Price, Thorpe emend to hi hine.

VI ÆTHELSTAN

Iudicia Civitatis Lundoniæ.

These are the ordinances which have been agreed upon and confirmed with solemn declarations in our association[1], by the bishops[2] and reeves[3] who belong to London—by both nobles and commoners—as a supplement to the decrees which were promulgated at Grately, at Exeter, and at Thundersfield (?)[4].

First of all:

§ 1[1]. No thief shall be spared [who has stolen goods worth] more than twelve pence, and who is over twelve years old. If we find him guilty according to the public law, and he cannot in any wise deny it, we shall put him to death and take all he possesses; and we shall first take the value of the [stolen] goods from his possessions, and afterwards what is left shall be divided into three. One part shall be given to the wife if she is innocent and not an accessory to the crime; and the remainder shall be divided into two, the king taking one half and the [slain man's] associates the other half. If he is a tenant on land held by title deed[2], or on land belonging to a bishop, the owner of the land shall share equally with the associates[3].

§ 2. And he who secretly harbours a thief and is accessory to his crime and guilt, shall receive the same treatment.

§ 3. And he who stands by a thief and fights on his side, shall be slain with the thief.

§ 4. And he who has been frequently and publicly convicted of theft, and who goes to the ordeal[1] and is there proved guilty, shall be slain, unless his kinsmen or his lord will ransom him by the payment of his wergeld and the full value of the [stolen] goods; and in addition, stand surety for him henceforth, that he will desist from every form of crime. If he steals again after this, his kinsmen shall give him back to the reeve to whose jurisdiction

út æt þam ordale namon, þam gerefan þe þar togebyrige[1], 7 slea man hine on þa þeofwráce. Gif hine
þonne hwa forene forstande 7 hine geniman wille, 7 he
wære fúl æt þam ordale, þæt hine man lecgan ne moste,
þæt he wære his feores scyldig, buton he cyng gesohte,
7 he him his féorh forgifan wolde, eall swa hit ær æt
Gréatanléa 7 æt Exanceastre 7 æt Þunresfelda gecweden
wæs.

§ 5. 7 se þe þeof wrecan wille 7 ǽhlip gewyrce oððe on stræte
togeliht, beo CXX scll. scildig wið þone cing. Gif he
þonne mann ofslea on þa wrace, beo hé his feores scyldig
7 ealles þaes þe he áge, buton se cing him arian wille.

Oðer:
Þæt we cwædon, þæt ure ælc scute IIII pǣng to ure gemæne
þearfe binnan XII monðum; 7 forgyldon þæt yrfe, þe syððan
genumen wǽre, þe we þæt feoh scuton; 7 hæfdon us ealle
þa ǽscean gemǽne; 7 scute ælc man his scll., þe haefde þæt
yrfe þæt wǽre XXX pænig wurð, buton earmre wúdewan, þe
nænne forwyrhtan næfde ne nán lánd.

Ðridde:
Þæt we tellan á X menn togædere, 7 se ýldesta bewiste þa
nígene to ælcum þara gelaste þara þe we ealle gecwǽdon;
7 syððan þa hyndena heora tógædere, 7 ænne hydenman, þe
þa X men mynige to ure ealre gemǽne þearfe; 7 hig XI
healdan þære hyndene feoh, 7 wítan hwæt hig[2] forð syllan,
þonne man gildan sceole, 7 hwæt hig eft niman, gif us feoh
arise ǽt ure gemǽnan[3] spræce; 7 witon eac, þæt ælc gelast
forðcume þara þe we ealle gecweden habbað to ure ealra
þearfe be XXX pǽn oððe be anum hryðere, þæt eall gelæst
sy, þæt we on urum gerædnessum gecweden habbað 7 on
ure forespæce stænt.

Feorðe:
Þæt ælc man wære oðrum gelastfull ge æt spore ge ǽt
midráde þara þe þa gebodu gehyrde, swa lánge swa þe man

---

[1] þar to gebyrige. Thorpe, Schmid.
[2] Altered from hig hwæt.
[3] em. Price. urum gemænum. H.

the case belongs, in as helpless a condition as he was when they delivered him from the ordeal; and he shall be slain in accordance with the punishment for theft. Further, if anyone stands up for him and wishes to rescue him in order to prevent his being killed, after he has been convicted at the ordeal, he shall forfeit his life unless he appeals to the king, and the king is willing to grant him his life, just as was declared at Grately, and at Exeter, and at Thundersfield[2].

§ 5. And he who wishes to avenge a thief and has recourse to violence, or comes to his aid on the high road[1], shall forfeit 120 shillings to the king. If, however, he slays anyone in the act of vengeance, he shall forfeit his life and all he possesses, unless the king is willing to pardon him.

Second:
We have declared that each one of us shall annually contribute four pence for our common benefit; and we shall pay compensation for property which is stolen after we have made our contributions; and quests [for missing property] shall be carried out by all of us together. And everyone shall pay his shilling[1] who has property which is worth thirty pence, except poor widows who have no land and no one to work for them.

Third:
We shall always count ten men together, and the chief man shall see that the [other] nine shall discharge all the dues which we have all agreed upon; and then [we shall count] them in groups of a hundred, with one official for the hundred[1] who will admonish those ten [chief men] for the common benefit of us all. And these eleven shall keep the money of the hundred-group and an account of what they disburse when money has to be paid; and again, of what they receive when money accrues to us through a plea we have made in common. And they shall see to it also that each of those dues is forthcoming on which we have all agreed for our common benefit, on penalty of[2] thirty pence or one ox; that everything may be fulfilled, which we have declared in our ordinances, and which stands in the terms of our constitution.

Fourth:
Every man who has heard a summons shall help the rest, both by following a trail, and by riding with them so long as the

spor wiste. 7 syððan him spór burste, þæt man funde ænne
man [swa of II teoðungum]¹, þær mare folc sig, swa of anre
teoðunge, þær læsse folc sy, to ráde oððe to gánge, buton má
þurfe, þider þonne mæst þearf sy, 7 hig ealle gecwædon.

Fifte:

þæt man ne forlǽte náne ǽscan naðer ne be norðan mearce
ne be suðan, ǽr ælc man hæbbe áne ráde geríden þe hors
habbe; 7 se þe hors nabbe, wyrce þam hlaforde þe him fore
ríde oððe gánge, oð ðæt² he ham cúme, buton man ǽr to rihte
cuman mæge.

Syxte:

§ 1. Émban ure³ ceapgild: hors to healfan punde, gif hit
swa gód sy; 7 gif hit mætre sy, gilde be his wlites
wyrðe 7 be þam þe se man hit weorðige þe hit áge,
buton he gewitnesse habbe, þæt hit swa god wære swa
he secge; 7 habbe þone⁴ oferéacan þe we þar abiddan.

§ 2. 7 oxan to mancuse 7 cú to XX 7 swyn to X 7 sceap to
scll.

§ 3. 7 we cwædon be urum þeowum mannum þa menn þa
men hæfdon; gif hine man forstæle, þæt hine man forgulde mid healfan punde; gif we ðonne gyld arærdon,
þæt him man yhte ufon on þæt be his wlites weorðe;
and hæfdon us þone oferéacan þe we þær abædon. Gif
he hine þonne forstalede, þæt hine man lædde to þære
torfunge, swa hit ǽr gecwedan wæs; 7 scute ælc man
þ[e]⁵ man hæfde swa pænig swa healfne be þæs gefer-
sápes mænio, swa man þæt weorð úparæran mihte. Gif
he þonne oðsceoce⁶, þæt hine man forgulde be his wlites
weorðe; 7 we ealle hine áxodan. Gif we him þonne
tócuman moston, þæt him man dyde þæt ylce þe man
þam Wyliscean þeofe dyde, oððe hine man anhó.

¹ em. Liebermann in accordance with Quadr. *inveniatur semper de duabus decimis unus homo.* Not in H.
² em. Price. *oðð.* H (for *oð*, Liebermann).
³ em. Price. *urne.* H.   ⁴ *þon̄.* H.
⁵ *þ.* H. em. Liebermann.
⁶ em. Toller. *oðsceote.* Liebermann. *oðseoce.* H.

trail can be followed. And after the trail is lost, one man shall be provided [from two tithings] where the population is large; and from one tithing[1] where the population is small[2]—unless more are needed—to proceed on horseback or on foot, in whatever direction there is most need, according to general consent.

Fifth:

No quest shall be abandoned either on the northern or the southern boundary[1], until every man who has a horse has ridden out once. And he who has not a horse shall go on working for his lord, when the latter is proceeding on horseback or on foot in his stead, until he [the lord] comes home—unless justice has already been obtained.

Sixth:

§ 1. With reference to indemnities for livestock[1], we reckon a horse at half a pound, if it is worth so much; but if it is less valuable it shall be paid for[2] according to the value suggested by its appearance, and what is approved by its owner[3], unless he can produce evidence that it is as good a horse as he says; in that case he shall have such additional sum as we are awarded in the suit.

§ 2. An ox[1] shall be valued at a mancus[2], and a cow at twenty pence, a pig at ten pence, and a sheep at a shilling.

§ 3. With reference to our slaves, those of us[1] who possess slaves[2] have declared: if anyone steals a slave, half a pound shall be paid for him. If we succeed in getting payment, he [the owner] shall receive an additional sum according to the appearance of the slave, and we shall keep the surplus of what we are awarded in the suit. If, however, a slave runs away, he shall be taken out and stoned as has already been decreed[3]. And each man who has a slave shall pay either a penny or a half-penny according to the numbers of the association, so as to make up the proper amount[4]. If, however, he gets clean away, his lord shall be paid for him according to his appearance, and we shall all search for him. Then, if we can catch him, he shall receive the same treatment as a Welsh thief[5], or he shall be hanged[6].

A.   11

§ 4. 7 þæt ceapgild aríse á ofer xxx pæñg oð healf pund, syððan we hit æscað, furðor, gif we þæt ceapgild arærað be fullan angylde; 7 beo sy æsce forð, swa hit ær gecweden wæs, þeah heo læsse sy.

Seofoðe:

Þæt we cwædon; dyde dæda se þe dyde þæt[1] úre ealra téonan wrǽce, þæt we wǽron ealle swa on ánum freondscype swa on ánum feondscype, swa hwæðer hit þonne wære. 7 se ðe þeof fylle beforan oðrum mannum, þæt he wære of úre ealra feo xii pæñg þe bétera for þære dæda 7 þon anginne. 7 se þe ahte þæt yrfe þe we foregildað, ne forlǽte he þa ǽscan be ure oferhyrnesse 7 þa mynegúnge þar mid, oð þæt we to þam gilde cuman; 7 we þonne eac him his geswinces geþancedon of urum gemænan feo, be þam þe seo fare wurðe wǽre, þy læs seo mynugung forlǽge.

Eahtoðe:

§ 1. Þæt we us gegaderian à emban ænne monað, gif we mágon 7 ǽmton[2] habban, þa hyndenmenn 7 þa þe ða teoþunge bewitan, swa mid byttfyllinge swa elles swa us tóanhágie, 7 witen[3] hwæt ure gecwydræddene gelæst sy; 7 habban þa xii[4] menn heora metscype tógædere 7 fedan hig swa swa hig sylfe wyrðe múnon, 7 dælon ealle þa metelafe Godes þances.

§ 2. 7 gif þonne þæt gebyrige, þæt ænig mægð to þan strang sy and to þam mycel, innon landes oððe uton landes, xii hynde oððe twyhynde, þæt us ures rihtes wyrnen 7 þone þeof foren[5] forstande, þæt we rídan be eallum mannum tó mid þam gerefan þe hit on his mónunge sy.

§ 3. 7 eac sendan on twa healfa to þam gerefum, 7 wilnian tó heom fultum be swa manegum mannum swa us þonne cínelic þince æt swa micelre spræce, þæt þam forworhtum mannum beo þe mara ége for ure gesomnunge; 7 we ridan ealle to 7 urne téonan wrécan 7

---

[1] þ. H. Liebermann emends to þe.   [2] Altered to ǽmtan.
[3] Altered to witan.   [4] Liebermann emends to xi.
[5] Altered to foran.

§ 4. When the value of the goods is more than thirty pence[1], the sum to be paid shall never be less than half a pound, when we have instituted a search. It shall rise to a larger amount, if we succeed in obtaining payment to the full value of the goods[2]. But a search must be continued, as has already been declared, even when the amount involved is less[3] [than thirty pence].

Seventh:

We have declared, whoever it be whose hands[1] avenge wrongs done to us all, we shall all stand together, both in friendship and in feud—whichever may result. And he who is before others in killing a thief, shall be the better off for his action and initiative by [the value of] twelve pence [taken] from our common property. And he who owns cattle for which we pay, shall not abandon the search nor the prosecution of the claim until we have obtained payment [from the thief], on pain of forfeiting the fine for disobedience to us[2]; and then we shall reward him also from our common property for his trouble, according to the expense incurred in his movements—lest the prosecution of the claim be neglected.

Eighth:

§ 1. We, the officials of the hundred-groups[1] and those who have charge of the bodies of ten[2], shall assemble once every month, if we have leisure and can do so—whether it be when the butts are being filled[3], or on any other occasion that may be convenient for us; and we shall take cognisance of how our various statutes are being observed. Twelve[4] men shall then have their dinners[5] together, and they shall have such food as they themselves think right, and they shall give away all the fragments, for the love of God.

§ 2. Again, if it happens that any group of kinsmen—whether nobles or commoners within or beyond the borders of our district[1]—become so strong and powerful as to prevent us from exercising our legal rights, and stand up in defence of a thief, we shall ride out against them in full force with the reeve in whose district the offence takes place.

§ 3. And in addition, we shall send to the reeves in both directions[1], requesting from them the help of as many men as seems desirable, according to the seriousness of the case, that wrongdoers may be the more afraid of us because of our numbers. And we shall all ride out against them, and avenge the wrong done to us, and

11—2

þone þeof lecgean 7 þa þe him midfeohtan 7 standan, buton hig him framgán willan.

§ 4. 7 gif man spór gespirige of scyre on oðre, fon þa menn tó þe þar nycst syndon 7 drifan þæt spór, oð hit man þam gerefan gecyðe: fó hé syððan tó mid his monunge 7 adrife þæt spór út of his scíre, gif he mage; gif he þonne ne mæge, forgylde þæt yrfe angylde. 7 habban þa gerefscypas begen þa fullan spæce gemæne, si swa hwær swa hit sy, swa be norðan mearce swa be suðan, á of scire on oðre—þæt ælc gerefa fylste oðrum to ure ealra friðe, be cynges oferhyrnesse.

§ 5. 7 eac þæt ælc oðrum fylste swa hit gecweden ís 7 mid weddum gefæstnod; 7 swilc mann swilce hit ofer þa mearce forsitte, beo XXX pæn scyldig oððe anes óxan, gif he aht þæs oferhæbbe, þe on urum gewritum stent 7 we mid urum weddum gefæstnod habbað.

§ 6. 7 we cwedon eac be ælcum þara manna þe on urum gegyldscipum his wédd geseald hæfð, gif him forðsið gebyrige, þæt ælc gegílda gesylle ænne gesúfelne hláf for þære sáule 7 gesinge án fiftig oððe begíte gesungen binnan XXX nihtan.

§ 7. 7 we beodaþ eac urum hiremannum, þæt ælc mann wite, hwænne he his yrfe hæbbe, oððe hwænne he næbbe, on his nehebura gewitnesse, 7 us spór tæce, gif he hit findan ne mǽg, binnon þrim nihton; forðam we wenað þæt mænige gimeléase menn ne reccean hú heora yrfe fare, for þam ofertruan on þam friðe.

§ 8. Ðonne beode we, þæt binnan III nihtum he his necheburan gecyðe, gif he þæs ceapgildes biddan wille. 7 beo seo[1] æsce þeah forð, swa hit ǽr gecweden wæs; forþan we nellan nán gymeleas yrfe forgyldan, buton hit forstolen sy: mænige men specað gemáhlice spræce. Gyf he nyte spór to tæcenne, gecyðe mid aðe mid his III

---

[1] *se.* H.

slay the thief and those who support him and fight on his behalf—unless they are willing to forsake him.

§ 4. And if anyone traces a trail from one district[1] to another, the men who are nearest shall take up the trail, follow it until it can be brought to the notice of the reeve. Afterwards, he, with the men under his jurisdiction, shall take up the trail and follow it, if he can, to the boundary of his district. If, however, he cannot, he shall pay the value of the cattle, and the whole case shall be undertaken by the authorities of the two districts in common[2], wheresoever it may happen that a trail passes from one district to another, whether to the north or the south of our borders—all reeves shall help one another to maintain the security upon which we are all dependent or pay the fine for insubordination to the king[3].

§ 5. And further, we shall all help one another as has been declared and ratified with solemn pledges. And every man who neglects to give such help[1] beyond the border[2], shall forfeit 30 pence or an ox[3]—if he disregards any of the provisions we have written down and ratified with our solemn pledges.

§ 6. And further, we have declared with regard to all those men who have solemnly pledged themselves as members of our association, that if any one of them chances to die, each associate shall give a *gesufel* loaf[1] for his soul, and sing, or cause to be sung, within thirty days, a third of the Psalter[2].

§ 7. And we further enjoin those under our jurisdiction[1], that every man should note, with the witness of his neighbours, when he has, and when he ceases to have, possession of his cattle[2]. If he cannot find them, he shall point out the trail to us within three days[3]; for we believe that many heedless men do not care where their cattle wander, owing to their excessive confidence in the public security [which now exists].

§ 8. Again we command, that if a man wishes to apply for the value of stolen cattle, he shall make their disappearance known to his neighbours within three days. Yet he must not desist from continuing the search, as has already been declared; for we will not pay for any stray cattle[1] unless it has been stolen—since many men bring impudent claims for compensation. If he cannot point out the trail, he shall declare on oath, with

necheburan, þæt hit binnan III nihtum wære forstolen,
7 bidde syððan his ceapgildes.

§ 9. 7 ne sy forspécen ne forswígod, gif ure hlaford oððe ure
gerefena[1] enig ús ænigne éacan geþæncean mǽge to
urum friðgildum, þæt we þærtó lustlice fón, swa hit us
eallum gerise 7 us þearflic sy. Ðonne gelyfe we to Gode
7 to urum cynehlaforde, gif we hit eall þus gelæstan
willað, þæt ealles folces þing byð þe bétere æt þam
þyfðum þonne hit ær wære. Gif we þonne aslaciað þæs
friðes 7 þæs weddes þe we seald habbað 7 se cyng us
beboden hafað, þonne mage we wénan oððe georne witan
þæt þas þeofas willað ríxian gýta swyðor þonne hig ær
dydon. Ac úton healdan ure wedd 7 þæt frið, swa hit
urum hlaforde lícige; us is micel þearf þæt we arédian
þæt he wile; 7 gif he us mare hǽt 7 tæcð, we beoð
eadmodlice gearawe.

Nígoðe :

Þæt we cwædon be þisum þeofum þe man on hrǽdinge fule
geaxian ne mæg 7 man eft geaxað, þæt he fúl bið 7 scildig;
þæt se hlaford hine oððe þa magas on þæt ilce geråd útniman, þe man þa menn útnimð, þe æt ordale fule weorðað.

Teoðe :

Þæt þa witan ealle sealdan heora wedd ealle togædere þam
arcebiscope æt Þunresfelda, þa Ælfeah Stybb 7 Brihtnoð
Oddan sunu cóman togeanes þam gemote þæs cinges worde,
þæt ælc gerefa náme þæt wedd on his agenre scire, þæt hi
ealle þæt frið swa healdan woldan, swa Æþelstan cyng hit
geræd hæfð 7 his witan ǽrest[2] æt Gréatanléa 7 eft æt
Exanceastre 7 syððan æt Fæfresham 7 feorðan syððe[3] æt
Þunresfelda beforan þam arcebiscope 7 eallum þam bisceopan
7 his witum, þe se cyng silf namode, þe þæron wæron, þæt
man þas domas healdan sceoldan, þe on þissum gemote
gesette wæron, buton þam þe þær ær ofadóne wæron; þæt
wæs Sunnandæges cyping, 7 þæt man mid fulre gewitnesse
7 getreowre moste ceapian butan porte.

---

[1] *gerefana.* H. [2] em. Thorpe. *ær east.* H.
[3] *quarta vice.* Quadr.

three of his neighbours, that the cattle have been stolen within the [previous] three days, and [then] he may demand their value.

§ 9. If our lord[1], or any of our reeves[2], can devise any additional rules for our association, such suggestions shall not be unheeded, nor passed over in silence; but we shall accept them gladly, as is fitting and beneficial for us all that we should. And if we are willing to act thus in all things, we may trust to God and our liege-lord, that everybody's property will be safer from theft than it has been. But if we are negligent in attending to the regulations for the public security, and to the solemn pledges we have given, we may anticipate—and indeed know for certainty—that the thieves of whom we were speaking will tyrannize over us still more than they have done in the past. But let us be as loyal to our pledges and to the regulations for the public security as will be pleasing to our lord; for it is greatly to our benefit that we should carry out his wishes. And if he issues further commands and instructions, we should be humbly ready to execute them[3].

Ninth:
With respect to those thieves who cannot be proved guilty on the spot, but who are subsequently convicted and proved guilty: we[1] have declared, that such a one may be liberated from prison by his lord or his relatives, on the same terms as apply to the liberation of men who have been proved guilty at the ordeal[2].

Tenth:
The councillors, all in a body, gave their solemn pledges to the archbishop[1] at Thundersfield, when Ælfeah Stybb[2] and Brihtnoth, the son of Odda[2], attended the assembly at the request of the king: that every reeve should exact a pledge from his own shire, that they would all observe the decrees for the public security which King Æthelstan and his councillors had enacted, first at Grately, and afterwards at Exeter, and then at Faversham, and on a fourth occasion at Thundersfield, in the presence of the archbishop and all the bishops and the members of the royal council nominated by the king himself who were present; [and] that the decrees should be observed, which were established at this meeting[3], except those which had been abrogated; namely, the decrees relating to trading on Sunday[4] and to bargaining outside a town in the presence of ample and trustworthy witnesses[5].

Endlyfte:

þæt Æþelstan[1] béot his bisceopum 7 his ealdormannum 7
his gerefum eallum ofer ealne minne ánweald, þæt ge þone
frið swa healdan swa ic hine gerǽdd habbe 7 mine witan. Gif
eower hwilc forgymeleasað 7 me hyran nelle 7 þæt wedd æt
his hyremannum níman nelle 7 he geþafað þa dyrnan ge-
þingo 7 emban þa stéoran swa beon nelle, swa ic beboden
haebbe, 7 on urum gewritum stent, þonne beo se gerefa
buton his folgoðe 7 buton minum freondscipe 7 gesylle me
cxx scll., 7 be healfum þam ælc minra þegna, þe gelandod
sy 7 þa stéore swa healdan nelle, swa ic beboden habbe.

Twelfte:

§ 1. þæt se cyng cwæð nú eft æt Witlanbyrig to his witan
7 het cyðan þam arcebiscope be þeodrede biscop, þæt
him to hreowlic þuhte, þæt man swa geongne man cwealde
oððe eft for swa lytlan, swa he geáxod hæfde, þæt man
gehwær dyde. Cwæð þa, þæt him þuhte 7 þam þe he
hit wiðrædde, þæt man nænne gingran mann ne sloge
þonne xv wintre man, buton he hine werian wolde oððe
fleoge 7 on hand gán nolde; þæt hine man þonne lede
swa æt maran swa æt læssan, swa hwæðer hit þonne
wære. 7 gif he þonne on hand gán wille, þonne dó hine
man on cárcern, swa hit æt Gréatanléa gecweden waes,
7 hine be þam ylcan lysige[2].

§ 2. Oððe gif he in cárcern ne cume, 7 man nán næbbe, þæt
hi hine niman be his fullan were on borh, þæt he æfre
má ælces yfeles geswice. Gif seo mægð him útniman
nelle ne him on borh gán, þonne swerige he, swa him
bisceop tæce, þæt he ælces yfeles geswycan wille, 7 stande
on þeówete be his were. Gif he þonne ofer þæt stalie,
slea man hine oððe hó, swa man þa yldran ær dyde.

§ 3. 7 se cyng cwæð eac, þæt man nænne ne sloge for læssan
yrfe þonne xii pæniġ weorð, buton he fleon wille oððe
hine werian, þæt man ne wándode þonne, þeah hit læsse
wære.

§ 4. Gif we hit þus gehealdað, þonne gelyfe ic to Gode, þæt
ure frið bið betera, þonne hit æror wæs.

---

[1] Æþelstanus rex. Quadr.   [2] em. Thorpe, etc. *lynige.* H.

Eleventh :

Æthelstan commands his bishops and his *ealdormen*[1], and all his reeves throughout his dominions[2] : You shall observe the provisions for the public security which I and my councillors have ordained. If any of you is neglectful and unwilling to obey me, and will not exact from those under his jurisdiction the [above-mentioned] pledge; and if he permits secret compacts[3], and is unwilling to attend to the duties of government, in accordance with what I have commanded and set down in writing[4]—the reeve shall be deprived of his office and of my friendship, and he shall pay me 120 shillings; and half this sum shall be paid by each of my thegns who is in possession of land[5], and is unwilling to attend to the duties of government in accordance with my commands.

Twelfth :

§ 1. Now again the king has been addressing his councillors at Whittlebury[1], and has sent word to the archbishop[2] by Bishop Theodred[3], that he thinks it cruel to put to death such young people and for such slight offences, as he has learnt is the practice everywhere. He has declared now that both he himself and those with whom he has discussed the matter are of opinion that no one should be slain who is under fifteen years old[4], unless he is minded to defend himself, or tries to escape and refuses to give himself up. Then, he shall be struck down whether his offence be great or small[5]—whichever it may be. But if he will give himself up he shall be put in prison, as was declared at Grately[6]; and he shall be liberated on the same conditions [as were laid down there].

§ 2. If he is not put in prison, none being available, they [his relatives] shall stand surety for him, to the full amount of his wergeld, that he shall desist for evermore from every form of crime[1]. If the relatives will neither redeem him, nor stand surety for him, he shall swear, as the bishop directs him, that he will desist from every form of crime, and he shall remain in bondage until his wergeld is paid[2]. If he is guilty of theft after that, he shall be slain or hanged, as older offenders have been.

§ 3. And the king has further declared, that no one shall be slain for the theft of property worth less than 12 pence[1] unless he is minded to flee or defend himself. But in that case there shall be no hesitation, even if the property is of less value.

§ 4. If we observe the provisions as stated above, I believe, before God, that the security of our realm will be better than it has been in the past.

APPENDIX I

BE BLASERUM AND BE MORÐ-SLIHTUM[1]

We cwædon be þam blaserum and be þam morð-slyhtum,
þæt man dypte þone að be þryfealdum and myclade þæt ordal-
ysen, þæt hit gewege[2] þry pund, and eode se man sylf to, þe
man tuge, and hæbbe se teond[3] cyre, swa wæterordal swa ysenordal, swa hwæðer [swa] him leofra sy. Gif he þone að forð-
bringan ne mæg, and he þonne fúl sy, stande on þæra yldesta[4]
manna dome, hweðer he lif áge þe nage, þe to þære byrig hyran.

APPENDIX II

DOM BE HATAN ÍSENE AND WÆTRE[1]

1. And of þam órdale we bebeodað Godes bebodum and þæs
   arcebiscopes and ealra bisceopa, þæt nán mann ne cúme
   innon þære ciricean, siððan man þæt fýr inbyrð, þe man þæt
   órdal mid hǽtan sceal, buton se mæssepreost and se þe
   þartó gán sceal; and béo þǽr gemeten nygon fét of þam
   stácan to þære mearce be þæs mannes fótan, þe þártó gæð.

   § 1. And gif hit þonne wæter sy, hǽte man hit oð hit hleowe[5]
   to wylme, and si þæt álfæt ísen oððe ǽren, léaden oððe
   lǽmen.

   § 2. And gif hit anfeald tyhle[6] sy, dúfe seo hand ǽfter þam
   stane oð þa wríste, and gif hit þryfeald sy, oð þæne
   élbogan.

   § 3. And þonne þæt ordal géara sy, þonne gan twegen menn
   inn of ægðre healfe, and beon híg ánrǽde, þæt hit swa
   hát sy, swa wé ær cwædon.

---

[1] Text from H. (App. I also in B.) [2] wége. B.
[3] se ðe tyhð. B. [4] yldestana. B.
[5] em. Thorpe. hleope. H. [6] Thorpe emends to tyhtle.

APPENDIX I

OF INCENDIARIES AND THOSE WHO SECRETLY COMPASS DEATH

With regard to incendiaries and those who secretly compass death[1], we have declared that the oath shall be augmented threefold and the weight of the iron used in the ordeal shall be increased until it weighs three pounds. And the man who is accused shall go to the ordeal, and the accuser shall choose either the ordeal by water or the ordeal by iron—whichever he prefers. If he [the accused] cannot produce the oath[2] and is proved guilty, the chief men of the borough shall decide whether his life shall be spared or not.

APPENDIX II

DECREE CONCERNING HOT IRON AND WATER[3]

1. And with regard to the ordeal, by the commands of God and of the archbishop and all the bishops, we enjoin that no one shall enter the church after the fire with which the iron or water for the ordeal is to be heated has been brought in, except the mass-priest and him who has to go to trial. And from the stake[4] to the mark, nine feet shall be measured by the feet of him who goes to the trial.

   § 1. And if the trial is by water, it shall be heated until it becomes so hot as to boil, whether the vessel (containing it) be made of iron or brass, lead or clay.

   § 2. And if the accusation is 'single,' the hand shall be plunged in up to the wrist in order to reach the stone; if it is 'threefold,' up to the elbow.

   § 3. And when the ordeal is ready two men shall go in from either party, and they shall be agreed that it is as hot as we have declared.

---

[1] See notes to E. and G. cap. 11.
[2] cf. I Edw 3; II As. 6.   [3] cf. Ine 37, note 1.
[4] cf. § 4. The iron had to be carried from the stake (post) to the mark which defined the distance.

§ 4. And gan inn emfela manna of ægðre healfe, and standen[1]
on twa healfe þæs órdales andlang þære cyricean, and
þa beon ealle fæstende and fram heora wífe gehealdene
þære nyhte; and sprænge se mæssepreost haligwæter
ofer hig ealle, and heora ælc abyrige þæs halig-wæteres,
and sylle heom eallum cyssan bóc and Cristes rode
tacn; and na béte nán man þæt fýr na læng, þonne man
þa halgunge ongínne, ac licge þæt isen uppan þam
gledan, oð ðæt þa æftemestan coll.; lecge hit man syððan
uppan þam stápelan, and ne sy þær nan oðer spǽc inne,
buton þæt hig biddan God Ælmihtig georne, þæt he
soðeste geswytelie.

§ 5. And ga he tó and in-seglige man þa hand, and séce[2]
man ófer þæne þriddan dǽg, swa hwæðer swa heo béo
ful swa clæne binnan þam in-segle.

§ 6. And se þe þás lag abréce, beo þæt órdal on him forad,
and gilde þan cyninge CXX scill. to wíte.

[1] em. Liebermann. *stande.* H.
[2] em. Price. *séte.* H. *inquiratur.* Quadr.

§ 4. And [then] an equal number of men from each party shall enter, and stand along the church on both sides of the ordeal, and all these shall be fasting and shall have abstained from their wives during the night; and the mass-priest shall sprinkle holy water over them all, and each of them shall taste the holy water. And [the mass-priest] shall give them all the book[1] and the symbol of Christ's cross to kiss. And no one shall continue to make up the fire after the consecration has begun, but the iron shall lie upon the embers until the last collect. Then it shall be laid upon the post, and no other words shall be spoken in the church, except that God be earnestly prayed to make clear the whole truth.

§ 5. And the accused shall go to the ordeal, and his hand shall be sealed up; and after three days it shall be inspected [in order] to ascertain whether it has become discoloured or remained clean within the sealed wrappings.

§ 6. And if anyone breaks these rules, the ordeal shall in his case be invalidated, and he shall pay a fine of 120 shillings to the king.

[1] The Gospels, according to Liebermann.

NOTES TO THE KENTISH LAWS

ÆTHELBERHT

1. The introductory words, like those of the following code, are obviously a later addition, made at some time after Augustine's death, the date of which is not certain—except that it took place on May 26th. Liebermann (notes, *ad loc.*) gives the year as 604; the *Saxon Chron.* (F) records it under ann. 614, while continental authorities (*Ann. Monas.*) assign it to 612. Augustine settled at Canterbury in 597.

2. 1. The word (*leudes*) was used in the same sense among the Franks.

4. 1. It is remarkable that the compensation due to the king is less than that due to a bishop (cf. cap. 1).

5. 1. To the king (Liebermann).

2. Presumably as breach of the king's *mundbyrd* (cf. cap. 2. 8).

6. 1. *To drihtinbeage.* Payment due to a lord for the loss of one of his men, and probably to be identified with the later *manbot* (see Ine, cap. 70. 76). Liebermann takes it as a fine due to the king for infraction of his sovereignty (zum Herrschergeld). He hesitates to believe that the king was the personal lord of every freeman. But it must not be assumed that conditions in Kent were the same as in Wessex; and the natural meaning of *dryhten* is 'personal lord' rather than king.

7. 1. The precise meaning of *laadrincmanna* is uncertain, as the word does not occur elsewhere; cf. *ladmann*, 'guide.'

2. The payment here specified is not, apparently, a wergeld proper but a sum equivalent to the wergeld of an ordinary freeman, *i.e.* 100 shillings (cf. cap 21 below), and double the compensation specified under cap. 6, owing to the fact that these are specially skilled servants. Liebermann suggests that the men referred to were of unfree birth, but were awarded a freeman's wergeld owing to their position in the king's service. But the context seems to me rather to suggest that this is a case of *manbot* (as in cap. 6) and that it was additional to any sum which was to be paid to the relatives as wergeld. We may refer to Wulfgar *Wendla leod*, who is described as King Hroðgar's *ar ond ombiht* in *Beowulf*, v. 336. The word *leod* would seem to indicate that he was a person of some position (cf. *v.* 331)—clearly not a slave.

8. 1. *Mundbyrd.* Literally 'protection'—then the amount to be paid for violation of protection (or guardianship).

9. 1. Liebermann takes *and* here as *or* (cf. cap. 87 below; Ine, cap. 27), since it would be pointless to exact a fine, where total confiscation was involved. He suggests that the choice between the two alternatives was determined by the gravity of the offence.

10. 1. Presumably the king's *mundbyrd* (cf. cap. 8).

12. 1. Liebermann translates 'Königskostgänger,' and refers to H. and E. cap. 15, and *Ethelwerd's Chronicle* 878 (*famuli qui regio pastu utebantur*). But the word *fedesl* occurs elsewhere only as a translation of *altilis*.

13. 1. The sum of 12 shillings specified in cap. 13 and 14 probably denotes the nobleman's *mundbyrd*.

2. The word *eorl* appears to be equivalent to *eorlcundman* in H. and E. cap. 1 (cf. *gesið* and *gesiðcundman* in Ine, cap. 50). Note that there is no evidence for different grades of nobility in Kent (cf. H. and E. cap. 1).

Apart from the laws of Æthelberht the word *eorl*, though frequent in poetry, scarcely occurs in prose except, (1) in such phrases as *ge eorl ge ceorl*, (2) as the translation of the Scandinavian *jarl* (from the time of Alfred onwards).

15. 1. For *mundbyrd*, see cap. 8, note 1 above.

2. It is difficult to find a satisfactory modern equivalent for the word *ceorl*, which denotes 'freeman' as distinct from 'noble.' 'Commoner' is less open to objection in the Kentish laws than in those of Wessex; but on the whole it seems preferable to 'peasant,' in both cases, although the latter would perhaps give a truer impression in general of the class specified.

16. 1. It is evident, especially from cap. 72 as compared with cap. 54 and 55, that 20 sceattas make a Kentish shilling.

The sceatt was the predecessor of the penny and was apparently intended to be of the same standard (21 grs.)—at all events, there is no clear evidence for any other standard. The Kentish shilling was consequently a (Roman) ounce of silver and therefore four times the value of the later West Saxon shilling, and five times that of the Mercian shilling.

There are some very early gold coins in existence, which may have been Kentish shillings, but we do not know whether they were in circulation at this time. These—or some of them at least—are of the same standard as the Roman *solidus* and the *mancus* of later times (70 grs.), and consequently represent a ratio of only 6 : 1 in the relative value of gold and silver.

18. 1. Liebermann takes the words, 7 *man nænig yfel ne gedeþ*, as referring to the lender, *i.e.* the lender takes no part in the fray, but this involves giving a different interpretation to *yfel gedon* from that which it bears in cap. 2 (cf. also H. and E. cap. 13. 15).

20. 1. The man robbed, in cap. 19; presumably also the man with whom the borrower of the weapons is quarrelling. Liebermann suggests that *þone* may be used for *þonne*, which would make the statement general: 'If however a man is slain (by the borrowed weapons), etc.' The rarity of *þonne* elsewhere in these laws is somewhat against Liebermann's view; for a similar use of the demonstrative, cf. cap. 28 below; for the whole passage cf. Alf. cap. 19 § 1.

21. 1. The *medume leodgeld* is obviously that of a freeman, as in cap. 7 (cf. H. and E. cap. 3, as compared with H. and E. cap. 1 and cap. 26 below).

22. 1. Cf. the document *Be Wergilde*, § 4. This is probably the payment known elsewhere as *healsfang* (see Wiht. cap. 11 and note).

23. 1. *i.e.* 'escapes.'

2. *i.e.* presumably from Kent.

25. 1. The word *hlafæta* ('breadeater') only occurs here. For the formation, we may compare *hlaford*.

2. Cf. cap. 15 above.

26. 1. The word *læt* does not occur except here. It is obviously identical with the term *litus, latus, lazzus* of the continental laws. The latter term denotes a class which is found among nearly all continental Teutonic peoples—intermediate between freemen and slaves, and consisting presumably of freedmen and their descendants, and perhaps also of subject populations. There is no trace of such a class in the other Anglo-Saxon kingdoms, where apparently manumitted slaves became equivalent to freemen in regard to wergeld, etc. We may however compare the *liesing* of A. and G. cap. 2 (Norse *leysingi*), and the wergelds of the Welsh population in Ine, cap. 23 § 3, 24 § 2, 32. For the rights of a lord in Kent over a manumitted slave, see Wiht. cap. 8. Nothing is known as to the qualification of the various classes of *lætas*. For similar classes in Norway see Seebohm's *Tribal Custom in Anglo-Saxon Law*, pp. 240—259, 260—267.

27. 1. Alf. cap. 40; Ine, cap. 45. The payment is presumably that which would be required when the offence was committed by one freeman against another, and amounts to breach of the latter's *mundbyrd* (cf. cap. 15 above).

29. 1. Presumably, ordinary trespass by one person, as against cap. 17 above, and cap. 32 below.

31. 1. The word *his* is ambiguous. Schmid and other scholars understand the word to refer to the wife's wergeld, in favour of which may be compared the Lex Baioariorum, cap. VIII, 1. 10: *Si quis cum uxore alterius concubuerit libera,...cum weragildo illius uxoris contra maritum componat.* Liebermann takes *his* to refer to the wergeld of the adulterer, and urges that otherwise the neuter *his* would not be used, but the changes of gender in cap. 11 and cap. 83 cited by him are hardly conclusive parallels, since in both cases the pronoun *hio* occurs in a new sentence.

It would seem that the injured husband in Kent was not difficult to please, unless we are to suppose, with Liebermann, that his consent in regard to the choice of the lady was secured beforehand—but the law, at all events, gives no hint of such a stipulation.

32. 1. Lit. 'pierces.'

2. See Liebermann's note *ad loc.* I do not feel any confidence as to the translation of this passage.

A. 12

36. 1. According to Liebermann, the *dura mater*; 'both' in cap. 37 refers to the *dura mater* and the *pia mater*.

46. 1. *sc.* 'that is pierced.'

49. 1. This law can hardly refer to the piercing of the nose, since this has already been mentioned in cap. 45 above, with a compensation of 9 shillings. Liebermann suggests that the word *þrotu* ('throat') has been omitted before *ðirel*.

63. 1. The meaning of *cearwund* is quite uncertain. Schmid translates 'Wenn jemand bettwund ist'; Liebermann, 'Wenn jemand schwer (?) verwundet ist.'

65. § 1. 1. Probably, the relatives of both parties, as suggested by Liebermann.

67. § 1. 1. *Gyfe ofer ynce*; sc. *man inbestinð*, as in cap. 64 § 2 above. Liebermann understands the reference to be to a stab an inch long, and compares the law to Alf. cap. 45; but, in the latter case, there is no mention of a stab. *Gyfe* is apparently a mistake for *Gyf*.

73. 1. The precise significance of *locbore* is uncertain. The usual interpretation is that the long hair denotes the freeborn woman as opposed to the slave.

2. Liebermann understands as the subject of *gebete* not the woman, but the man with whom she misconducts herself.

74. 1. Or possibly, the compensation to be paid *by* an unmarried woman (cf. *mægþbot*, B. and T.).

75. 1. The meaning of *mund* is not clear. But from cap. 76 below it would seem that the *mund* belongs, not to the widow herself, but to a person responsible for her (*mundbora*)—i.e., that it is a value of guardianship, though the sums are higher than we should expect in view of cap. 8 and cap. 15 above. It is conceivable that *mund* may be used here in the sense of Norse *mundr* and may mean the marriage price of a widow. In that case, however, *gebete* must have been inserted by mistake.

81. 1. The gift made by the bridegroom to the bride after the wedding (cf. II Can. cap. 73). Henr. II. 13. 70 § 22. Among wealthy people, it often took the form of a gift of land; cf. Harmer, *Historical Documents*, p. 31.

82. 1. Liebermann understands *þam agende* to mean the person who possesses right of guardianship over the girl. It seems clear from the context that a free girl (not a slave) is meant. See also Pollock and Maitland, *History of English Law*, ii. p. 363.

83. 1. *sc.* to the bridegroom, in addition to what is specified in cap. 82 above.

84. 1. Presumably to the guardian or 'owner.'

85. 1. Liebermann (see ii. p. 690) thinks there is probably no difference in meaning between *esne* in cap. 85—88, and *þeow* in cap. 89. 90, and compares Wiht. cap. 9. 10, with *ib.* cap. 13 ff. The original meaning of *esne* appears to have been 'harvester' (cf. Gothic *asans*, 'harvest'), and in general the word seems to have a wider meaning than *þeow* (cf. *þeuwne esne*, Wiht. cap. 23). The title to Ine, cap. 29, certainly uses *þeow* as synonymous with *esne*, while in Alf. cap. 43 we find the phrase *butan þeowum monnum ך esnewyrhtan*. It seems to me not impossible that in the Kentish Laws *esne* may mean a half-free servant, presumably of the *læt* class.

87. 1. Liebermann translates *and* as meaning 'or' (cf. cap. 9 above, Ine, cap. 27, etc.).

89. 1. Liebermann understands the law to mean 'robbery *by* a slave.'

HLOTHHERE AND EADRIC

For Hlothhere and Eadric see p. 2.

1. 1. The sentence *þane ðe sio þreom hundum scll' gylde* is probably merely explanatory—three hundred shillings being the wergeld of a Kentish nobleman. For the meaning of *esne* see note 1, Abt. cap. 85.

2. Not the wergeld of 3 freemen (which is the amount of the nobleman's wergeld), but the value of 3 slaves (see Liebermann's note *ad loc.*). This would be a much smaller sum. In Wessex (see Ine, cap. 74) the master of a Welsh slave who murders an Englishman is bound only to give up the slave, or pay his value (60 shillings).

Cap. 1. 3 are misunderstood by Schmid and Seebohm (*Tribal Custom in A.S. Law*, p. 467 ff.).

5. 1. For the 'number' we may possibly compare Wiht. cap. 21.

2. Liebermann takes this sentence to mean that every witness must belong to the same village as the accused (er habe solcher Freier eine Anzahl [als] Eidesmannen und [zwar] einen mit im Eide, jeglichen [Eides]mann aus dem Ortsbezirk, welchem er [selbst] zugehört); but *æghwilc* is nominative, not accusative.

3. Lit. 'one [of those] in oath with [him].'

4. The order of words is awkward, as not unfrequently in Anglo-Saxon, *e.g. Sax. Chron.* ann. 878 : ך *hiene mon þær ofslog*, ך *dccc monna mid him.* ך *xl monna his heres.*

5. *i.e.* produce such witnesses.

6. 1. *i.e.* 'remain with.'

2. Cf. Ine, cap. 38.

3. Cf. Ine, cap. 7 § 2.

7. 1. More literally 'attaches'; cf. cap. 16 § 1 below; Ine, cap. 53, etc (*befo*).

8. 1. *mote.* The verb *motan* is not found elsewhere with this meaning. Perhaps *mote* may be due to a misunderstanding of *moete* (i.e. *mete*) in an earlier MS.

2. The precise difference between the meaning of the two words is unknown; *þing*, in this sense, occurs elsewhere only in poetry, while *meðel* (*mæðel*) is found only in early glossaries and poetry.

3. I have adopted the usual interpretation of this passage, though the form of the sentence *he þane mannan*, etc. rather suggests a change of subject, and consequently, that the man required to

12—2

provide a surety is the accuser—*i.e.* the action involved is one for slander.

9. 1. *sacy*, presumably for *sacu*.

10. 1. So Liebermann. Other editors understand 'the accuser.'

11. 1. Cf. Seebohm, *Tribal Custom in A.S. Law*, p. 240.

12. 1. For *eald riht* cf. Wiht. cap. 5, note 4.

13. 1. Cf. Abt. cap. 18.

15. 1. It is uncertain whether *mearc* means the frontier of Kent or the border of a.district (cf. Wiht. cap. 8).

2. *i.e.* the householder.

16. 1. No doubt the law, as usual, applies primarily to cattle stealing.

§ 1. 1. Liebermann suggests that London was under the king of Kent when this law was drawn up. We have no evidence elsewhere to this effect. For *ætfo* see cap. 7 above, and note.

2. *wic*—an abbreviation for *Lundenwic* (Liebermann).

§ 2. 1. Or perhaps 'the king's reeve in London.'

2. Or rather, perhaps, 'in a public transaction.'

§ 3. 1. *i.e.* that he bought the property openly, etc.

For a detailed account of the procedure involved in vouching to warranty see B. and T. *s.v.* team (III.); see also Pollock and Maitland, *History of English Law*, I. p. 34 f.

WIHTRED

1. See p. 2 f. above.

2. Cf. Plummer, *Baedae Opera Historica*, II. p. 38 f.

3. *i.e.* perhaps, the month of the rye harvest (August?).

4. *Berghamstyde* has been variously identified with Berkhampstead, Barham (near Canterbury), and Berstead (near Maidstone). See Liebermann's note *ad loc.*; Chadwick, *Anglo-Saxon Institutions*, p. 252.

1. 1. sc. *sie*; literally, 'the Church shall be in freedom of,' etc.

§ 1. 1. *i.e.* the clergy (in their services).

2. 1. See note on Abt. cap. 8.

4. 1. *i.e.* Kent.

5. 1. The word *gesiðcund*, which is used in the Laws of Ine and Alfred, now takes the place of the antiquated word *eorlcund*, which is used in the earlier codes.

2. For the construction ðæs geweorþe cf. *Beowulf*, 1598, 2026, etc. Liebermann would emend to ðæt geweorþe.

3. The reference is presumably to ecclesiastical law—perhaps, as Schmid suggests, to those laid down at the Council of Hertford (cap. 10); cf. Bede, *Hist. Eccl.* IV. 5.

4. Liebermann suggests that *eald* cannot have its ordinary meaning here, since the provision cannot be more than two generations old. It may, however, denote what had already been established by custom, in contrast with an injunction ordered for the first time

in a decree; or possibly the *eald riht* may refer to the amount of the fine to be paid to a lord for serious disobedience, without specific reference to this particular offence.

7. 1. For the meaning of *steorleas* Liebermann refers to Stubbs, *Councils*, III. 234.

2. Possibly for one night only.

8. 1. The word occurs elsewhere only in II Can. cap. 45 § 1.

For *ofer mearce* cf. H. and E. cap. 16 and note; II Can. cap. 45 § 3.

9. 1. The slight emendation of 'shilling' to 'sceatt' (possibly due to a misunderstanding of the abbreviation *sc.*) gives an intelligible sense. Liebermann emends *ofer* to *of* and *dryhtne* to *dryhten*, and thus makes the lord liable to the penalty of 80 shillings, while in cap. 10 he takes *rade* in the sense of *ræde*, which really seems to necessitate a third emendation. His explanation however involves too great a discrepancy between cap. 9 and Ine, cap. 3; for then a fine of 1600 coins would be required for an offence for which contemporary West Saxon law prescribes a fine of only 120 (or 150) equivalent coins. Even if the value of the slave is added the total sum will only be 360 (or 450) coins. Moreover the *healsfang*, specified as a fine due from a freeman for a similar offence, must have been far less than 80 shillings, whether we equate it with the sum specified in Abt. cap. 22, or not, whereas in Ine, cap. 3 § 2 the freeman is liable to a heavier penalty.

10. 1. See note on cap. 9 above. Add 'to his lord' (*wið dryhten*) after 'he shall pay.'

11. 1. *healsfang* is the name given, apparently, to the first instalment of the wergeld—a sum which is to be paid only to the nearest relatives (see *Be Wergilde*, cap. 4 and 5). In Kent the payment to be made before the grave is closed (see Abt. cap. 22) is probably to be regarded as *healsfang*. The origin of the term is uncertain, but the Norse *halsfang* ('embrace') suggests the possibility that this payment denoted the re-establishment of peace between the families involved in the vendetta. On the other hand, cap. 12 f. below would seem rather to favour the idea that it was a redemption from imprisonment (enslavement).

12. 1. (With Liebermann) *and* is to be understood as 'or' (cf. Abt. cap. 9, etc.).

19. 1. *gemacene*, a late (12th cent.) form for *gemacena*. For *feowra sum* see note on II As. cap. 11.

2. *ane* may possibly stand for *ana*; but cf. cap. 24 below, where *ane* appears to be instr.

3. *abycgan*, perhaps 3rd pl. conjunct. Schmid suggested the insertion of *and* before *aþ*.

23. 1. All editors emend to *Godes*. But it is difficult to understand why, if such a scribal mistake had been made, it should not have been corrected. *Heora* also presents a difficulty. Liebermann understands the expression to refer to a religious community. But is it

likely that the head of such a community would not be a communicant? The word *gæd* occurs in the sense of 'union,' 'association'
(abstract) in *Salomo and Saturn*, v. 449 (cf. *gegada*, etc.); and it
seems to me not impossible that this may be the same word (with
Kentish *e* for *æ*) used in a concrete (collective) sense. But I do not
feel any confidence in the suggestion.

2. *i.e.* without oath-helpers.

3. See note 1 above.

4. The oath of the communicant was worth double that of a
non-communicant in Wessex (cf. Ine, cap. 15 § 1).

24. 1. *i.e.* without oath-helpers.

26. § 1. 1. The sum (70 shillings) specified here and in cap. 27 seems
hardly credible, but it is not easy to suggest what the right sum
should be.

27. 1. The alternative is given, awkwardly enough, in the following
sentence.

2. The word properly means 'owner'; but, as Liebermann
points out, the context here requires that the man who possesses his
person at the moment must be meant.

28. Cf. Ine, cap. 20.

NOTES TO LAWS OF INE AND OF ALFRED

INE

1. Of Cenred nothing certain is known, though his name occurs (sometimes with the title *rex*) in several spurious charters; see Liebermann's note, III. p. 68. Hedde was bishop of Wessex (Winchester) 676—705 (cf. Bede, *Hist. Eccl.* IV. 12 ; v. 18). For Erconwald, see p. 34 above, and Bede, *Hist. Eccl.* IV. 6.

2. The *ealdorman* in Wessex was the head of a county down to the time of Edward the Elder (900?—925?), after which several counties were usually grouped under one *ealdorman*. (In Canute's time the title was changed to *eorl, i.e.* Scand. *jarl*.) They were the chief persons in the kingdom after the king and, sometimes at least, members of the royal family. The royal council consisted of *ealdormen*, king's thegns (corresponding to the barons of later times), and ecclesiastics.

3. *Godes þeowas* denotes the whole of the clergy. both secular and regular. In V Athlr. cap. 4 *Godes þeowas* are defined as *biscopas and abbudas, munecas and mynecena, preostas and nunnan.*

4. 1. To the king (Liebermann).

2. To the church (Liebermann).

6. § 1. 1. To the monastery (Liebermann). For *mynster* in the text read *mynstre*.

§ 2. 1. It is difficult to believe that a smaller fine was exacted for fighting in the house of an *ealdorman*, etc., than for fighting in the house of a person of humbler position (see the following clause). The Latin in § 3 has XXX for CXX, and Liebermann suggests that 30 sh. may have been the penalty laid down by Ine, and that the reading of our MSS is due to a change introduced by Alfred, to bring the penalty into conformity with that laid down elsewhere for insubordination to the king. This explanation however would only shift the anomaly from the time of Ine to that of Alfred. Is it possible that the *wite* of 60 shillings was paid not to the king, as Liebermann assumes, but to the *ealdorman* himself—with or without an additional payment of 120 shillings to the king (see Chadwick, *Anglo-Saxon Institutions*, p. 118)?

§ 3. 1. One of the commonest Latin terms for 'hide' is *tributarius*, which strictly speaking appears to be a translation of *gafolgelda*. It would seem, therefore, that a *gafolgelda* was, whether in Ine's time or at some time not long previously, a peasant who held a hide of land. If we compare cap. 23 § 3 with cap. 32 we are brought to the same conclusion. The word *gafolgelda* does not occur elsewhere in the laws.

6. § 3. 2. For the *gebur* of later times see *Rect.* cap. 4. In Domesday Book the word is translated by *colibertus*. In Ine's time it may have had a wider significance. The presumption is that the terms *gafolgelda* and *gebur* together comprise the whole peasant population, and that, in contradistinction to the former term, *gebur* denotes one who did not possess a holding of his own (see Chadwick, *Anglo-Saxon Institutions*, p. 87 ff.).

3. Liebermann adds, 'to the king,' both here and in § 4 and § 5.

4. The *gafolgelda* is presumably to be included with the *gebur*.

7. 1. There is an apparent contradiction between this law and Ine, cap. 12. Liebermann understands that in the latter case, in contradistinction to this, the reference is to a thief caught in the act (cf. Wiht. cap. 26 ; II As. cap. 1).

8. 1. *i.e.* apparently, fulfilment of a legal debt or obligation.

2. If the word *scir* is used in its technical sense, *i.e.* 'county,' the official indicated is presumably an *ealdorman*, since each county was under an *ealdorman* at this time (cf. Preamble, note 2). *Scir-gerefa* (sheriff) does not appear before the 10th century. It is possible however, that *scir* is here used in a wider sense.

3. To the king (Liebermann).

9. 1. To him whom he has outraged (Liebermann).

2. To the king, as also in cap. 10 below (Liebermann).

11. 1. *i.e.* only a West Saxon.

2. *i.e.* a freeman who has been reduced to slavery.

3. Liebermann translates—'löse er sich mit seinem Wergeld.' Grammatically *his* could refer to 'the countryman bond or free,' but this interpretation would be open to the objection that the slave has no wergeld. At this time an export trade in slaves was carried on in London by Frisian merchants ; see the case of Imma mentioned by Bede (*Hist. Eccl.* IV. 22). For earlier evidence of a similar practice see the account of Gregory and the English slaves given by Bede (*op. cit.* II. 1).

12. 1. *i.e.* taken in the act (cf. note 1 to cap. 7 above).

13. This clause curiously breaks the connection between cap. 12 and 13 § 1.

14. 1. The expression of the value of the oath in hides is found only in the laws of Ine (cf. cap. 19. 46. 52. 53. 54), together with Alf. cap. 11, and the *Dialogue of Archbishop Egbert: Presbiter secundum numerum cxx tributariorum ; diaconus vero juxta numerum lx manentium ; monachus vero secundum numerum xxx tributariorum, sed hoc in criminali causa.* (Cf. Seebohm, *Tribal Custom in A.S. Law*, p. 379 f.) Elsewhere, the value of the oath is expressed in money. The expression of the oath in hides has never been satisfactorily explained, but it may be observed that the number of hides required seems to correspond to the number of shillings involved in the compensation or fine (see Ine, cap. 52 ; cap. 46. 7. 43 ; cap. 54.

23 ; and, for a discussion of this subject, Chadwick, *Anglo-Saxon Institutions*, p. 134 ff.). See Liebermann, *Die Eideshufen bei den Angelsachsen*, in the *Festschrift für Zeumer*.

15. § 1. 1. Cf. cap. 19 below, where the oath of a communicant appears to be of greater value than that of a non-communicant. For the privileged position of communicants see Wiht. cap. 23.

16. 1. Lit. 'those associated with him in payment' (of the wergeld). The word probably refers primarily to relatives (cf. cap. 74 § 2), though in Alf. cap. 27 it would seem to be otherwise. See B. and T. for other references.

2. In order to exculpate him (cf. cap. 21 and 21 § 1 below).

18. 1. The repetition of this law in cap. 37, together with the discrepancy between cap. 23 § 3 and cap. 32, suggests the possibility that the present code is a combination of two (see Chadwick, *Anglo-Saxon Institutions*, p. 10 ; but cf. note on cap. 23 § 3 below).

19. 1. It would seem that the number of hides for which a 'twelvehynde' man was entitled by his birth to swear was thirty at this time. In that case, the value of the oath is doubled if he is a member of the king's household, and is at the same time a communicant (see Chadwick, *Anglo-Saxon Institutions*, p. 136 f.). According to Liebermann all *twelfhynde* men were assumed to be communicants (see Liebermann, *Die Eideshufen bei den Angelsachsen*).

The expression *Cyninges geneat* occurs in the *Sax. Chron.* ann. 897, where the death in battle is recorded of *Æðelferð cynges geneat* —a fact which would seem to indicate that these men were persons of some position (see Chadwick, *Anglo-Saxon Institutions*, p. 137).

20. For the significance of this cap. see the introduction to the Laws of Ine and Alfred, p. 34.

21. 1. See note 1, cap. 16 above.

§ 1. 1. Presumably because, by doing so, the homicide will give the relatives of the dead man a *prima facie* case for exculpating their kinsman.

23. 1. Including probably, as Liebermann suggests, a subject of one of the English kingdoms other than Wessex.

§ 1. 1. *i.e.* the man under whose protection he has been. Liebermann connects this law with Alf. cap. 31, and understands *se gesið* to be equivalent to *þam gegildan* (Alf. cap. 31), but the two cases are not really parallel. There is no previous reference here to *gegildan* as there is in Alf. cap. 30, while in the latter case it is not stated that the person under discussion is a foreigner. Further, *Gif hit ðonne abbod sie* of the following clause (23 § 2) clearly carries on the sense of *healf se gesið*, and must refer to the person in authority over the dead man. For the use of *gesið* cf. cap. 50. 'Squire' might be a better trans. but the authority implied is over persons rather than land.

§ 3. 1. There is perhaps a certain discrepancy, though not an actual contradiction, between this law and cap. 32, which may point to a composite origin (cf. cap. 18, note 1) or to additions having been made after the time of Ine; though this cannot be regarded as certain.

23. § 3. 2. The principle that the head of the household is valued at a greater amount than his son, seems to represent Welsh custom —though the amount of the wergelds here given is far less than those stated in the Welsh laws themselves (cf. Seebohm, *Tribal System in Wales*, p. 106). No such principle is to be found in the Anglo-Saxon Laws. Cf. Seebohm, *Tribal Custom in A.S. Law*, p. 308.

3. *i.e.* probably a pound (cf. cap. 59)—the ordinary price of a slave (cf. cap. 3 § 2, 74; IV As. cap. 6 § 6; II Athlr. cap. 5 § 1; *Duns.* 7).

4. The context here seems to suggest that slaves in a Welsh community or household are meant.

5. Cf. Ine, cap. 54; Alf. cap. 35.

24. § 2. 1. An Englishman who possessed 5 hides of land was, in later times at any rate, entitled to the privileges of a thegn, and consequently to a wergeld of 1200 shillings; cf. *Northleoda Laga*, cap. 9 f., *Rect.* cap. 2 f. For a discussion of the Social System see Chadwick, *Anglo-Saxon Institutions*, Chap. III.

25. § 1. 36 shillings is an unusual fine (cf. cap. 45). For an explanation and discussion see Chadwick, *Anglo-Saxon Institutions*, p. 128.

26. 1. It is not clear to me what is meant—whether a strong healthy child needs more sustenance, or whether more should be paid for a child which appears to be of aristocratic origin. Schmid translates 'Gestaltnis der Person'; Liebermann, 'Körperbeschaffenheit.'

27. 1. Liebermann suggests that *and* should be translated 'or,' and that the king obtains the wergeld when there is no lord. It is possible, however, that the intention is to divide the sum, as in cap. 23 § 1, where (as against Liebermann's view) *se gesið* may correspond to *his hlaford* here (cf. also note 1 to cap. 50 below).

28. 1. *i.e.* his captor.

§ 1. 1. The reference is presumably to the captor, and not to the thief, for the next paragraph clearly refers to the same person, and allows the possibility of a denial of culpability, which would be hardly feasible in the case of a thief caught in the act (cf. cap. 36. 72. 73).

29. 1. Perhaps a slave rather than a servant. The word *þeowa* is used in the title (cf. note to Abt. cap. 85).

31. 1. This, substantially, is the rendering given by Thorpe and Liebermann. Price and Schmid, following the Latin version, understand *gyft* as 'bride-price,' and interpret the law to mean that if the price to be paid by the bridegroom is not forthcoming, the bridegroom must not only pay this, but he must also make amends, etc.

32. 1. Cf. *Northleoda Laga*, cap. 7 f. From a comparison between this law and cap. 23 § 2 above, it may perhaps be inferred that the *gafolgelda* still commonly possessed a hide of land.

33. 1. It has been doubted whether *horswealh* means anything more than 'horse-servant,' 'marshal'; but the evidence of the preceding law is against this interpretation. Reference may be made to the *radmen* or *radchenistres* of later times (*Pseudoleges Canuti*, cap. 6) where these words are used to translate the *syxhynde* of Alf. cap. 30 and 39 § 2 (cf. Maitland, *Domesday Book and Beyond*, pp. 44, 56, 66, 305). If this identification is correct, then the Welsh horseman is to be equated with the English *syxhynde* man, though with a reduced wergeld, as in the case of the Welsh *gafolgelda* and the Welshman who own 5 hides (cf. cap. 23 above). The man Wulfric described as *cynges horsðegn, se wæs eac Weath gerefa* (*v.l. gefera*), whose death is recorded in *Sax. Chron.* ann. 897 *ad fin.*, was evidently a person of higher position than the people referred to in this law. Reference may also be made to *Eyrbyggja Saga*, chap. 4: *Til hofsins skyldu allir menn tolla gjalda, ok vera skyldir hofgoða til allra ferða, sem nú eru þingmenn höfðingjum* etc.

34. 1. Cf. Alf. cap. 29 and 31; *þæt* is possibly final—'for the purpose of.'

35. § 1. 1. The amount to be paid is not clear. Liebermann suggests 2 × 60 shillings, Schmid 2 × 36 shillings, others 2 × 30 shillings.

36. § 1. 1, 2. See note 2 to the preamble; note 2 to cap. 8.

37. 1. Lit. 'cauldron,' a reference to the ordeal, as was first pointed out by Liebermann; see *Kesselfang bei den Westsachsen im 7ten Jahrh.*, *S.B.A.W.* 1896, II. 829—835; Hastings, *Encyclopædia of Religion and Ethics*, s.v. Ordeal.

The commonest forms of the ordeal resorted to by the Anglo-Saxons were the hot-iron ordeal, the hot and cold water ordeal, and *corsnæd*. There is no evidence that trial by battle was an Anglo-Saxon institution (see Pollock and Maitland, *History of English Law*, I. p. 16; H. C. Lea, *Superstition and Force*, p. 105),— a curious fact since the duel was exceedingly common among the Teutonic peoples of the continent. It was introduced into England by the Normans, and though the Laws of William allow Englishmen to resort to the duel in their suits with Frenchmen, they expressly allow them to decline it (II Wm. cap. 1. 2. 3; III Wm. cap. 12; cf. Henr. cap. 75 § 6). Pollock and Maitland (*op. cit.* p. 28) explain the absence of trial by battle from Anglo-Saxon procedure by the persistence of extra-judicial fighting, due to the feebleness of the central executive power.

Trial by *corsnæd* in which the accused had to swallow a morsel of barley bread or cheese (sometimes but not always consecrated), is most frequently mentioned in the laws in connection with ecclesiastics, though it was not confined to them. It was resorted to when they were without friends, or kindred, or associates, who would act as oath-helpers, unless the accused chose to clear himself by an oath taken on the sacrament (VIII Athlr. cap. 22. 24; I Can. cap. 5 § 2)—a form of ordeal definitely religious and almost entirely confined to the clergy (see Liebermann, *Glossar*, s.v. Geweihter Bissen, Abendmahlsprobe).

The chief sources of information about the ordeal are II As. cap. 23, III Athlr. cap. 6. 7, *Be blaserum and be morð-slihtum* (p. 170), *Dom be hatan isene and wætre* (p. 170), and *Exorcismus* (Schmid,

Appendix XVII; Liebermann, I. p. 401). According to this last document, every man who proceeded to the ordeal had to prepare himself by fasting for three days (cf. II As. cap. 23). He was then led into the church by the officiating priest (cf. *Dom*, cap. 1), and after the mass had been sung the Eucharist was administered. Before the sacred elements were given to him the priest addressed him thus: *Adiuro uos N. per Patrem et Filium et Spiritum Sanctum et per uestram christianitatem, quam suscepistis, et per unigenitum Dei Filium et per Sanctam Trinitatem et per sanctum euangelium et per istas sanctas reliquias, quae in ista ecclesia sunt, et per illud baptismum, quo uos sacerdos regenerauit, ut non presumatis ullo modo communicare neque accedere ad altare, si hoc fecistis aut consensistis aut scitis quis hoc egerit.* If the accused remained silent, the priest partook of the Eucharist and administered it to the accused also (cf. II As. cap. 23). Then the trial proper began. If it was by hot iron the proceedings were as follows. After the iron had been heated two representatives from each party entered the church to see all was in order (cf. *Dom*, cap. 1 § 3, Edw. Conf. cap. 9). Then an equal number from each party entered the church to watch the trial (cf. II As. cap. 23 § 2; *Dom*, cap. 1 § 4). If the ordeal was a threefold one, an iron ball weighing three pounds had to be carried nine feet (cf. *Be Blaserum*); if simple, the iron weighed one pound and had to be carried three feet. The hand was then bound up and unwrapped after three days. If it proved to be septic the defendant was pronounced to be guilty. If the trial was by boiling water, a stone was suspended therein—a span deep if the ordeal was simple, an ell deep if threefold (cf. *Dom*, § 2)—which the accused had to lift out. The preliminary and final proceedings were similar to those of the hot iron ordeal (cf. *Dom*, § 5).

If the trial was by cold water, the priest consecrated it, and gave some of it to the accused to drink. Then he called on God to receive the innocent into the holy water, and reject the guilty: *ut nullo modo suscipias hunc hominem N., si in aliquo sit culpabilis de hoc quod illi obiicitur, scilicet aut per opera, aut per consensum vel per conscientiam, seu per ullum ingenium, sed fac eum super te natare* etc. The defendant was then undressed. After kissing the gospels and the crucifix he was sprinkled with the consecrated water and cast in. According as he sank or swam he was judged to be innocent or guilty. It is uncertain if this form of the ordeal was very common in England, but II As. cap. 23 refers to one form of it.

Trials by ordeal were resorted to (1) when the suit was between Welshmen and Englishmen (see *Duns.* cap. 2. 8); (2) when strangers and foreigners had neither friends nor associates to act as oathhelpers (II Can. cap. 35, III Can. cap. 13, Henr. cap. 65 § 5); (3) when perjurers or men frequently accused were the defendants (I Edw. cap. 3; II As. cap. 7, VI As. cap. 1 § 4; I Athlr. cap. 1, III Athlr. cap. 3; II Can. cap. 22 § 1, 30; I Wm. cap. 14; Henr. cap. 65 § 3, 67 § 1); (4) when very serious offences were committed:— plotting against a lord (II As. cap. 4); breaking into a church

(II As. cap. 5); practising witchcraft (II As. cap. 6; *Be Blaserum*); coining false money (II As. cap. 14 § 1; III Athlr. cap. 8; IV Athlr. cap. 5. 7); incendiarism (*Be Blaserum*; II As. cap. 6 § 2). According to III Athlr. cap. 6 and *Be Blaserum* the accuser could choose whether the ordeal should be by water or iron, but whether it was simple or threefold depended on the offence committed, and the reputation of the accused. According to III Athlr. cap. 6 all trials by ordeal had to take place in a royal borough, but they were forbidden on Sundays and during fasts (see E. & G. cap. 9; V Athlr. cap. 18; VI Athlr. cap. 25; I Can. cap. 17, Henr. cap. 62 § 1). For the conditions under which women were tried see Edw. Conf. cap. 19.

For a discussion of the origin, prevalence, and variety of forms of the ordeal, see Hastings, *Encyclopædia of Religion and Ethics*, s.v. *Ordeal*, and the bibliography appended.

38. 1. Presumably a cow is to be given if the husband dies in summer, an ox, if he dies in winter. The husband, judging from the amount of the maintenance allowance, would be a commoner (cf. cap. 26 above).

2. Liebermann translates 'den Hauptsitz (das Stammgut).' 'Maturity' is reached apparently at the age of ten (cf. Ine, cap. 7 § 2, H. and E. cap. 6).

39. 1. See note 2 to cap. 8.

42. 1. An obvious reference to the open field system of agriculture Each field was divided into parallel acre strips (normally a furlong long and a chain wide) of which each *ceorl* had a number, though these, as a rule, were not adjacent. Doubtless the whole of the available arable was not cultivated every year, though it is uncertain whether the 'three field system' was already in existence. Neither the land nor the produce was communally owned; the *ceorls*, to borrow Vinogradoff's phrase, resembled 'a community of shareholders.' Since individual *ceorls* would seldom possess eight oxen—the number used to draw the wooden plough of the Anglo-Saxons—ploughing could only be done by hiring the oxen of neighbours (cf. Ine, cap. 60); there was no communal team to call into service.

2. Round the arable land lay the common meadows and pasture lands, enclosed by a strip of forest which provided mast pasture for the swine (cf. Ine, cap. 43. 44. 49) and served as a means of defence (cf. Ine, cap. 20). The fencing of the arable land was obviously a necessary precaution.

3. As stated above, crops were not owned communistically. Each *ceorl* would take the produce of his own strips. For an exhaustive treatment of this subject see Seebohm, *The English Village Community*; Cunningham, *Growth of English Industry and Commerce*, I. p. 30 ff.; Vinogradoff, *The Growth of the Manor*, p. 165 ff.; Maitland, *Domesday Book and Beyond*, p. 337 ff.; Hodgkin, *Political History of England*, p. 219 ff.

§ 1. 1. *i.e.* perhaps the difference between its value alive and dead.

44. § 1. 1. For 'rents in linen, cloth' in later times see Vinogradoff, *The Growth of the Manor*, p. 329; Neilson, *Customary Rents*, p. 191.

2. *hiwisc* is apparently used in the *Northleoda Laga*, cap. 7, for *hid*, the original meaning of which was the portion of land appertaining to a household (Lat. *familia*). It is very likely that *hiwisc* has the same meaning here, *i.e.* as Liebermann suggests, the tax would not be paid by the cottager who held little or no land.

45. 1. Lit. 'breaking through the fortifications of,' etc. It would seem that the residences of the higher classes were usually surrounded by some kind of stockade. Stones or earth can hardly have been used; otherwise such residences would frequently be traceable now.

2. *i.e.* within his diocese.

3. From a comparison of this law with Alf. cap. 40, it seems probable, that in spite of the slight difference in the amount stated, the phrase *gesiðcundes monnes landhæbbendes* is equivalent to the more usual *twelfhynde man*; though this identification is not allowed by Liebermann.

46. 1. For the loss of the right to produce an oath see I Edw. cap. 3; II As. cap. 25; II Can. cap. 36.

47. 1. By him in whose possession it is attached. The disability was removed later; see II As. cap. 24.

48. 1. *i.e.* the oath required for this purpose shall be no more than the value of the goods stolen.

49. § 1. 1. For the value of a pig see VI As. cap. 6 § 2, *Duns.* cap. 7.

§ 3. 1. That is to say, if payment for the pasturage of pigs is paid in kind.

50. 1. *i.e.* before the case passed out of his jurisdiction. Note that a *gesiðcund man* has a lord. *Gesið* is here used for *gesiðcund man* (cf. cap. 23 § 1 above). Liebermann translates *his inhiwan* by 'seine Gutsinsassen' ('inhabitants of his estate'). If this translation is correct, the last words of the law imply something like the existence of a court leet.

51. 1. The original meaning of this word was 'journey' (cf. Norse *ferð*), then (military) 'expedition'; and in view of the fact that the Latin translation is nearly always *expeditio*, it would possibly be better to translate the sentence, 'if a nobleman etc. neglects to go on a (military) expedition.' The custom arose, perhaps, not from state conscription but from the obligation of a dependant to accompany his lord on journeys (cf. reference to the *Eyrbyggja Saga* given in note to cap. 33). I take *gesiðcund man landagende* to be equivalent to *twelfhynde man* (cf. cap. 45), and the *gesiðcund man unlandagende* to be equivalent to *syxhynde man*.

52. *i.e.* an illicit compact by which a case is settled out of court, the judge and king thus being deprived of their fines (see V As. note to cap. 3 § 1).

53. 1. *i.e.* the declaration was presumably to be made at the dead man's grave.

§ 1. 1. In this clause *ierfe* appears to be used in two different senses. In the first three instances, it denotes the whole of the estate of the dead man; in the last, the particular piece of property which is in dispute.

2. *i.e.* the slave or any other article which is in dispute.

54. 1. *i.e.* in each 100 hides required in the oath (cf. note, cap. 14).

2. The expression *kyningæde* is obscure, but 30 hides was probably the value of the oath of a *twelfhynde man* (cf. cap. 19 above) If this is correct, it would mean that each 100 hides of the oath required must contain the oath of a *twelfhynde man* (see Liebermann's note *ad loc.* and Chadwick, *Anglo-Saxon Institutions*, p. 148). 'Whichever he may be,' refers most probably to the man slain, but this is not absolutely certain.

§ 1. 1. Lit. 'if he need' that is to say, if he has not the value at hand, in money or other articles.

2. The value of the slave in Wessex was 60 shillings (cf. note 3 to Ine, cap. 23 § 3); a mailcoat and sword together would probably be worth quite 40.

3. Or possibly 'or'; see the following note.

4. Swords were sometimes worth much more than this, see Harmer, *Historical Documents*, p. 4: *Freoðomund foe to minum sweorde ⁊ agefe ðeræt feower ðusenda, ⁊ him mon forgefe ðeran ðreotene hund pending*; and Thorpe, *Diplomatarium Anglicum* (*Will of the Atheling Æthelstan*). For the value of arms etc. in later times, see II Can. cap. 71 f.

§ 2. 1. The figure is curious. One MS of Quadr. has *xx quatuor*. The meaning is 'shall not be compelled...by less than.'

55. 1. The value of a sheep alone is given at a shilling (cf. note 1 to cap. 59 below) in VI As. cap. 6 § 2, and *Duns.* cap. 7.

56. 1. The subject of *swerie* must be the man who sold the beast; but the text can hardly be right as it stands. It would seem as if a number of words after *to honda* had fallen out. For the form of the oath sworn by the buyer and seller of the cattle see *The Formulae for Oaths*, cap. 7, 9.

57. 1. It would seem that two-thirds of the property—that is all except the one-third which could be claimed by the wife—was to be forfeited. See Liebermann, *Glossar*, *s.v.* 'eheliches Güterrecht,' 2—4; Pollock and Maitland, *History of English Law*, II. p. 362 ff.

59. 1. Liebermann assumes that the shilling in Ine's time contained five pence, as it did in Wessex in later times; but it is difficult to believe that the terms 'shilling' and 'five pence' used in this law signify identical amounts. That the West Saxon shilling contained four pence at this time (like the Mercian shilling) seems to be shown by the *Sax. Chron.* ann. 694, where the sum paid for the slaying of Mul is identical with the wergeld of a king stated in the fragment *Be Myrcna Lage*. It is probable also that the *wite* of 60 shillings originally meant a pound of silver (see Chadwick, *Anglo-Saxon Institutions*, p. 12 f.).

§ 1. 1. The wey of barley is now 6 quarters, that of other grains 5 quarters; but the exact amount in Ine's time can hardly be determined with certainty. For a discussion of the wey see Liebermann's note *ad loc.*, and Harmer, *Historical Documents*, p. 73.

61. 1. The meaning of *to þam healme* is uncertain ; *healm* means lit. 'stalk, straw,' *i.e.* 'crop.' Schmid and Liebermann (in his notes) translate *to* by ' nach Verhältnis von,' *i.e.* 'in proportion to (the size of).'

62. *beforan ceace* may also be translated 'when faced with the ordeal' (lit. 'cauldron ') ; or more probably 'in place of undergoing the ordeal' (see Liebermann's note *ad loc.*). For 'ordeal' see note to cap. 37 above.

63. 1. With B. and T. and Liebermann I have taken *-festran* as fem. (nom. *-festre*). It might however be a masc. noun (nom. *-festra*) meaning 'fosterer.'

64. 1. The object of cap. 64. 65. 66 is, according to Seebohm (*Tribal Custom in A.S. Law*, p. 421 f.), to ensure provision for the payment of the king's food-rent.

67. 1. The *gyrd* ('virgate') was no doubt, as in later times, a quarter of a ploughland. It is more or less the normal holding of the *villanus* in Domesday Book (see Maitland, *Domesday Book and Beyond*, p. 36 ff.). It is not clear that the hide was identified with the ploughland in the time of Ine.

2. Thorpe and Kemble (*Saxons in England*, I. p. 310) understand this to mean that the tenant shall not be deprived of the results of his labour. Liebermann translates 'so braucht der [Bauer] es nicht anzunehmen wenn jener [Herr] ihm nicht [auch] eine Hofstätte giebt, und entbehre der Äcker.' He says *æcer* means not 'korn' but 'saatflur' ; but see *æcer*, B. and T. Suppl.

68. 1. It is not clear to me what this law means. B. and T. (*s.v. seten*, p. 866) suggest 'the ejected tenant was not to be deprived of what he had planted ?' or 'that he was to be compensated for the cultivation of the land ?' *Seten* may possibly be used in the sense of *land-seten*, 'land in occupation,' *i.e.* land occupied by tenants (cf. cap. 64 above). Seebohm (*Tribal Custom in A.S. Law*, p. 432 f.) suggests that *seten* refers to the *gesiðcundman's* own cattle and crops (see also Liebermann's note *ad loc.*). Is it possible that *'ordrifan* can here mean 'to undertake hostilities against'?

69. 1. *i.e.* by anyone who sells a sheep which has been shorn before that date. This would mean that two pence would be deducted from the price of the sheep.

70. 1. For *manbot, i.e.* compensation paid to a lord for the death of one of his men, cf. Abt. cap. 6 ; Ine, cap. 76 ; II Edm. cap. 7 § 3, 3 ; I Can. cap. 2 § 5 ; I Wm. cap. 7 ; and Maitland, *Domesday Book and Beyond*, pp. 31, 54, 70.

§ 1. 1. The amber was apparently half a mitta, but in neither case can the capacity be determined at this time. In the 13th century the amber contained 4 bushels (see Harmer, *op. cit.* p. 73).

2. Similar payments are not unfrequently mentioned in charters (see Harmer, *Historical Documents*, I. II. etc.; Maitland, *Domesday Book and Beyond*, pp. 234, 318, 324). In Birch, *Cart.*

Sax. 1010, a payment very much less than this is described as one day's *feorm* for Christchurch, Canterbury, in the middle of the 10th century.

71. 1. It is not clear whether the reference is to homicide, in which case the wergeld would be that of the man slain, or to some serious crime which involved the payment of the perpetrator's own wergeld (see note 1 to cap. 72, below). Liebermann takes the former view; but it is possible to take this law in connection with cap. 72, which would mean the payment of the perpetrator's own wergeld.

72. 1. According to Liebermann *wergildþeof* denotes not only a thief, but any criminal who has forfeited his wergeld. He gives a complete list of over twenty offences by which this penalty was incurred; see *Glossar, s.v.* Wergeld, 30.

2. 60 shillings, according to Liebermann (cf. cap. 43).

3. Liebermann takes *him* to be singular—referring to the thief; but cf. cap. 28 § 1 and cap. 36.

73. 1. *i.e.* before the thief is recaptured.

74 § 2. For *frige* read *frigea* (with H, B, and Ld). 1. Thorpe translates 'unless he be desirous to buy off from himself,' etc. Schmid, 'ausser wenn er ihn von der Feindschaft los kaufen will.' In the MSS *mæg gieldan* is written as one word, and in Henr. cap. 70 § 5, where this clause is translated, *mæggieldan* is rendered by *megildare*. Such compounds are unusual, though not unknown; Liebermann, III. p. 81, cites *dædbetan*. It is perhaps better to read thus than to trans. *mæg* as 'Sippenzahlung' (with Liebermann) or to take it as nom.

75. 1. Schmid translates 'Vieh (Gut).' The law relates primarily, no doubt, but not exclusively to cattle.

76. 1. For the importance attached to this form of relationship cf. *Sax. Chron.* ann. 755, where a solitary survivor of the defeated force is excused for his surrender, on the ground that he was the godson of the leader of the victorious party.

2. For *manbot* see note to cap. 70 above.

ALFRED

The Laws of Alfred are preceded by a long introduction (cap. 1—48) which contains the ten commandments (cap. 1—10), and many other precepts from the Mosaic law (cap. 11—48). These are followed by a brief account of Apostolic history and of Church law, as laid down by ecclesiastical councils, both ecumenical and English (cap. 49 § 1—§ 7). The concluding words of cap. 49 § 8 state that compensations for misdeeds on the part of men were ordained at many councils, and written in their records, with varying provisions.

Introd. 1. Lit. 'and (*i.e.* 'or') ordered to be observed in a different way,' *i.e.* I have annulled some laws, and changed others.

2. The laws of Offa, who reigned 757—796, have not been preserved.

1. § 2. 1. This is perhaps the most satisfactory translation of the expression *cyninges tun*. (Quadr. translates *ad mansionem regiam*.) The usual meaning of *tun* is 'village.'

2. 1. See note 2 to Ine, cap. 70 § 1.

2. [Read 'free²......endowed']. 'Free,' *i.e.*, exempt from certain payments to the king (see Liebermann's note *ad loc.*), or, perhaps, more generally, 'privileged.'

3. Lit. 'he shall have a space of three days to protect himself etc.'; cf. cap. 5 and 42, below.

§ 1. 1. Liebermann understands this to mean, 'he (the pursuer) shall not have obtained the sum due to him': *i.e.* by violating the right of asylum, he will lose what the fugitive owes him. But *forfon* does not seem to have this meaning elsewhere, while the syntax too is peculiar. Is it possible that in the archetype MS the reading was *his agenne forfong*, and that owing to an error of omission and a subsequent marginal correction, the *en* of *ag[en]ne* has been transposed to the end of the sentence? It is not stated that the pursuer has been robbed by the fugitive.

3. 1. *i.e.* commits an offence against any person (or place?) under the special protection of the king. The word *borg* seems to be used not, as usually, in the sense of bail, but as more or less equivalent to *mund*. Cf. *Be Griðe*, cap. 11, and the note to Abt. cap. 8.

2. Anglo-Saxon coins are seldom debased, but it is worth noting that the most debased are those of the Mercian king Burgred (852—874), who was still reigning when Alfred came to the throne.

4. 1. *i.e.* men in the king's service, who are plotting secretly against the king's life. Schmid and Liebermann take *his* in connection with *wreccena*, and translate 'their men' or 'men belonging to one of them'; but such a construction seems hardly possible.

§ 1. 1. The value of the wergeld of the King of Wessex is never stated in the laws. In the fragment *Be Myrcna Lage*, cap. 2, the king's (simple) wergeld is stated to be equal to the wergeld of six thegns, *i.e.*, 30,000 sceattas or 120 pounds, while an equal amount, called *cynebot*, has to be paid to the *leode* (*i.e.* the men in the personal service of the king). As this is the sum stated to have been paid for the West Saxon prince Mul (see *Sax. Chron.* ann. 694), it would seem that the wergelds of the West Saxon and Mercian kings were originally identical. A different and somewhat larger sum is specified in the *Northleoda Laga*, cap. 1 (see Chadwick, *Anglo-Saxon Institutions*, p. 17 f.).

5. 1. Liebermann and earlier editors take *ut* and *feohte* together as a compound verb, but as no such verb is recognised by Bosworth-Toller it would be safer perhaps to take *ut* as an adverb—equivalent to *ute*, in which sense it occurs, though rarely, elsewhere.

2. The words from *gif hit...ofgefo* form a parenthesis which can hardly be rendered in modern English, without transposition of the sentences.

§ 1. 1. Lit. 'greater need,' *i.e.* too great for it to be spared.

§ 5. 1. According to Liebermann *Sunnanniht* means 'Sunday,' which is no doubt correct for this passage. On the other hand two of the instances of the use of this word given in B. and T. clearly indicate the night between Saturday and Sunday.

§ 5. 2. According to Liebermann the expression *ðone halgan Þunresdæg on Gangdagas* is used in order to distinguish this day from Thursday in Holy Week. In some MSS (cf. p. 66, note 17) *and* has been inserted (as a correction) between *dæg* and *on*, which would seem to show that the expression was not understood. Rogation Days are the three days before Ascension Day.

7. 1. So also Liebermann. Possibly, however, the words may mean 'on such terms as the king is willing (to forgive him).'

§ 1. 1. If a man is slain.

2. *i.e.* such a fine as he may have incurred by his original offence.

8. 1. It is not certain whether *and* should be translated here by 'or' or 'and.' If it is translated 'or,' the *hlaford* would, usually at least, be a woman.

2. The word *munuc* is not elsewhere used for a woman, though *munuc had* is used to indicate the monastic life both of men and women (cf. cap. 18, below). H, B, and Ld read *þa nunnan*; So, *þone mynecenne*. The discrepancy seems to show that *þone munuc* was the original reading and was not understood by later scribes.

9. § 1. 1. *i.e.* the value of the article stolen, or the damages incurred for an offence. Note the complete change of subject.

11. § 2. 1. So Liebermann.

2. In addition to the legal fine (Liebermann).

§ 5. 1. In H *bett* is written above the line, while later MSS read *æþel*, which shows that the uncompounded *borenran* was not understood in later times. I know of no exact parallel for its use, and it is a question whether some word has not been omitted in the MS from which all our copies are derived (see Liebermann's note *ad loc.*).

12. 1. The explanation (in B) *id est half pund* is incorrect. The scribe was reckoning in Mercian shillings which contained four pence. The West Saxon shilling at this period contained five pence (cf. note to Ine, cap. 59).

14. 1. According to Liebermann, *oððe* should be translated 'and.'

17. 1. Primarily, no doubt, children are referred to.

18. § 1. 1. Quadr. translates *LX solid. emendetur marito*.

2. *feogodum* may be taken as a definition (possibly added later) of *cwicæhtum*. This is preferable to supposing that *and* has been omitted, which Liebermann suggests as another possibility.

19. 1. *i.e.* the lender and the borrower.

§ 2. 1. *i.e.* the lender.

§ 3. 1. Lit. 'they shall both give it back in such condition as either of them has received it in.' The object of this cap. according to Pollock and Maitland (*History of English Law*, I. p. 31) was to prevent men, intent on homicide, from obtaining another man's weapons and so obscuring incriminating evidence or permitting the homicide to swear an oath that it was with no weapon of his that the dead man was slain.

21. 1. This cap. presents much difficulty. Liebermann adds 'ihn' after *to handa*, keeps *and*, reads *mid him* (following H, B, Ld, So), and *bohte* in preference to *brohte* (H and B). He translates *weorpe... agife* 'liefere man (ihn) und alles, womit er sich eine Stelle kaufte, aus, und der Bischop degradire ihn, indem man ihn aus der Kirche herausgiebt.' *Hames* (for *mynsterhames*, cf. cap. 2, above) however may be partitive genitive after *þæt*. *Brohte* (in H and B) seems to show that the meaning of the original was not clear.

22. 1. H adds here 'and he shall receive the fine.' Presumably, the king's reeve is the subject of the sentence, and the fine (for bringing a groundless accusation) must be paid by the plaintiff.

23. 1. The word *abitan* usually indicates a fatal bite, and Liebermann understands it thus here. But in that case, the payment seems rather inadequate. And would it be permitted to keep a dog which had killed three people?

2. Lit. 'if he gives it food.'

§ 2. 1. Schmid and apparently Liebermann take *be* etc. to mean 'in proportion to' etc. (with reference to the various wergelds of 200, 600, and 1200 shillings). But can *fullan* mean this? Quadr. has *emendetur plena wera sic malum sicut inflixerit.*

25. 1. Liebermann adds 'to the king.'

26. 1. For a definition of *hloþ*, see Ine, cap. 13 § 1.

2. Cf. Ine, cap. 34 § 1, where the penalties are somewhat different.

27. 1. It is not clear whether the full fine is 60 or 120 shillings (see Liebermann's note *ad loc.*).

28. § 1. 1. Liebermann understands as the subject of *oðswerian wille*, not the band of marauders, but a single member of it who has been accused.

30. 1. In Ine, cap. 16 and 21, *gegildan* seems to denote those who are associated with the defendant for purposes of payment, and the presumption is that relatives are meant. Here it would seem that persons who had no relatives, or relatives only on one side (in general, presumably manumitted slaves or their sons), had other such persons associated with them, in place of relatives, for the same purpose. Liebermann (see his *Glossar*, *s.v.* Genossenschaft, 3 ff.) takes a different view.

2. Lit. 'shall flee.' B. and T. and Liebermann translate *he fleo* as 'he shall go into banishment.' But do not the words rather mean, that in default of payment, the relatives of the dead man shall have the right of taking vengeance; cf. Ine, cap. 74 § 1.

32. 1. *i.e.* one-third of the wergeld; cf. cap. 52 and 47, below.

33. 1. The term *god borg* only occurs here. It is to be contrasted presumably with *mennisc borg* (cap. 1 § 8); with an appeal to God instead of a human surety. Pollock and Maitland suggest that the giving of such a solemn promise would be confined to persons of high social rank, and would probably relate to marriages, family settlements,

and the reconciliation of standing feuds (*Hist. of Eng. Law*, I. p. 35). Thorpe quotes as a comparison the following extract from Welsh law: 'If a person pledge his baptismal vow for a debt, let him either pay or deny it, as the law requires. The church and the king ought to enforce the baptismal vow; for God is accepted in lieu of security' (*Ancient Laws*, p. 82). With Thorpe, too, we may compare Fleta, Lib. II. c. 63: *Inter quos (sc. mercatores) vero habetur talis consuetudo, quod si tallia proferatur contra talliam, allegando per eam solutionem rei petitae, si ex parte adversa dedicatur, tunc considerandum erit quod ille, cuius tallia dedicitur eam probet hoc modo; quod adeat novem ecclesias, et super novem altaria iuret, quod talis querens talliam dedictam sibi fecit nomine acquietantiae debiti in ea contenti, sic ipsum Deus adiuvet et haec sancta.*

2. This repetition of the *fore-aðˇ* and the oath of denial would involve one or other of the parties in manifold perjury, and contempt of the saints and the church.

The *fore-aðˇ* which had to precede every suit (II As. cap. 23; Henr. cap. 64 § 1) was distinct from the definitive oath of proof, though where there were manifest grounds for an accusation, *e.g.* where a man could show a wound in court, or where the trail of lost cattle could be traced to the accused man's estate (see V As. cap. 2), the *fore-aðˇ* was rendered unnecessary. Often the *fore-aðˇ* was merely an oath of integrity; a declaration that the party bringing the suit entered it not out of malice etc., but solely to procure the rights to which he was entitled by law (see Ine, cap. 56; II As. cap. 9, 11; I Wm. cap. 14; *Formulae for Oaths*, cap. 2, 7). The *fore-aðˇ* might be sworn by the plaintiff alone or by him and his oath-helpers (see passages already cited); once only, or more frequently (Henr. cap. 64 § 1; Alf. cap. 33). According to *Be leod-geþincðˇum*, cap. 3 and II Can. 22 § 2 a *fore-aðˇ* may be sworn by proxy, but the same cap. in II Can. states that a *fore-aðˇ* shall never be remitted.

35. § 2. 1. For *hengenne* see B. and T. *s.v.*, and Liebermann, *Glossar, s.v.* gefongniss. The translation 'stocks' is due to Schmid.

§ 4. 1. *i.e.* if he tonsures him.

§ 5. 1. Quadr. *decem sol*, which is probably merely a scribal error.

§ 6. 1. All the MSS read *LX (sixtig)*, but Liebermann suggests that the emendation to *feowertig* (40) in B is probably correct— 40 shillings being the total of the two fines specified in cap. 35 and cap. 35 § 4.

36. § 1. 1. 'his' refers to the man carrying the spear.

§ 2. 1. The words 'supposing the point...fingers' obviously belong to the preceding section; the spear point would thus be on a level with the face (see Pollock and Maitland, *Hist. of Eng. Law*, I. p. 31).

2. *Butan pleo*; lit. 'without danger.' Quadr. translates *sine culpa*.

37. 1. Lit. 'collection of habitations.' Liebermann (III. 58) understands *boldgetæl* to mean 'county.' In Alfred's time each county

had an *ealdorman* of its own. The word *ealdorman* (like *scir*) is sometimes used in a more general sense, but it is rather difficult to believe that Alfred would use the word in his laws, otherwise than in its technical meaning.

37. 2. Lit. 'a lord.'

§ 1. 1. Liebermann notes the growth of the authority of the state in this respect, as compared with Ine, cap. 39.

2. Lit. 'serving.'

38. § 2. 1. Schmid and Kemble understand *gingran* to mean sheriff; but there is no evidence that such an official was in existence at this time.

39. 1. Cf. Ine, cap. 6 § 3. In Kent the fine for a similar offence was 6 shillings, but the Kentish shilling contained 20 sceattas; cf. Abt. cap. 15, and the note to Abt. cap. 16.

40. 1. Note the distinction between *burg-* and *edor-* (cf. Ine, cap. 45 and note 1).

§ 2. 1. Quadr. has *sanctum velum* which is evidently based on the same reading as Ld (*halig rift*) and refers probably to the hangings of the altar; but, as Liebermann remarks, this would not have been permitted, even exceptionally.

41. 1. *bocland* was land acquired by title deed (often in reality a deed of purchase). The owner had the right of disposing of such estates by will. On this subject see Maitland, *Domesday Book and Beyond*, p. 244 ff.; Pollock and Maitland, *History of English Law*, I. p. 37 f.; Vinogradoff, *English Historical Review*, vol. VIII. 1 ff., and *Growth of the Manor*, pp. 142—144, 244—248, 209.

42. § 4. 1. I understand *hwa* (7 *hwa ofer ðæt* etc.) to refer to a third person, a relative of the man who has surrendered. Liebermann takes the sentence differently, understanding *on him*, as against the man who surrenders, while as subject of *gielde*, *hæbbe* he understands the pursuer, whom he regards as exacting vengeance for a kinsman not previously mentioned. Quadr. reads *Si uelit in manus ire et arma sua reddere, et aliquis super hoc impugnet eum, soluat sic weram sic uulnus sicut egerit, et witam et perdat quod de cognatione sua requirebat.*

2. *i.e.* he who uses violence.

3. *i.e.* the man who has surrendered his weapons.

4. Lit. 'and (thereby) he shall have brought about his kinsman's undoing.'

§ 5. 1. The word *orwige* here evidently denotes a man who, having committed homicide (under the circumstances specified), is protected from vengeance at the hands of the relatives of the man he has slain. In later times the meaning of *orwige* was not understood —hence *on wige* ('in fight') in H, and *sine wita* ('without fine') in Quadr.

§ 7. 1. See note to § 5. 1, above.

43. 1. Liebermann, in his notes (III. p. 60), translates *esnewyrhtan* as 'knechtischen Arbeitern'; see also note to Abt. cap. 85, above.

'Free men,' Liebermann explains, includes 'Hintersassen im Herrschaftsgut, Bauern und Kötter, die Fron leisten,' and 'Landarbeiter ohne Grundbesitz, die im Gutshofe, auch des Bauern, wohnen.'

43. 2. 15th February.

3. 12th March.

4. 29th June.

5. 15th August (Liebermann). Quadr. reads *et in Augusto plena ebdomada ante festum beate Marie.*

6. 1st November.

7. Ember days were days of fasting appointed by the Church to be observed in the four seasons of the year. Each fast occupied three days which, since the Council of Placentia A.D. 1095, have been the Wednesday, Friday and Saturday next following (1) The first Sunday in Lent, (2) Whitsunday, (3) Holy Cross Day (14th Sept.), (4) St Lucia's Day (13th Dec.) (see *N.E.D.*).

8. The words *þam þe him..for Godes noman* are taken differently by Schmid, Liebermann, and previous editors, who place a comma after *forgifen* and interpret *þam* as dative singular, and *þe* as nominative to *sie*. The translation would then be 'in order to give to him who is dearest to them etc.' I take *þe him* to be dative plural of the relative.

9. Lit. 'in their fragments of time.'

47. 1. Obviously a third of the wergeld (200 shillings) is the amount intended—*i.e.* 66 shillings, 3 pence and a third part of a penny.

48. 1. Liebermann points out that the word *neb* may mean more than the nose, and that injury to the mouth is not elsewhere provided for.

49. 1. For a different classification of the teeth see Abt. cap. 51.

§ 1. 1. Lit. 'cheek-tooth.'

§ 2. 1. Note the different relative values in Abt. cap. 51. Quadr. mistranslates *wongtoð* as *caninos* and *tux* as *molares dentes*.

51. 1. Not merely the larynx. Thorpe translates 'windpipe.'

52. 1. Lit. 'head.'

2. Cf. cap. 47.

55. 1. According to Liebermann, 'both bones' refers, not to the radius and the ulna, but to the bones both above and below the elbow.

57. 1. *scyte-finger; digitus secundus quo sagittatur* (B. and T.).

2. According to Liebermann, the reading of H (v shillings) is probably correct.

59. 1. Lit. 'ring-finger'; *auricularis,* Henr. cap. 93 § 19.

66. § 1. 1. Cf. Abt. cap. 59 and 60.

67. 1. *forslean* means 'to strike with violence, smite, break, etc.' (see B. and T.). Liebermann translates 'Wenn die Lendenseite zerschlagen ist etc.' The translation given is Thorpe's. He suggests the law refers either to the maiming of the lower false ribs, or the posterior part of the haunch-bones, or the spinous processes of the lumbar vertebrae.

68. 1. There appears to be a discrepancy between this law and cap. 53. Either the word *eaxle* is a mistake, or (as Liebermann suggests) some words may have been lost. The mistake, whatever it may be, is common to all MSS.

69. 1. This translation is taken from Thorpe, with whom Schmid ('an der Aussenseite zerschlägt') and Liebermann ('die Hand aussen zerschlägt') practically agree. I do not understand what kind of an injury is meant.

70. 1. For *gehaldre* read *gehalre* (B and H). Lit. 'within the whole (unbroken) skin.'

§ 1. 1. 'Taken out,' Thorpe; 'herausreisst,' Liebermann; cf. cap. 74, below.

71. 1. Cf. cap. 47, note.

73. 1. For the use of the plural (ða *sculdru*), see Liebermann's note (III. p. 62).

74. 1. Quadr. reads *Si quis intro plagietur, ut os extrahatur*—the removal of the bone being the result of the wound; this is also, perhaps, the meaning of the original.

77. 1. ða *geweald* can hardly be used in the abstract sense of *geweald* ('power,' 'strength,' 'efficiency'). Liebermann compares the word to *wælt* in Abt. cap. 68; he suggests the reference here is to the spine.

2. *i.e.* the judges of the court in which the case is tried. Some of the MSS of Quadr. add at the end of this cap., *hoc est, ut reddantur afflictiones liberorum per plenum, seruorum autem per dimidium.*

NOTES TO TREATIES WITH THE DANES

ALFRED AND GUTHRUM

Preamble. 1. This, no doubt, practically means the royal council, as in *Sax. Chron.* ann. 823.

2. From cap. 1 it is clear that in addition to East Anglia proper, Essex and South-east Mercia are included.

3. Among the subjects of Guthrum there would be freemen of English origin.

2. 1. Scandinavian payments are regularly reckoned by marks (A.S. *marc*, O. Norse *mörk*) and ores (A.S. *ora*, O. Norse *eyrir*, pl. *aurar*), which are standards of weight, 8 of the latter being equal to one of the former. In England 20 pence were commonly reckoned to the (silver) *ora*, though an *ora* of 16 pence is not unfrequently found. As the payment here is to be made in gold, the question of the relative values of gold and silver is involved (see Chadwick, *Anglo-Saxon Institutions*, pp. 24 f., 47 f.). The sum specified may represent a recognised Scandinavian wergeld, which is probably not very far from that of the West Saxon thegn (1200 shillings).

3. 1. The oath of a king's thegn was equal to that of 12 commoners (see Chadwick, *op. cit.* p. 134 ff.).

2. The *mancus* was a gold coin weighing about 70 grains. It contained 30 pence. The earliest belongs to the reign of Offa and in addition to the legend *Offa Rex* it bears a long Arabic inscription, copied from a Mohammedan coin. The name is Arabic in origin, and is derived from *man-kush*, lit. 'stamped' (cf. Chadwick, *op. cit.* p. 10 ff.).

5. 1. In the 10th century the word *here* is frequently used (like O. Norse *herr*), without military significance; cf. IV Edg. cap. 15. It is not unlikely that here the expression *in ðone here faran* denotes simply a journey into Danish territory.

2. Lit. 'that one has a clean back.'

EDWARD AND GUTHRUM

Preamble. 1. The fact that no king is mentioned here or in cap. 4, 5 § 1, may indicate, as Liebermann suggests, that the laws were enacted at a provincial (East Anglian) assembly (cf. III As. Preamble), after the kingdom had ceased to exist. On the other hand, reference may be made to IV As. Preamble, where the laws are attributed to the action of a council, though the king is mentioned. We may also compare the Preamble to the Laws of Wihtred.

2. 1. Scand. Lit. 'a breach of the law,' then the fine incurred thereby.

3. § 1. 1. Three half-marks, *i.e.* 12 *oran,* probably a pound (240 pence). This agrees with the *wite* of 60 shillings (strictly speaking Mercian shillings), found elsewhere; but not with the fine of 30 shillings here imposed. This offence was apparently less costly among the English than among the Danes (see also A. and G. cap. 2, note 1).

§ 2. 1. Maundy Thursday.

2. Probably a pound; see note 1, cap. 3 § 1, above.

4. 1. Both here and in cap. 5 § 1, below, Liebermann attaches significance to the absence of a reference to any king; cf. note 1 to the Preamble, above, and note to cap. 12, below.

5. § 1. 1. See note 1 to cap. 4.

6. § 2. 1. According to Schmid and Toller 'light-dues' were paid to provide the church with lights (cf. VIII Athlr. cap. 12 § 1; V Athlr. cap. 11 § 1; I Can. cap. 12).

§ 3. 1. Apparently dues paid from each plough; cf. I As. 4; I Edm. 2; II Edg. 2; V Athlr. 11; VI Athlr. 16; VII Athlr. 7; VIII Athlr. 12; I Can. 8: see Liebermann, *Glossar, s.v.* Pflugalmosen.

§ 5. 1. According to Liebermann the reference here is to the man who uses violence against the person who is collecting the dues of the Church. Quadr. reads *Si contrastet, ut hominem uulneret qui Dei rectitudines exigat, de hoc uita componat.*

§ 6. 1. Lit. 'if he strikes anyone dead,' but the reference is obviously to the same person mentioned in the preceding clause.

2. The word *hearme* occurs in all MSS, both here and in II Can. cap. 48 § 2. Schmid (followed by Liebermann) suggested that *hearme* stands for *hreame* ('hue and cry'); cf. Quadr. *et prosequatur eum cum clamore.* But the actual reading of the MSS gives at least intelligible sense.

7. 1. See note 1 to cap. 3 § 1, above.

§ 2. 1. The Danelagh was the region within which Danish Law prevailed (cf. O. Norse *Gulaþings Lög, Frostaþings Lög,* etc., which denote not only the Laws of the Gulaþing and Frostaþing, etc., but also the districts within which these laws were enforced). The reference here, no doubt, is to the Danish kingdom of East Anglia, though elsewhere the term embraces other parts of England which were occupied by Danes (cf. Chadwick, *Anglo-Saxon Institutions,* p. 198 f.).

9. 1. See note to Ine, cap. 37.

11. 1. Quadr. translates *Si sortilege uel incantatrices,* etc. *Wiccan* may be either masculine or feminine, but *wigleras* must be masculine. With this law may be compared a passage in Wulfstan's *Sermo ad Anglos* (printed in Sweet's *Anglo-Saxon Reader,* 8th Ed. p. 95): *and her syndan manswaran and morðorwyrhtan, and her syndan hadbrecan and æwbrecan,...and her syndan wiccan and wælcerian,* etc.

2. Birch, *Cart. Sax.* 1131 affords an interesting comparison. It describes how land at Ailsworth had belonged to a widow and her son who practised pinsticking witchcraft upon Ælsie; but she was drowned at London Bridge and her son was outlawed : *7 þæt land æt Ægeleswyrðe headde an wyduwe 7 hire sune ær forwyrt for þan þe hi drifon iserne stacan on Ælsie Wulfstanes feder 7 þæt werð æreafe 7 man teh þæt morð forð of hire inclifan. Ɖa nam man þæt wif 7 adrencte hi æt Lundene brigce, 7 hire sune ætberst 7 werð utlah*, etc.

12. 1. As mentioned above (see p. 96), Liebermann regards this passage as showing that the East Anglian kingdom had already come to an end, and that the province was now under the charge of an earl. The concluding words however, *þe cyning sy on ðeode*, are not easy to reconcile with this interpretation ; in particular, the expression *on ðeode*, which is used above of the bishop, would seem more naturally to refer to the kingdoms of England and East Anglia respectively, than to the succession of the kings of England alone. Before the extinction of the East Anglian kingdom, there were earls in Bedford, Huntingdon, Northampton, and doubtless also, in the other chief Danish centres ; and the reference in the text might well be to these, rather than to a later earl of the whole province—for which indeed we have no satisfactory evidence. The *Ealdorman* Æthelstan ('Half king') seems to have been in office in 932. On the other hand there is a difficulty in regard to the mention of a bishop. We have no trustworthy record of an East Anglian bishop between 870—933, though presumably some provision must have been made for episcopal jurisdiction from the time when the Danes accepted Christianity.

NOTES TO THE LAWS OF EDWARD
THE ELDER AND OF ÆTHELSTAN

I EDWARD

Preamble. 1. *domboc*, according to Liebermann, refers to the Laws of Alfred and Ine (cf. II As. cap. 5).

2. Liebermann points out that a similar phrase is used in King Alfred's Will (see Harmer, *Historical Documents*, p. 17), and suggests that it may have been a regular formula unless Edward had borrowed it from the will.

3. Cf. II Edw. cap. 8.

1. 1. *i.e.* the reeve in charge of a town (*port*). For 'port' see Maitland, *Domesday Book and Beyond*, p. 195 f. (cf. note 1 to II As. cap. 14; note 2 to II As. cap. 14 § 2).

§ 1. 1. 120 shillings (see cap. 2 § 1, below).

2. Lit. 'where it comes to a standstill.' When a man could not produce witnesses to prove his rightful possession of property, he was held guilty of theft (see II Athlr. cap. 9). Later, vouching to warranty was necessary to three removes only (see II Can. cap. 24).

§ 2. 1. Liebermann suggests that the form of the oath is perhaps given in *The Formulæ for Oaths*, cap. 3 § 3.

§ 3. 1. When a suitor was free (as here) to produce his own oath-helpers, the combined oath was known as an unselected (*un-gecoren*) oath (cf. I Athlr. cap. 1 § 2; II Can. cap. 30 § 7. 44). When (as in § 4) he was compelled to select oath-helpers from men nominated either by the judge or the defendant, the combined oath was known as a selected (*cyre*) oath (cf. II As. cap. 9; III Athlr. cap. 13; II Can. cap. 65; Henr. cap. 66 § 6, etc.). In *Norðhymbra preosta laga*, cap. 51 we have a combination of both oaths, and in Henr. cap. 66 § 10 the selection of oath-helpers is to be made by lot.

When it was necessary to produce the oaths of all the nominated witnesses the combined oath was known as a *rim-að*.

§ 4. 1. *geburhscipe* (H and Quadr.) may, according to Liebermann, mean an administrative district with a borough as its centre.

2. For the value of the cow see VI As. cap. 6 § 2; *Duns.* cap. 7.

§ 5. 1. Quadr. adds an explanatory parenthesis after *wiðer-tihtlan*: '*id est pro iniusta accusatione.*' Liebermann following Quadr. translates 'kraft widerrechtlicher Klage.' Thorpe explains it as 'a cross action resorted to for purposes of delay and oppression'; it was forbidden by II Can. cap. 27.

2. The form of the oath, Liebermann suggests, may be that given in *The Formulæ for Oaths*, cap. 2.

2. 1. For 'bookland,' 'folkland' see references quoted in the note on Alf. cap. 41.

2. This passage might also be translated 'that he (the defendant) shall appoint a day when he shall do him (the plaintiff) justice,' etc.

3. 1. *i.e.* if an oath of sufficient value to clear the accused has not been obtained.

2. See note to Ine, cap. 37.

II EDWARD

Preamble. 1. Lit. 'how their peace might be better than it had been.'

2. Lit. 'that which he had commanded.' The reference is to the previous code.

§ 3. 1. Cf. I Edw. cap. 2 § 1.

2. 1. Liebermann takes this to mean that a number of men are nominated to act as witnesses for the reeve when he exacts the fines mentioned in § 3, above. According to II As. cap. 25 § 1, the fine incurred by the reeve is to be exacted by the bishop.

3. 1. Cf. II As. cap. 2; Henr. 82 § 2.

§ 1. 1. II As. cap. 20 § 5.

§ 2. 1. See note to Ine, cap. 37.

4. 1. The duty of assisting to trace stolen cattle falls in later times on the Hundred (see I Edg. cap. 5).

5. 1. Probably, as Liebermann suggests, the two words express only one idea.

2. For *domboc*, see note 1 to I Edw. Preamble. Liebermann points out that as there is nothing in the Laws of Ine or of Alfred about tracing stolen cattle, the reference to the *domboc* can be relevant only to the breaking of a man's oath and pledge (cf. Alf. cap. 1 § 2; cap. 7). *ðis* (*Gif hwa ðis oferhebbe*) probably refers to all the preceding sections (cf. II As. cap. 25), and not to cap. 4 only.

§ 2. 1. Cf. Ine, cap. 30, etc. (see Index, *s.v.* 'fugitive').

2. Edward's dominions at his accession comprised Wessex, together with Kent, etc. and English Mercia (*i.e.* the south-western half of the Midlands). Before his death he had carried his frontier as far as Nottingham and Manchester.

3. *i.e.* East Anglia and Northumbria. The former kingdom was conquered by Edward after the battle of Tempsford, in which the East Anglian king was killed. The date is uncertain; the *Saxon Chronicle* (A) gives it under the annal 921, but the dates of this text are, in general, three or four years in advance of those of B and C.

4. These treaties are now lost, the Laws of Edward and Guthrum containing no provisions of this kind. This passage seems to me (as against Liebermann's view) to point to a date before the conquest of the East Anglian kingdom, since this kingdom is treated on a par with the Northumbrian kingdom which was still in existence at Edward's death, though it had already recognised his supremacy.

6. 1. B. and T. translate 'let him have such servile work assigned to him as pertains thereto'; but this translation seems to be pointless. Does not the sentence mean that the thief must do as much servile work as will equal the value of the fine which is not forthcoming?

7. 1. *i.e.* 120 shillings; cf. cap. 2, above.

8. 1. This would seem to be a meeting comparable to the meeting of the hundred in later times, cf. I Edg. cap. 1. It is doubtful however if the hundred itself as an organised unit was in existence at this time, since the first reference to it is in III Edm. cap. 2.

I ÆTHELSTAN

Preamble. 1. Archbishop of Canterbury 925—940 (cf. As. Ord. Pr.; II As. Epilogue).

2. Liebermann translates 'in jeder Stadt,' but in his notes he says that it would be better to translate 'in jedem Gericht (Amtsprengel)'; adding that the reference is not merely to town officials, but in the great majority of cases to public officials in charge of country districts and royal officials in charge of crown estates. The use of the word *byrig* would seem to imply that primarily the reeves of boroughs with dependent districts are meant—perhaps as the most important of their class. For a general discussion of the borough see Maitland, *Domesday Book and Beyond*, p. 172 ff. Cf. II As. cap. 13—18 and notes.

1. 1. 29th August.

2. 1. 2. The references seem to be to Gen. xxviii. 22 and Ex. xxii. 29; but neither of the quotations is exact.

3. 1. Liebermann refers to *Mon. Germ., Epist. Karol.* ii. 25 (a Synod of the year 786, cap. 17) *De decimis dandis...Sapiens ait: qui decimam non tribuit, ad decimam revertitur*; and to the Blickling Homilies 51, 49, where the same doctrine is enunciated.

4. 1. Cf. VI As. cap. 8 § 6.

2. See E. and G. cap. 6 § 3.

5. 1. 120 shillings (see I Edw. cap. 2 § 1).

ORDINANCE RELATING TO CHARITIES

As stated on p. 113 the Anglo-Saxon text is preserved only in Lambarde's edition, and contains many incorrect forms: *Æþelstane* (nom.), *mine* (dat.), *mina* (gen. pl.), *an earm* (acc. sing. masc.), *him* (acc. sing. masc.), *hine* (dat. sing. masc.); so also *monaþ, ane, ambra, an sconc, monþa, ðæs ealle, lufu, it, gereafa, oferheald, ða tun.*

Preamble. 1. Wulfhelm, Archbishop of Canterbury 925—940.

2. See Ine, Pr. note 3.

3. Quadr. adds *et adquisitionem vitæ æternæ.*

1. 1. *i.e.* from the rents of two of my estates. Quadr. has *nihtfirmis.* For *feorm* see Ine, cap. 70 § 1, note 2.

2. See Ine, cap. 70 § 1, note 1.

3. Quadr. has *et casei quattuor et in tercia die pasche triginta denarii ad vestitum duodecim mensium unoquoque anno.*

II ÆTHELSTAN

1. § 1. 1. According to Liebermann the wergeld is that of the thief.

§ 2. 1. The words added in So (p. 126, n. 10) mean, according to Liebermann, 'whether he is younger or older than twelve.'

§ 3. 1. According to Liebermann, this section and the following one refer to persons who are minors (cf. VI As. 12 § 1); but it is difficult to see how such a restriction could have been understood unless some word has been omitted.

§ 4. 1. *i.e.* in prison.

§ 5. 1. *i.e.* the thief's wergeld.

2. According to Liebermann, some private authority (either nobleman or prelate) who is entitled to receive fines.

2. 1. Or 'in conformity with public law.'

§ 2. 1. 'his' refers to the outlaw.

3. 1. The reference, according to Liebermann, is not to a person who had a court of his own, but to one who was influential enough to shield his men from the operation of the law. He points out also that in case of appeal there is no mention here of an appeal to a county court such as we find in later times (cf. II Can. cap. 18).

2. Three times, according to later laws (cf. II Can. cap. 19).

§ 1. 1. 'his' refers to the lord. A slave had no wergeld.

§ 2. 1. *i.e.* financial officials of the king in the various districts (Liebermann); cf. III Edm. cap. 5.

4. 1. See note to Ine, cap. 37.

5. 1. Cf. note to Ine, cap. 37.

2. Cf. Alf. cap. 6; I Wm. cap. 15; Edw. Conf. cap. 6.

6. 1. See E. and G. cap. 11, note.

§ 1. 1. See note to Ine, cap. 37.

§ 2. 1. The reference is to those who seek vengeance for a relative or friend who has been put to death for thieving.

7. 1. See note to Ine, cap. 37.

8. 1. For 'shire' see note to Ine, cap. 36 § 1.

9. 1, 2. See note to I Edw. cap. 1 § 3.

3. For the live stock which 20 pence would purchase see VI As. cap. 6 § 2.

10. 1. See note to cap. 3 § 2, above.

2. To the king (Liebermann).

11. 1. There is a curious ambiguity about the use of *sum* with the genitive of cardinal numbers. According to what was no doubt the original use, the subject is included in the number—as is probably the case in Wiht. cap. 19. Here, however, the subject seems not to be included and there are clear cases elsewhere of the same use; *e.g.* II Athlr. cap. 4 *gange feowra sum to 7 oðsace 7 beo him sylf fifta.*

For further examples of both constructions see B. and T. *s.v. sum*; cf. also J. E. Wülfing, *Englische Stu.* XVII. p. 285 f., XXIV. p. 463.

11. 2. Apparently a reference to a lost law.

12. This cap. refers primarily to cattle (cf. cap. 9, note 3; I Edw. cap. 1, note).

13. 1. For the significance of this introductory formula (*we cweðaþ*), see p. 113, above.

2. Rogation Days are the Monday, Tuesday and Wednesday before Ascension Day.

14. 1. Besides being a military centre the *burh* was the natural centre of trafficking. According to Maitland (*Domesday Book and Beyond*, p. 195), when in the laws there is a desire to emphasise the fact that the *burh* is a centre of trade, it is called a *port*, though not every 'port' was necessarily a *burh*.

§ 1. 1. See Ine, cap. 37, note.

§ 2. 1. Of St Augustine's.

2. Athelstan's coins commonly bear the name of the place where they were minted. Of the boroughs here mentioned, London, Winchester, Wareham, Exeter, along with 14 other boroughs, are represented in the Brit. Mus. Catalogue of English Coins (vol. II. p. 105 ff.).

16. 1. Elsewhere we find that one man was required for the *fyrd* (*expeditio*) from every five hides (see Maitland, *Domesday Book and Beyond*, p. 156). Since by this time the hide and the ploughland were probably identical, the requirement stated here is exceptionally heavy; but the explanation probably is that cap. 13—18 seem to have been intended for *burgware*, who may be regarded as primarily a military caste (see Maitland, *op. cit.* p. 190 f.).

19. 1. See note to Ine, cap. 37.

20. 1. *i.e.* 120 shillings, cf. I Edw. cap. 2 § 1. The assembly is probably that which met every four weeks (cf. II Edw. cap. 8).

§ 2. 1. *i.e.* 120 shillings.

§ 8. 1. 'his' refers to the fugitive.

21. 1, 2. Instead of going to the ordeal, the guilty man may come to terms with the prosecutor for any payment. But for the fine, he must settle with the authority to whom the court belongs.

22. § 1. 1. See note to cap. 20, above.

23. 1. Cf. Ine, cap. 37, note 1. The religious aspect of the ordeal is especially emphasised here. Indeed Karl von Amira (Paul, *Grund. der germ. Phil.* vol. III. pp. 218—220) contends that the ordeal was unknown to the Teutonic peoples until it was introduced by the Church. But there is evidence to show that the ordeal was generally practised in pre-Christian times, and the probability is that the Church after trying hard to abolish the ordeal was compelled to adopt and adapt it; see Lea, *Superstition and Force*, p. 355; Maitland, *Collected Papers*, II. p. 448 f.; Hastings, *Encyclopædia of Religion and Ethics*, p. 530 f.

2. *i.e.* to the ordeal.

§ 1. 1. According to a document given by Liebermann (I. p. 418, cap. 21) an ordeal by cold water is referred to here. The accused man was tied up with his hands below his knees, and let down gently into the water. If he sank to the depth specified he was judged to be innocent, the assumption being that there was a natural antipathy between the consecrated water and anything evil. A guilty man would not be taken into the water, but would float on the surface (see also note to Ine, cap. 37).

§ 2. 1. Apparently a reference to a lost law.

2. *i.e.* those in excess of 12 (cf. *Dom be hatan isene,* cap. 1 § 4).

24. 1. And with it, the responsibility for proving whence he obtained it (see II Athlr. cap. 8, 9).

2. Contrast Ine, cap. 47.

25. 1. Thorpe and Schmid, following Ld, and in accordance with a logical sequence, place cap. 26 before cap. 25. It is probable that this rearrangement is also in accordance with the original MS, and that the sequence in H is due to a mistake on the part of the scribe. *þis* refers apparently to the whole code, and not to cap. 24 only (cf. *ðis* in the last section below, and *Gif hwa ðis oferhebbe,* etc., II Edw. cap. 5).

§ 2. 1. Five pounds is a sum greater than the wergeld of a commoner (200 shillings), so the law can refer only to people of a higher social rank.

Epilogue. 1. South-west of Andover, Hampshire.

2. See I As. Pr., note 1.

III ÆTHELSTAN

Preamble. 1. Liebermann dates this document *c.* 928—*c.* 938. The 'bishops' would then be Wulfhelm of Canterbury (see I As. Pr.; As. Ord. Pr.; II As. Epilogue) and Cyneferth (or his successor Burgric), Bishop of Rochester.

2. If *comites et uillani* is a definition of *thaini,* we may (with Liebermann) compare *mine þegnas twelfhynde 7 twihynde* which occurs in a writ of Cnut's 1017 (Kemble, *Cod. Dipl.* 731). This use of the word is Scandinavian rather than English (see Kemble, *Saxons in England,* II. p. 234 f.).

1. § 1. See I As. Preamble.

2. 1. Grately, Hampshire, S.W. of Andover; cf. also VI As. Preamble, cap. 1 § 4, 12 § 1; III As. cap. 5, 7 § 3; IV As. cap. 2. The references to the Council of Grately (II As.), here and in cap. 5 and 6, appear to be of a general character rather than to specific chapters.

2. Faversham in Kent; cf. also VI As. cap. 10; III. cap. 2; IV. cap. 1.

3. 1. *misericorditer* is evidently a mistranslation—of *arlice* according to Liebermann.

2. Lit. 'that the *wite* should be excused to all.'

4. 1. Cf. Ine, cap. 39; Alf. cap. 37; II As. cap. 22; IV As. cap. 5.

§ 1. 1. Cf. V As. cap. 1 § 1.

2. *eum,* apparently for *se,* probably through a misunderstanding of *hine.*

A. 14

5. 1. Cf. II As. cap. 25 § 2.
6. 1. Cf. IV As. cap. 3 ; VI As. cap. 8 § 2.
    2. *i.e.* at Exeter ; cf. V As. Preamble, § 1.
7. 1. Cf. III Edm. cap. 7 ; I Athlr. cap. 1 ; II Can. cap. 31 ;
I Wm. cap. 52 ; Henr. cap. 8 § 3.
8. 1. Cf. II As. cap. 15.

IV ÆTHELSTAN

1. 1. See V Æthelstan, Pr. § 1.
    2. See III As. cap. 2 ; VI As. cap. 10.
    3. Thundersfield in Surrey ? In VI As. cap. 10 reference is
made to the same three councils together with that held at Grately.
Cf. also VI As. Preamble.
2. 1. See II As. cap. 12, 13 § 1.
    2. See II As. cap. 24 § 1. In later times trading on Sunday
was again forbidden (see VIII Athlr. cap. 17).
3. 1. Cf. III As. cap. 6.
    2. Cf. V As. Pr. § 1.
    3. According to Liebermann the Latin is not quite a correct
translation ; the original Anglo-Saxon was presumably a sentence
beginning with *man*.
    4. Cf. V As. Pr. § 2 ; Wiht. cap. 25, 26 ; Ine, cap. 12, 16, etc.
    § 1. 1. 'his' refers to the subject of the sentence and not to
the outlaw.
Cf. V As. Pr. § 3.
    § 2. 1. Liebermann suggests that *superinfracta* (Lond.), which he
adopts, is either a corruption of *superexcepta et infracta*, V As. Pr. 3,
Quadr., or that the original Anglo-Saxon MS had *oferbrocen*. But may
it not be a scribal error for *semper infracta* ?
        2. Cf. V As. Pr. § 3.
4. 1. Cf. III As. cap. 4.
    2. Presumably the border of his district ('Provinzgrenze,'
Liebermann).
    3. Cf. V As. cap. 1 ; I Edw. cap. 2 § 1 ; II As. cap. 22, etc.
5. Cf. III As. cap. 4 § 1 ; V As. cap. 1 § 1.
6. 1. Cf. Ine, cap. 5 ; Alf. cap. 2, 5, etc.
    2. Cf. II As. cap. 1 § 3 ; VI As. cap. 12 § 1.
    3. For Lond. in note 10 (p. 148) read Lieb. The MSS have
adlata (R), *aplata* (T, Co, Or), *awlata* (M, Hk), *aplata* (K). Liebermann's emendation is suggested by *to nanan andsæce ne mæge*, VI As.
cap. 1 § 1. For earlier explanations of the various MS readings see
Liebermann, III. p. 114.
    4. See Ine, cap. 37, note.
    § 2. 1. In the Anglo-Saxon fragment preserved in H the bishop
shares with the king the privilege of granting a respite of 9 days.
Liebermann suggests that this elevation of the bishop is due to the
Rochester scribe's desire to increase his bishop's dignity.

§ 3. 1. Apparently a formula for describing a loyal subject; cf. V As. cap. 3 : *for ealle þe willaþ ðæt he wile.*

§ 5. 1. Obviously the number meant both here and in § 7 is eighty, but I do not know the reason for the periphrasis.

§ 6. 1. Apparently to make up the price of a slave, which was a pound (240 pence); cf. Ine, cap. 3 § 2, 74, 23 § 3.

§ 7. 1. See note on § 6.

      2. See Wiht. cap. 10, 13 ; Ine, cap. 3 § 1, etc.

7. 1. See I Edw. cap. 2 § 1.

      2. See II As. cap. 25 ; V As. cap. 1 § 2, § 3.

Fragment of IV Æthelstan

This fragment is found only in H, where it is appended to V As. It differs considerably from the Latin text. In § 1 the bishop is placed alongside the king as being able to grant a respite of nine days (see note to IV As. 6 § 2)—a privilege granted only to the archbishop in the Latin version. There is nothing in the Latin version corresponding to § 3, and this, with the comparative mildness of the punishment (cf. Alf. cap. 2 § 1, II Edm. cap. 4), suggests that § 3 is a later insertion. For a discussion of the relationship between the Latin and A.S. texts see Liebermann, III. p. 112.

V ÆTHELSTAN

Preamble. The reference (Grately) is to II As.

§ 1. 1. Or, perhaps, 'are with me,' if, as seems probable, this meeting was being held at the time when the laws were promulgated (Liebermann).

      2. Implied in the previous section (cf. III As. cap. 6 ; IV As. cap. 3).

      3. Perhaps 'cattle' (cf. cap. 2, below, etc.).

§ 2. 1. Cf. IV As. cap. 3.

      2. Cf. Wiht. cap. 26 ; Ine, cap. 29 ; II As. cap. 11, etc.

§ 3. 1. Cf. IV As. cap. 3 § 1, 6 § 3.

      2. At Grately.

1. 1. Note that this refers to a case different from those of Ine, cap. 39, II Edw. cap. 7, II As. cap. 22 (cf. IV As. cap. 4).

      2. Cf. II Edw. cap. 2.

§ 1. Cf. IV As. cap. 5 ; III As. cap. 4.

§ 2. 1. *i.e.* 120 shillings ; see II Edw. cap. 20 (cf. cap. 1, above).

§ 3. § 4. 1. Cf. IV As. cap. 7 ; II As. cap. 26 ; VI As. cap. 11.

§ 5. 1. According to Liebermann a fresh nomination of witnesses would not be made in each new case. The persons specified were a permanent body who served as co-swearers as well as witnesses (cf. II Edw. cap. 2 ; IV Edg. cap. 3, 4, 5).

      2. Cf. I Edw. cap. 1 § 3, note 1.

2. 1. This, I take it, is the significance of *ut.*

      2. *i.e.* the evidence of the trail renders the oath of accusation unnecessary (see Alf. cap. 33, note).

3. 1. See Ine, Preamble, note 3.

2. *i.e.* one of the three sections into which the Psalms were divided (see Plummer, *Baedae Op. Hist.* II. 137 ; Harmer, *Historical Documents*, pp. 9, 23, 75 ; and cf. Wiht. cap. 1 § 1).

3. *i.e.* as Liebermann suggests, all true subjects (cf. *qui uelit quod rex*, IV As. cap. 6 § 3).

4. Their merits being measured by their benefactions to the Church.

§ 1. 1. That is to say, that the suit might be settled privately out of court, and then no fine would be paid to the judge. Ine, cap. 52, expressly forbids such private settlements. 'These secret compositions,' says Thorpe (p. 134), 'are forbidden by nearly every early code of Europe; for by such a proceeding both the judge and the crown lost their profits' (cf. III As. cap. 3).

2. Cf. Alf. cap. 5 § 5 ; II As. cap. 13.

VI ÆTHELSTAN

This document is of considerable importance as the first example of what may be called the by-laws of an association. It may be compared in some respects with the laws of the Association of Thegns at Cambridge, which, however, seem to be nearly a century later. It is written in a curiously unliterary style—frequently ungrammatical[1]—which presents many difficulties. There is some incongruity also between the various sections. The last few sections seem to be decrees of the king, and their relationship to the rest of the document is not quite clear. It is curious too that cap. 1 § 1, which treats of theft by young persons, should be abrogated by the royal decree contained in cap. 12 of the same code. It is not clear from the laws themselves what was the extent of territory over which they were to be enforced. Liebermann infers from cap. 10 that they applied to the whole county of Middlesex, and perhaps to Surrey and Essex as well. They were evidently intended for a population engaged in agriculture, rather than in occupations which we associate with town life. It is a natural inference that the people for whom the code was compiled were the *burgware* of London, who are frequently mentioned in the *Sax. Chron.* But the word *burg* itself nowhere occurs in the actual code. Many important points are not made clear, *e.g.* whether the associations included the whole population of both sexes, and how it was possible to preserve the groups of ten and a hundred referred to in cap. 3, etc. The relationship of these associations to the frankpledges of later times is altogether obscure.

Preamble. 1. Lit. 'peace-associations'; Liebermann takes *friðgegyldum* to be a plural noun with singular meaning.

---

[1] There are several false concords (*e.g. urum gemænum spræce*, cap. 3; *urne ceapgild*, cap. 6 § 1); but Liebermann suggests these may be due to the scribe of H.

2. According to Liebermann, this means the bishops who had property in London; viz. the Archbishop of Canterbury and the Bishops of London, Worcester, Rochester and Elmham.

3. According to Liebermann, the reeves of noblemen and ecclesiastics who had property in London are meant.

4. The references are to the codes II, V and IV of Æthelstan. The identification of *þunresfeld* is uncertain (cf. IV As. cap. 1).

1. § 1. 1. This chapter consists of regulations which were enforced throughout the whole nation and not merely in the locality of London. The by-laws proper of the association begin with cap. 2.

2. See note 1 to Alf. cap. 41. The case taken here is not that of a man who holds land by title deed, but that of a farmer who is a tenant on land which the landlord himself holds by title deed.

3. Liebermann understands this to mean that the landowner and the association each receive one-sixth of the property.

§ 4. 1. See note on Ine, cap. 37.

2. Cf. II As. cap. 1 §4; V As. Preamble§3; IV As. cap. 6§3.

§ 5. 1. Quadr. translates *uel ad eum liberandum in uia descendet*. On *stræte* is probably to be understood as the road along which the thief is being taken under arrest.

2. 1. The shilling mentioned here seems to be the Mercian shilling, which contained four pence (see note 1 to Ine, cap. 59). Down to 911 London had been a Mercian town.

3. 1. This group of a hundred associates (*hynden*) is, of course, quite distinct from the territorial hundred.

2. Thorpe and Schmid understand '*be* xxx *p.*' to mean 'after the rate of 30 pence' (cf. cap. 2); but I have followed Liebermann's suggestion (III. p. 119) that a better translation would be 'bei Strafe von 30 P. oder einem R.' (cf. cap. 6 § 2, below), 30 pence being the fine for insubordination enacted by the guild (cf. cap. 8 § 5, below).

4. 1. 'Tithing' (*teoðung*) would seem from the context to mean the bodies of ten men specified in cap. 3, above.

2. Quadr. reads *Et postquam vestigium deerit, inveniatur semper de duabus decimis unus homo, ubi magis populi sit, sic de una decima, ubi minus populi sit* etc.

5. 1. *be norðan mearce ne be suðan* probably means 'in all directions,' although only specifying two of them.

6. § 1. 1. Liebermann understands *ceapgild* to mean here the compensation paid by the guild to one of its members who has been robbed; but in § 4, below, he takes it to mean the compensation accruing to the guild. Quadr. reads *de nostro ceapgildo, id est de nostro captali persoluendo*, and apparently takes *ceapgild* in the same sense in § 4, below.

2. Liebermann adds *we*, or following Quadr. *man*, as the subject of *gilde*. Quadr. reads *Si sit metre (betre, id est melior), reddatur secundum pretium appreciatum*.

3. Schmid (following Thorpe) and other early editors suggest-

ed the insertion of *ne* before *be þam*. Liebermann accepts the emendation and translates *weorðige* as [*eidlich*] *bewerthet*; in the last sentence he adds 'we' (or 'us') and understands *habbe* to be for *habben*, following the reading of Quadr. (*habeamus nobis superplus*). The introduction of the oath (*eidlich*) scarcely seems to be justified by the original, and I am inclined to think that the text as it stands may be correct, although the meaning is neither clearly nor logically expressed. I would suggest that the passage *be þam þe se man hit weorðige* really implies some process of haggling.

6. § 2. 1. Cf. *Duns.* cap. 7, which among other valuations gives that of the horse to be 30 shillings; the ox, 30 pence; the cow, 24 pence; the pig, 8 pence; and the sheep, a shilling.

2. Quadr. inserts *id est* xxx *den.* after *una manca*, and v *den.* after *ouis solido*. This is the value of the West Saxon shilling (see note 1, cap. 2, above). For mancus see note 2 to A. and G. cap. 3.

§ 3. 1. I take the first *þa men* of the Anglo-Saxon text to be nominative in apposition to *we*; the second *þa* as nominative of the relative and the second *men* as accusative, meaning 'slaves.' Thorpe and Schmid regard the repetition of *þa men* as a scribal error, Liebermann emends the first *þa men* to *þam*. Quadr. reads *Diximus de seruis nostris, eis qui men habent*.

2. With Liebermann I take 'our slaves' as referring not to slaves of the association, but to the slaves owned by individual members.

3. See IV As. cap. 6 § 5.

4. *i.e.* the full value of a slave which was usually a pound (240 pence); cf. Ine, cap. 23 § 3, 74, 3 § 2; IV As. cap. 6 § 6.

5. This means he would be stoned to death (cf. IV As. cap. 6 § 5).

6. Cf. Ine, cap. 24.

§ 4. 1. Liebermann interprets this differently. He understands *ofer* xxx *pæñg* as the minimum to be paid by the convicted thief and translates the first clause: 'Und das [uns zukommende] Ersatzgeld, sobald wir [den Dieb gerichtlich nachweisen und] es einklagen, steige jedesmal über [mindestens] 30 Pfennig bis zu einem halben Pfund und ferner hinauf etc.' But ought not *ofer* xxx *pæñg* to be interpreted like *ofer* xii *pæningas* in cap. 1 § 1, above, and 'half a pound' to be taken as the minimum payment to be made by the thief? The clause *furðor gif we* etc. seems to contain an ellipsis—'when the value of the goods stolen exceeds half a pound etc.'

2. This clause, *gif we þæt...angylde*, seems to imply that the thief may not be able to pay to the full value of the goods.

3. A literal translation of the clause *þeah heo læsse sy* would be 'though it is a smaller one,' it (*heo*) referring to *æsce* (search).

7. 1. Liebermann's textual emendation of *þ[æt]* to *þ[e]* is in accordance with Quadr. which reads: *Diximus faciat quicumque faciat, qui omnium nostrum molestiam vindicet*, etc.; but the emendation does not seem to me to be necessary.

2. 30 pence, according to Liebermann (cf. cap. 8 § 5, and note 2 to cap. 3, above).

8. § 1. 1. Cf. cap. 3, above

2. Cf. cap. 4, note 1, above.

3. Liebermann interprets this as referring to preparations for a coming feast of the guild.

4. The arithmetic is rather difficult to understand. Quadr. also has *duodecim homines*. Liebermann emends to XI and takes *þa* (Quadr. *ipsi*) as nominative plural of the pronoun.

5. Lit. 'food.'

§ 2. 1. Probably the (burghal) district attached to London. No such district is mentioned in the text of the Burghal Hidage which has come down to us. But the *burgware* of London are frequently mentioned in the *Sax. Chron.*, and the existence of a burghal district is implied in the preamble to this code.

§ 3. 1. Liebermann takes *on twa healfa* to mean 'to north and south.' But does it not rather mean 'in all directions' (cf. note to cap. 5, above)?

§ 4. 1. *scyre* is clearly the sphere of jurisdiction of a *gerefa* (cf. cap. 10, below). It is not clear whether the *gerefa* mentioned here and in the two preceding paragraphs is what was later called *scir-gerefa, i.e.* sheriff. If that were the case it might be inferred that the *scir* was a county. It may, however, denote a smaller division of territory, possibly the divisions belonging to the reeves mentioned in the preamble.

2. Cf. Alf. cap. 37 § 1.

3. *i.e.* 120 shillings (cf. II Edw. cap. 2).

§ 5. 1. *i.e.* in pursuing the trail beyond the border.

2. Cf. cap. 8 § 4, § 2, above.

3. Cf. cap. 3, note 2, and cap. 7, note 2, above.

§ 6. 1. *gesufel* is obviously connected with *sufl*, the term denoting cheese, beans or whey. Zupitza and Kluge in their glossaries give *gesufel*, 'zur Zukost gehörig.' Cf. Harmer, *Historical Documents*, p. 74.

2. See Harmer, *op. cit.* p. 75.

§ 7. 1. It is not clear whether *hiremannum* denotes 'persons under our jurisdiction,' or 'personal dependants.' In the former case the word *urum* must refer to the reeves and bishops, in the latter to the community in general, with special reference to the wealthier members of it. In his notes, Liebermann takes the passage in the latter sense.

2. Presumably this means that he should acquaint his neighbours with the time when he last saw it in his possession.

3. Maitland (*Collected Papers*, I. p. 421) suggests a connection between this cap. and the *Lex Salica* where 'the burden or rather the benefit of proof' depended on whether a man who was tracing cattle could overtake them before three nights had elapsed.

§ 8. 1. Quadr. reads *quia nolumus aliquod pecus incustoditum et per inobservantiam perditum reddere.*

8. § 9. 1. *i.e.* the king.

    2. *i.e.* 'the royal reeves who are set over us' (Liebermann).

    3. This admonition apparently forms the conclusion to the by-laws proper of the association. What follows appears to be in the nature of a national ordinance.

    9. 1. 'we' here seems to mean the king's council assembled at *Witlanbyrig* (cf. cap. 12, below), though their decrees have been incorporated among the by-laws of the London association.

    2. Cf. cap. 1 § 4, above.

    10. 1. Wulfhelm, Archbishop of Canterbury 925—940.

    2. These names are met with among the *ministri regis* (barons) who sign King Æthelstan's charters; and two grants of land to Ælfeah Stybb are recorded in Birch, *Cart. Sax.* 648, 707. Odda is the name which usually comes first in the list of the *ministri*.

    3. 'this meeting' refers to the one first mentioned above, viz. Grately (II As.).

    4. Cf. IV As. cap. 2; II As. cap. 24 § 1, 12, 13.

    5. Cf. IV As. cap. 2; II As. cap. 24 § 1.

    11. 1. Cf. Ine, Preamble, note 2.

    2. Lit. 'my dominions,' with change to the first person.

    3. See note to V As. cap. 3 § 1.

    4. Lit. 'in accordance with what...stands in our documents.'

    5. *i.e.* the possession of land which involves private jurisdiction (Liebermann).

    12. § 1. 1. *Witlanbyrig* has not been certainly identified. Price suggested Whittlebury, Northants.

    2. Wulfhelm of Canterbury.

    3. Theodred was bishop of London from 926 (or earlier) to 951.

    4. Cf. cap. 1 § 1, above, and the introductory note.

    5. Lit. 'whether for [something] greater or [something] smaller—whichever it may be.'

    6. Cf. II As. cap. 1 § 3.

    § 2. 1. Cf. cap. 1 § 4, above.

    2. Cf. II Edw. cap. 6.

    § 3. 1. Cf. VI As. cap. 1 § 1, II As. cap. 1.

INDEX

A comma between the number of the chapter and the section mark indicates a reference both to the chapter and the section.

Archbishop, *continued*
  If anyone breaks into his premises, Alf. 40
  In Canterbury there shall be two moneyers for the archbishop, II As. 14 § 2
  Of fasting, at the ordeal, according to his commands, II As. 23 § 2
  Of the respite granted by an archbishop to a thief, IV As. 6 § 1
Arm. Of injuries to the arm, Abt. 53, § 1; Alf. 54, 55, 66
Army '*fierd*'
  Of nobles and commoners who neglect military service, Ine 51
  Of *burgbryce* and *edorbryce* when the army is in the field, Alf. 40 § 1
Associates '*gegildan*'; of a slain man, Ine 16, 21; Alf. 31; VI As. 1 § 1: of a
    homicide, Alf. 30 § 1; cf. Wiht. 19, 21
Association '*friðgegyldan*'. The by-laws of the association of London, VI As.
Asylum. See *Fierst, Frið*
Attachment '*ætfon*,' '*befon*,' '*gefon*'
  If the owner attaches stolen property, H. & E. 7
  If property bought in London is attached in Kent, H. & E. 16 § 1, § 2, § 3
  If stolen property is attached, Ine 25 § 1, 47, 75
  If a stolen slave is attached, Ine 53
  If a stolen beast is seized in a house, Ine 57
  Of the two courses to be adopted when cattle is attached, I Edw. 1 § 5
  He who attaches livestock shall have witnesses nominated to him, II As. 9

Bacon '*spic*'
  Of the bacon when pannage is paid in pigs, Ine 49 § 3
  A shank of bacon to be given to a poor Englishman, As. Ord. 1
Bail. See *Borg*
Bana 'murderer'; Abt. 23; H. & E. 1-4. See *Slaying*
Baptism '*fulluht*'
  If a priest neglects the baptism of a sick man etc., Wiht. 6; E. & G. 3 § 2
  Of the baptism of children, Ine 2, § 1
  Æthelberht the first king to be baptised, Alf. Introd.
Barley. See *Gafol*
Beard. If anyone cuts off a commoner's beard, Alf. 35 § 5
Beast. See *Cattle*
Bees. The fine for stealing bees, Alf. 9 § 2
Befon. See *Attachment*; Ine 25 § 1, 47, 53, 57, 75; II As. 9
Belly. If one is wounded in, Abt. 61, § 1; Alf. 61, § 1
Biddan 'to ask,' 'entreat,' 'order,' 'command'; Ine 8, 9, 21, 53 § 1; Alf. 42 § 3;
    II As. 3, 11; VI As. 8 § 8
Birele 'serving-maid'
  Of lying with the *birele* of a noble or commoner, Abt. 14, 16
Bishop
  Of stealing his property, Abt. 1
  Of his commands against illicit unions, Wiht. 5
  Of his decision in the case of a negligent priest, Wiht. 6
  His word shall be incontrovertible, Wiht. 16
  If his servant is accused, Wiht. 22
  Of bearing false witness in his presence, Ine 13
  Of breaking into his premises, Ine 45; Alf. 40, § 1
  Of slaying his godson, Ine 76 § 3
  Of his sentence when a man proves false to his pledge, Alf. 1 § 2
  Of violating his protection (*borgbryce*) or guardianship (*mundbyrd*), Alf. 3
  Of the sanctuary of a church consecrated by a bishop, Alf. 5
  Of taking a nun from a nunnery without his permission, Alf. 8
  Of fighting in his presence, Alf. 15
  The bishop shall unfrock a priest guilty of homicide, Alf. 21
  The bishop shall be a witness to suits about land, Alf. 41
  Of the amends to the church, determined by the bishops, E. & G. Pr. § 2
  In cases of incest, the bishop shall take the woman, E. & G. 4
  Of the bishop's decision when a man in orders commits a capital crime, E. &
    G. 4 § 2

Bishop, *continued*

Of his permission to tend a mutilated criminal, E. & G. 10

The bishop shall act as kinsman of strangers and ecclesiastics, E. & G. 12

Bishops shall order the payment of tithes, I As. Pr., 1

Bishops shall superintend the distribution of charities, As. Ord. 1, 2

The bishop of Rochester shall have one moneyer, II As. 14 § 2

The fine for insubordination shall be exacted from a reeve by the bishop, II As. 25 § 1

Of the bishop, when a man swears a false oath, II As. 26, § 1

Of the decrees of the bishops and other councillors in Kent, III As. Pr.

If a fugitive seeks a bishop, IV As. 6 § 2

Of a slain thief who was a tenant on land belonging to a bishop, VI As. 1 § 1

Boc 'book'; Wiht. 5; I As 3: *domboc* ; I Edw. Pr.; II Edw. 5 § 2; II As. 5

Bookland '*bocland*'

Of *bocland* bequeathed conditionally by kinsmen, Alf. 41

Of him who withholds from another his rights in 'bookland,' I Edw. 2, § 1

Of a slain thief who was a tenant on 'bookland,' VI As. 1 § 1

boldgetal 'collection of houses; district,' Alf. 37

Bonds '*bend*'; vb. *gebindan*

If a man lays bonds on a freeman, servant, Abt. 24, 88; Alf. 35, § 6

If a perjurer has to be bound, Alf. 1 § 4

If one who has right of asylum is put in fetters, Alf. 2 § 1

Bones. Injuries to, Abt. 34, 35; (chin) Abt. 50, Alf. 50; (collar) Abt. 52; (thigh) Abt. 65, 67, § 1; Alf. 62, § 1; (rib) Abt. 66; Alf. 70, § 1; (shin) Alf. 63, § 1; (shoulder) Alf. 73, 74

Border '*mearc*'; H. & E. 15; Wiht. 8; IV As. 4; III As. 4; VI As. 5, 8 § 4, § 5 : *gemære* ; Ine 10: *landg-* ; A. & G. 1

Borg. See *Surety*

Borough '*burg*'

The reeves in every borough shall render tithes, I As. Pr.

Of the repairing of boroughs, II As. 13

There shall be a moneyer in every borough, II As. 14 § 2

Of the chief men of the borough when anyone neglects the *gemot*, II As. 20 § 1, § 4

Bot 'amends,' 'compensation.' See also *Mægbot, Manbot*. Abt. 33, 72; Ine 76 f.; Alf. 2 § 1, 11 § 3, § 4, § 5, 23 § 1, 26, 39 § 2, 52; E. & G. Pr., 2; II Edw. 1 § 1; II As. 26 § 1

Botl 'dwelling-place'; Ine 67, 68

Boundary '*landgemære*.' See also *Border*

The boundaries between the kingdoms of Alfred and Guthrum, A. & G. 1

Bribe '*medsceat*'

Of receiving bribes to prevent the tracing of lost cattle, II Edw. 4

Of him who takes bribes from a thief, II As. 17

Of a reeve who takes bribes, V As. 1 § 3

Bride, -groom; Ine 31. See *Marriage*

Bruise, '*dynt*.' The compensation to be paid for inflicting a bruise, Abt. 58, 59, 60

Burgbryce. Of compensation for *b*. to be paid to the king, archbishop, etc., Ine 45; Alf. 40, § 1

Burial. See *Grave*

Burning. Of the burning of a female slave, IV As. 6 § 7

Butts. Of filling the butts, VI As. 8 § 1

Byrigea. See *Surety, Guardian*

Castration. Alf. 25 § 1

Cattle '*æht*,' '*ceap*,' '*feoh*,' '*ierfe*' (q.v.) ; '*cu*,' '*cealf*,' '*hryðer*,' '*neat*,' '*oxa*,' '*orf*'

Of payment of the wergeld in livestock (*feoh*), Abt. 30

Of Kentish men who buy *feoh* in London, H. & E. 16—§ 3

If a man is vouched to warranty for livestock (*feoh*), Ine 35 § 1

A cow and an ox shall be given to maintain an orphan, Ine 38

Cattle, *continued*

Of a stray beast (*ceap*) on another man's premises, Ine 40

Of stray beasts (*hryðer*) which eat up the common grass and crops, Ine 42, § 1

Of stealing and harbouring stolen cattle (*ceap*), Ine 46

If one buys a beast (*ceap*) and finds any blemish in it, Ine 56

If a husband steals a beast (*ceap*) and takes it into his house, Ine 57

Of the values of horn, tail and eye, of a cow and an ox, Ine 58, 59

Of hiring a yoke of oxen, Ine 60

Of the cattle (*hriðer*) to be paid in the food-rent from 10 hides, Ine 70 § 1

If anyone steals a cow and a calf, Alf. 16

Of the compensation to be paid in cattle (*cwicæht, feoh*), when a betrothed woman commits fornication, Alf. 18 § 1

If a beast (*neat*) injures a man, Alf. 24

Of trading in cattle (*ierfe*) between Englishmen and Danes, A. & G. 4, 5

Of vouching cattle (*hryðer, orf*) to warranty, I Edw. 1 § 3, § 4, § 5

Of the provisions for tracing stolen cattle (*yrfe*), II Edw. 4; V As. 2

Of him who attaches livestock (*yrfe*), II As. 9

Of the witnesses when cattle (*yrfe*) is exchanged, II As. 10

If anyone buys cattle (*yrfe*) in the presence of a witness, II As. 24

The trail of lost cattle (*yrfe*) shall serve for the *foraþ*, V As. 2

An ox or thirty pence is the fine exacted by the association, VI As. 3, 8 § 5

Of the provisions made by the association for tracing cattle (*yrfe*), VI As. 4, 5, 7, 8 § 4

An ox shall be valued at a mancus, a cow at twenty pence, VI As. 6 § 2

The trail of lost cattle (*yrfe*) must be pointed out within three days, VI As. 8 § 7

If a man wishes to apply for the value of stolen cattle (*ceapgild*), VI As. 8 § 8

Ceap 'cattle,' 'goods,' 'property' (*q.v.*); Abt. 77; H. & E. 16 § 2; Ine 37, 40, 42, 46, 47, 48, 49 § 1, 53 § 1, 56, 57, 60, 62, 74 § 1, 75; E. & G. 7; I Edw. 1 § 4; I As. Pr.; II As. 12, 24 § 1

Ceapgild 'the value of goods'; II As. 3, 19, 21; VI As. 1 § 1, 1 § 4, 6 § 4, 8 § 8

Cearwund; Abt. 63

Ceorl. See *Commoner, Husband*

Charge. See *Accusation*

Cheek. Of injuries to, Abt. 46, 47

Cheese; Ine 70

Child 'bearn,' 'cild,' 'cniht'

Of provision for children, Abt. 78, 79, 80, 81

If a man dies leaving a wife and child, H. & E. 6; Ine 38

A child shall be baptized within 30 days, Ine 2

If anyone steals with and without the cognisance of wife and children, Ine 7, § 1

A ten year old child can be an accessory to theft, Ine 7 § 2

The maintenance of a foundling, Ine 26

The wergeld of an illegitimate child, Ine 27

A nobleman may take his children's nurse with him when he moves, Ine 63

If an abducted nun bears a child, Alf. 8 § 2, § 3

If anyone slays a woman with child, Alf. 9

If a child is born deaf or dumb, Alf. 14

Of a child which dies in the keeping of its guardian, Alf. 17

If anyone rapes a girl who is not of age, Alf. 29

See also II As. 1 f., IV As. 3; VI As. 1 § 1, 12 § 1 f.

Chrism. If a priest does not fetch it on the appointed day, E. & G. 3 § 2

Christ; Alf. 1 § 7, 43; E. & G. Pr. § 2, 12

Christianity

If anyone offends against the Christian religion, E. & G. 2

Of the adoption of Christianity by the Danes, E. & G. Pr. § 1, § 2

Christmas 'Gehhol,' 'midwinter'

Of payment of church dues at Christmas, Ine 61

He who steals during Christmas, Alf. 5 § 5

Freemen shall have twelve days' holiday at Christmas, Alf. 43

Of the *gemot* held at Exeter at Christmas, V As. Pr. § 1

Church '*cirice*,' '*ciricsceatt*,' '*ciricfrið*,' '*ciricgrið*,' '*ciricbryce*'
  Compensation for theft of church property, Abt. 1
  Breach of church *frið*, Abt. 1
  The church shall not be taxed, Wiht. 1
  The *mundbyrd* of the church, Wiht. 2
  Excommunication from, for adultery, Wiht. 3, 4 § 1
  Of the church's prerogatives with regard to expurgation, Wiht. 21 § 1 f.
  When church dues shall be paid, Ine 4, 61
  The sanctuary of the church, Ine 5, § 1
  A prisoner who escapes shall be excommunicated from all churches, Alf. 1 § 7
  Compensation for violation of sanctuary of the church, Alf. 2, § 1
  Of sanctuary granted to a church consecrated by a bishop, Alf. 5—§ 4
  The *ealdor* of a church shall not feed a fugitive, Alf. 5 § 2
  If anyone steals anything from a church, Alf. 6
  Of the oaths of accusation to be made in churches, Alf. 33
  If anyone publicly disregards the laws of the church, Alf. 40 § 2
  If an adversary flees to a church, Alf. 42 § 2
  Of legislation to secure amends due to the church, E. & G. Pr. § 2
  Of sanctuary within the walls of a church, E. & G. 1
  Of ecclesiastical dues, E. & G. 5 § 1, 6—§ 7 ; I As. 4
  Of breaking into a church, II As. 5
Clerk
  Of compensation for stealing a clerk's property, Abt. 1
  How a clerk shall clear himself, Wiht. 19
Cliff. A free woman who is a thief shall be thrown from a cliff, IV As. 6 § 4
Clothes. Clothing '*hrægl*,' '*scrud*,' '*wæd*'
  Of bruises inflicted under and outside the clothes, Abt. 59, 60
  If a nun is lustfully seized by her clothes, Alf. 18
  Of the clothing to be given to a poor Englishman, As. Ord. 1
  Of a priest standing in his holy garments before the altar, Wiht. 18
Coat of Mail '*byrne*'; Ine 54 § 1. See *Weapons*
Commoner '*ceorl*.' See also *Freeman, Twyhynde*
  A commoner's *mundbyrd*, Abt. 15
  Fines for lying with his slaves, Abt. 16
  If his premises are forcibly entered, Abt. 17
  If a dependant (*hlafætan*) of a commoner is slain, Abt. 25
  If a commoner enters into illicit union, Wiht. 5 § 1
  How a commoner may clear himself at the altar, Wiht. 21
  If a commoner is caught after having been often accused, Ine 18, 37
  If a commoner is accused of harbouring a fugitive, Ine 30
  If a commoner is slain on a foray, Ine 34, § 1
  Of a commoner proved guilty in the ordeal or caught in the act, Ine 37
  A commoner's premises shall be fenced winter and summer, Ine 40
  Of commoners who have partible land to fence, Ine 42
  If a commoner neglects military service, Ine 51
  If anyone is accused of homicide and wishes to deny the deed, Ine 54
  Of a commoner who hires another's yoke of oxen, Ine 60
  Of commoners who plot against their lord, Alf. 4 § 2
  Of adultery with a commoner's wife, Alf. 10
  Of outrage against a woman of the commons, Alf. 11—§ 4
  If a commoner's slave is raped, Alf. 25
  If a commoner is killed by a band, Alf. 26, 28 § 1
  Of various forms of outrage against an unoffending commoner, Alf. 35—§ 6
  If anyone fights in his house, Alf. 39, § 1
  The fine for breaking through a commoner's fence, Alf. 40, § 1
  Of commoners who occupy tributary land, A. & G. 2
  Of a commoner belonging to too powerful a kindred to be punished, III As. 6; IV As. 3
Communicant '*huslgenga*'
  Of the oath of one who is a communicant, Wiht. 23; Ine 15 § 1, 19

Communicant, *continued*
He who is going to the ordeal shall attend communion, II As. 23
Compact, Compounding. See *Geþing*
Confession, Confessor '*scriftspræc*,' '*scrift*'; vb. '*geandettan*'
Of one who confesses an act previously denied, Ine 71
A man's confessor shall prescribe the compensation to be paid for *wedbryce*, Alf. 1 § 8
Of one who confesses committing a secret offence, Alf. 5 § 4
Of a deaf mute who cannot confess his wrongdoings, Alf. 14
Of one of a *hloð* who slays an unoffending man, Alf. 26
If a man condemned to death desires confession, E. & G. 5
Of confession for perjurers, II As. 26, § 1
Councillors '*witan*'; Ine Pr., 6 § 2; Alf. Introd., 77; A. & G. Pr.; E. & G. Pr., 4, 5 § 1; II Edw. 1; III As. Pr., 1; IV As. Pr.; V As. Pr.; VI As. 10, 11
Country. See *Land*
Cow, Calf. See *Cattle*
Crime, Criminals '*facn*,' '*ful*,' '*laþ*,' '*tiht*'
Of crime committed against one under the king's protection, Alf. 3
Of one accused of criminal intention against a child, etc., Alf. 17
If a crime is committed with borrowed weapons, Alf. 19 § 2
Of a man in orders who commits a capital crime, E. & G. 4 § 2
Of tending a mutilated criminal, E. & G. 10
Of shielding crime and harbouring criminals, II Edw. 4; IV As. 3, 6 § 3; VI As. 1 § 2
Of the crime of coining false money, II As. 14 § 1
Of the favour granted to criminals, III As. 3
A lord shall stand surety for a man charged with crime, III As. 7
A man free from crime may seek any lord he wishes, V As. 1 § 1
Of the wife's share of the goods of a slain criminal, VI As. 1 § 1
Of relatives who shall stand surety for a kinsman against crime, VI As. 1 § 4, 12 § 2
Of a thief who shall swear to desist from crime, VI As. 12 § 2
Crops '*æcer*'; Ine 42, § 1, 67
Cultivation. See *Land*
Custom. See *Riht*

Dæd; Alf. 36 § 1; E. & G. 2, 4 § 1, 12; VI As. 7: *misdæd*; Alf. 14, 23, § 1, 24: *morðdæd*; II As. 6
Dæl '*share*,' '*part*'; Ine 23, 29, 42, 57; Alf. 8 § 3, 19 § 1, 47 § 1, 71; I As. 3; VI As. 1 § 1
Dane
If a Dane is slain, A. & G. 2
Slaves and freemen shall not pass over to the Danish host without permission, A. & G. 5
Of the peace and friendship between the English and Danes, E. & G. Pr. f.
Of the fines to be paid in a Danish district, E. & G. 3 § 1, 6 f.
If a slave in the Danelagh works during a festival, E & G. 7 § 2
Day '*dæg*.' See also *Night*; Abt. Pr.; Wiht. Pr.; Ine 3 § 2, 72; Alf. 43; A. & G. 5; E. & G. 7; I As. 1; II As. 23; IV As. 6 § 1, § 2; IV As. Frag. 6 § 1, § 2, § 4; VI As. 8 § 6—§ 8
Deacon
If his property is stolen, Abt. 1
How a deacon shall clear himself, Wiht. 18
Dead
Of an oath on behalf of a dead man, Ine 21, § 1
Of a vendetta on behalf of a dead man, Ine 35
Of vouching the dead to warranty, Ine 53, § 1
How payment may be made for a dead man, Ine 54 § 1
Of charging a dead man with guilt, II As. 11
Of singing for the souls of the dead, VI As. 8 § 6; I As. 4

Esne, continued
If the *esne* of the king or bishop is accused, Wiht. 22
If the *esne* of a company is accused, Wiht. 23
If a layman's *esne* accuse the *esne* of an ecclesiastic, Wiht. 24
If anyone provides another's *esne* with a sword, spear, or horse, Ine 29
The holidays granted to *esne wyrhtan*, Alf. 43
Ewe. Ine 55
Excommunication
For living in illicit union, Wiht. 3, 4 § 1
If a perjurer escapes from prison, Alf. 1 § 7
Exculpation. See also *Denial, Oath, Laðleas*
Of him who allows a homicide to escape, H. & E. 2, 4
Of him who is charged with stealing a man, H & E. 5
Of him in whose possession property is attached, H. & E. 16 § 3
How the head of a monastery shall clear himself, Wiht. 17
Of the Church's prerogatives with regard to expurgation, Wiht. 21 § 1
How the servant of a bishop or the king shall clear himself, Wiht. 22
(ge)clænsian
How a priest, or clerk, or stranger, or commoner shall clear himself, Wiht. 18, 19, 20, 21
Of those the reeve shall exculpate or deliver up to be scourged, Wiht. 22
Of those a lord may clear by his own oath, Wiht. 23, 24
'*gecyþan*'
Of declarations when property is attached, H. & E. 16 § 2, § 3
Of the declaration on oath of him who kills a thief, Ine 16, 21, 35
Of the declaration on oath of him who finds stolen meat, Ine 17
Of a trader's declaration when stolen property is attached in his hands, Ine 25 § 1
Of a declaration on oath with regard to intruding swine, Ine 49 § 1
Of a wife's declaration on oath with regard to stolen meat, Ine 57
Of a declaration of him who attaches stolen property, Ine 75
Of the declaration demanded of an evil man who brings a counter-charge, i Edw. 1 § 5
(ge)ladian
How a commoner harbouring a fugitive shall clear himself, Ine 30
How one accused of making an illicit compact shall clear himself, Ine 52 (H)
How a young woman shall clear herself, Alf. 11 § 4
How a king's thegn, etc., shall clear himself, A. & G. 3
How one who spares a thief shall clear himself, ii As. 1 § 1
How one who harbours an outlaw, etc., shall clear himself, ii As. 2 § 2; 20 § 8; iv As. 6 § 3
How a moneyer shall clear himself, ii As. 14 § 1
'*geswican*'
How he who is accused of belonging to a *hloþ* or *here* shall clear himself, Ine 14, 15, § 1
Of a thief who shall not have the right of clearing himself, Ine 15 § 2
How one accused of making an illicit compact shall clear himself, Ine 52
geswican 'to desist,' 'cease from'; Alf. 22; E. & G. 11; i Edw. 2 § 1; ii As. 1 § 3, 6 § 1, 20 § 4; v As. Pr. § 1; vi As. 1 § 4, 12 § 2
(ge)treowian, (ge)treowsian
Of one who has been on a foray, Ine 34
How he who plots against the king or his lord must clear himself, Alf. 4, § 1, § 2
Of him who is charged with causing the death of a dependant, Alf. 17
Of him who lends weapons with which murder is committed, Alf. 19 § 2
Of him who must clear himself in 12 churches, Alf. 33
Of the owner of a spear when a man is transfixed on it, Alf. 36 § 1
Of one who, having been found a lord, commits theft, ii Edw. 3
ungereccan'
Of a reeve who is accused and cannot clear himself, v As. 1 § 2

Ge þing, continued
If a nobleman comes to terms with the king, Ine 50
He who is accused of making an illicit compact, Ine 52
On compounding for one who is being forced to the ordeal, Ine 62
If a man comes to terms for a yard of land, Ine 67
On coming to terms for allowing a thief to escape, Ine 73
Of a fugitive who comes to terms with his enemy, Alf. 2
If a sword-furbisher comes to terms with the owner of a weapon, Alf. 19 § 3
Of coming to terms for injuries inflicted by a beast, Alf. 24
Of one who utters a public slander, Alf. 32
Of compounding for an ordeal, II As. 21
Of reeves who allow secret compacts, VI As. 11
(Ge)ðolian. Wiht. 4 § 1; Ine 3 § 1, § 2, 36 § 1, 40, 42 § 1, 51, 62, 67; Alf. 1 § 4,
    11 § 4, 20, 22, 42 § 1; E. & G. 7; II Edw. 5 § 1; I As. 4; II As. 3 § 1, 24 § 1,
    25 § 2
Getreowian. See *Exculpation*
Gift
Of a wife's 'morning-gift' when she bears no child, Abt. 81
Gingra (of an *ealdorman*), Alf. 28
God (God's *feoh*), Abt. 1; Ine Pr. 11; Alf. 43; A. & G. Pr.; E. & G. Pt. § 1, 3,
    4, 5 § 1, 6 § 7; I As. Pr. 3, 5; II As. 23 § 2; VI As. 8 § 1; (*Godes þeow*) Ine
    Pr., 1; As. Ord. Pr.; V As. 3; (*Godborg*) Alf. 33; (*Godcund*) E. & G. Pr.
    § 2, 6 § 4; I As. 4 § 1
Godfather, Godson
Of the compensation (*mægbot*) and the wergeld when a godfather or a godson,
    a king's godson, or a bishop's godson is slain, Ine 76–§ 3
Gold (half marks of pure gold); A. & G. 2; 'gold finger,' Abt. 54 § 4, Alf. 59;
    'gold thief,' Alf. 9 § 2
Goods (Chattel). See also *Property, Possessions*
Of the king's right to the goods (*æht*) of a thief, Abt. 9
Of the wife's share of the goods (*scæt*) left by her husband, Abt. 78, 79, 80, 81
Twice the value of stolen goods shall be paid by a slave, Abt. 90
Of purchasing property with goods (*ceap*) known to be the purchaser's, H. & E.
    16 § 2
Of the goods (*æht*) of men living in irregular unions, Wiht. 4, § 1
Of forfeiture of all goods (*æht*) for idolatry, Wiht. 12
Of rendering an oath equivalent to the value of stolen goods (*feoh*), Ine 28 § 2
A man may clear himself from the charge of harbouring stolen goods, Ine 46 § 2
If a stolen chattel (*ceap*) is attached, Ine 47
Of driving a penal slave to a scourging for stealing goods (*ceap*), Ine 48
Of suits concerning a dead man's goods (*ceap*), Ine 53, § 1
Of payment in goods (*ceap*) for the hire of oxen, Ine 60
Of one who gives his goods (*ceap*) to save another from the ordeal, Ine 62;
    VI As. 1 § 4
Of refusing to accept a stolen chattel (*ceap*) when it is vouched to warranty,
    Ine 75
Of trading in goods (*æht*) between the English and Danes, A. & G. 5
He who bargains on Sunday shall forfeit the goods (*ceap*), E. & G. 7
Of attempting to deprive a stranger or a man in orders of his goods (*feoh*),
    E. & G. 12
Of stealing goods worth more than 8 pence, II As. 1
Of a lord's obligation to pay the value of goods (*ceapgyld*) in dispute, II As. 3
Of buying goods (*ceap*) worth more than 20 pence outside a town, II As. 12
He who trades on Sunday shall lose the goods (*ceap*), II As. 24 § 1
Powerful wrongdoers shall be banished with all their goods, etc., IV As. 3;
    V As. Pr. § 1
Oaths shall be proportionate to the value of the disputed goods (*feoh*), V As.
    1 § 5
Of obtaining the value of stolen goods (*ceapgyld*) from a thief's property (*yrfe*),
    VI As. 1 § 1, § 4

Goods, *continued*
Of a wife's share of the goods of a slain thief, vi As. 1 § 1
Of the fine for stealing goods worth more than 30 pence, vi As. 6 § 4
Grave
20 shillings shall be paid before the grave is closed, Abt. 22
Of vouching to warranty at a grave, Ine 53
A perjurer shall not be buried in a consecrated burial ground, ii As. 26
Griđ 'sanctuary,' 'protection.' See also *Friđ*
The *griđ* of a church and the *handgriđ* of the king shall be inviolate, E. & G. 1
Guardian '*byrga*'
Of a child's guardian when the father dies, H. & E. 6
Of a guardian's neglect to have a child baptised, Ine 2
Of a bride's guardian when the marriage does not take place, Ine 31; Alf. 18 § 1, § 2, § 3
Of the guardian of a child or helpless person, Alf. 17
Guardianship. See *Mundbyrd*
Guilty. See *Scyldig*
Gylt; Alf. 5 § 4

Hærfest; Alf. 43
Hair
Of seizing a man by the hair, Abt. 33
Of cutting of another man's hair, Alf. 35 § 3–§ 6
Of wounds inflicted under, or outside, the hair, Alf. 45, § 1, 66 § 1
Ham. See *House*; *Hamfæst*, i Edw. 1 § 4
Hand
If a blow is received with uplifted hand, Abt. 58 § 1
Of expurgation with the hand on the altar, Wiht. 19–21; by the hand of the reeve, Wiht. 22
The hand of a thief caught in the act shall be cut off, Ine 18, 37; Alf. 6
Of compensation for the hand, Alf. 66, 69, 71
The hand of a coiner of false money shall be cut off, ii As. 14 § 1
Of the hand in the hot iron and hot water ordeal, ii As. 23 § 1; App. ii; *habbendre handa*, Wiht. 26; ii As. 1; iv As. 6; v As. Pr. 2; *to handa, etc.*, Ine 53, 56, 62, 74, 75; Alf. 21, 22, 24, 42 § 1; ii Edw. 6, 7; vi As. 12 § 1
Hanging
An English penal slave who absconds shall be hanged, Ine 24
An absconding slave shall be hanged, vi As. 6 § 3
Harbouring '*feormung*'; vb. (*ge*)*feormian*
If a stranger is entertained for three days, H. & E. 15
If a vagrant tonsured man is entertained, Wiht. 7
If a commoner harbours a fugitive, Ine 30
If a man is charged with harbouring stolen cattle, Ine 46 f.
If anyone harbours outlaws or traitors, Alf. 4, § 1; ii As. 2 § 2
If anyone harbours a man from another district, Alf. 37 § 1; iii As. 4
Of shielding crime and harbouring criminals, ii Edw. 4; iv As. 3
If anyone harbours a perjurer, ii Edw. 5 § 2
Of harbouring a landless man from another shire, ii As. 8
Of harbouring a thief, etc., ii As. 20 § 8; iv As. 6 § 3; vi As. 1 § 2
Of harbouring a banished man, iv As. 3 § 1; v As. Pr. § 3
Harm. See *Yfel*
Head '*heafod*.' Of injuries to, Alf. 44, 47 § 1, 49
Healm, Ine 61
Healsfang. Payment of *healsfang* for serious offences, Wiht. 11, 12, 14; cf. Abt. 22
Heathen practices; E. & G. Pr. § 1, 2. See also *Devil*
Hedge. See *Fence*
Heorđ. See *House*
Here
A band of more than thirty-five is a *here*, Ine 13 § 1

Here, continued
He who is accused of belonging to a *here*, Ine 15, § 1
Of slaves and freemen who wish to trade with the Danish host (*here*), A. & G. 5
Hide (skin). See also *Scourging*
If a rib is broken but not the skin, Alf. 70
If the skin is broken and a bone removed, Alf. 70 § 1
Of the hide and flesh when a stray beast is killed, Ine 42 § 1
A shield shall not be covered with sheep-skin, II As. 15, cf. III As. 8
Hide (of land)
The wergeld of a Welshman holding 5 hides, 1 hide, etc., Ine 24 § 2, 32
Of the number of hides to be kept under cultivation, Ine 64, 65, 66
Of the food rent from 10 hides, Ine 70 § 1
Of oaths expressed in hides, Ine 14, 19, 46, 52, 53, 54, § 2; Alf. 11 § 4
Highway '*weg*,' '*strǣt*'
If highway robbery is perpetrated, Abt. 19
Of robbing a slave on the highway, Abt. 89
If a man from afar or a stranger quits the road, Wiht. 28; Ine 20
Of coming to the aid of a thief on the highroad, VI As. 1 § 5
Hiwan | See *House*
Hiwisc |
Hlaf 'loaf,' 'bread'; Ine 70 § 1; II As. 23; VI As. 8 § 6
Hloþ, -slihte, -bot
A band of from seven to thirty-five thieves is called a *hloþ*, Ine 13 § 1
He who is accused of belonging to a *hloþ*, Ine 14
If one of a *hloþ* slays a commoner, or a noble, Alf. 26, 27, 28, § 1
Home. See *House*
Homicide. See *Slaying, Wergeld*
Homola, Alf. 35 § 3
Honey, Ine 70 § 1
Hor-cwene. See *Adultery*
Horn
If a stranger quits the road and does not blow his horn, Wiht. 28; Ine 20
An ox's horn is worth 10 pence, a cow's 2 pence, Ine 58, 59
Horse. Mare, Foal
If a horse is lent to an absconding *esne*, Ine 29
The fine for stealing horses, Alf. 9 § 2
If anyone steals a mare or foal, Alf. 16
If a man buys a horse, A. & G. 4
Two well-mounted men shall be provided for every plough, II As. 16
Of sending horses across the sea, II As. 18
Every man who has a horse shall ride after lost cattle, VI As. 5
Of the indemnity to be paid for a horse, VI As. 6
Horseback
If an *esne* makes a journey on horseback on Sunday, Wiht. 10
If a fugitive reaches a church on foot or horseback, Alf. 5
Horseman
The wergeld of a Welsh horseman in the king's service, Ine 33
Hostages '*gislas*'; A. & G. 5
House, Household, Home. See also *Frumstol*
If the king is feeding at anyone's house (*ham*), Abt. 3
Of purchasing a second wife for another man and bringing her to his home (*ham*), Abt. 31
Of returning a betrothed maiden to her home (*ham*), Abt. 77 § 1
If a man entertains a stranger in his own home (*ham*), H. & E. 15
If a man is abused or called a perjurer in another's house (*flett*), H. & E. 11
Of offences committed while drinking in another's house (*flett*), H. & E. 12, 13
If a house (*flett*) is stained with blood, H. & E. 14
Of the *mund* of an emancipated slave's household (*hiwan*), Wiht. 8
If a man gives meat to his household (*hiwan*) during a fast, Wiht. 14

House, *continued*

Of fighting in the house (*hus*) of the king, an *ealdorman*, etc., Ine 6–§ 3 ; Alf. 39, § 1, § 2

Of the value of the oath of a member of the king's household (*cyninges geneat*), Ine 19

If a member of your household (*ðin geneat*) commits a theft, Ine 22

The blanket paid as rent from each household (*hiwisc*), Ine 44 § 1

If a nobleman comes to terms on behalf of his *hiwan*, Ine 50

If a man steals a beast and carries it into his house (*ærn*), Ine 57

Of the house (*heorð*) from which church dues shall be paid, Ine 61

Of compensation to the *hiwan* for violation of the sanctuary of their church, Alf. 2 § 1

Of a fugitive when the *hiwan* need their church, Alf. 5 § 1

Of besieging an adversary in his home (*hamsittend*), Alf. 42–§ 4

Of the *ham* of a priest who slays a man, Alf. 21

Of a man who must work till his lord comes home (*ham*), vi As. 5

Hrægl. See *Clothing*

Hundred '*hynden*'; (100 hides) Ine 54; (100 shillings) Ine 54 § 1; (100 men) vi As. 3; *hyndenman* (an official in charge of 100 men) vi As. 3

Hus. See *House*

Husband '*ceorl*'

Of the compensation to be paid to a husband for lying with his wife, Abt. 31

Of the division of property between husband and wife, Abt. 78–81

If a man lies with a woman during the lifetime of the husband, Abt. 85

If a husband makes offerings to devils, Wiht. 12

If a husband dies leaving a wife and child, Ine 38; H. & E. 6

If a husband steals a beast, Ine 57

Of compensation to the husband for adultery, Alf. 10

Hynden. See *Hundred*

Ierfe 'property,' 'cattle' (*q. v.*); Wiht. 8; Ine 6, 53 § 1; Alf. 1 § 4, 8 § 1, § 2; A. & G. 5; i Edw. 1 § 5; ii As. 9, 10, 24; v As. Pr. § 1, 2; vi As. 1 § 1, 2, 7, 8 § 4, 12 § 3

Incendiaries; ii As. 6 § 2; Append. i

Informer '*melda*'

If a freeman steals a man who returns as informer, H. & E. 5

Of him who informs against a freeman's working on Sunday, Wiht. 11

Of him who traces stolen meat, Ine 17

The axe is an informer and not a thief, Ine 43 § 1

Injuries. Wounds. See also *Head, Arm, Bones,* etc., Abt. 32–72; Alf. 44–77

Of lending weapons during a quarrel, Abt. 18; H. & E. 13

If anyone who has the right of sanctuary is injured, Alf. 2 § 1

If a dog tears or bites a man, Alf. 23

If a beast injures a man, Alf. 24

If a man is transfixed on a spear, Alf. 36 § 1

If one wounds a defenceless man, Alf. 42 § 4

If anyone wounds a collector of church dues, E. & G. 6 § 5

He who tries to avenge a thief but wounds no one, ii As. 6 § 3

If one of the king's lieges is molested, Abt. 2

Of a quarrel when no injury is inflicted, Abt. 18; H. & E. 13

If a house is stained with blood, H. & E. 14

Of a maimed and mutilated criminal, E. & G. 10

Insubordination '*oferhiernes.*' Fines for, i Edw. 1 § 1, 2 § 1; ii Edw. 1 § 3, 2, 7; i As. 5; ii As. 20, § 1, § 2, 22 § 1, 25, § 1; iv As. 7; v As. 1, § 2, § 3; vi As. 7, 8 § 4

Insult

If one man insults another, H. & E. 11

If one man cuts another's hair to insult him, Alf. 35 § 3

Iron. See *Ordeal*

Nied 'need,' 'necessity,' 'compulsion'

If a man forcibly carries off a maiden, Abt. 82

If anyone is wrongfully constrained to promise to betray his lord etc. Alf. 1 § 1, § 4

If anyone rapes a slave (*to nedhæmde*), Alf. 25, § 1

If anyone rapes a girl (*to niedhæmde*), Alf. 29

Of Danes and Englishmen trading to satisfy their wants, A. & G. 5

Niednæme 'seizing with violence,' Ine 10

Night. (Day) '*niht*'

Of payment of the wergeld within 40 days, Abt. 22

Of finding an arbitrator within 3 days, H. & E. 10

Of entertaining a stranger for 3 days, H. & E. 15

A child shall be baptised within 30 days, Ine 2, § 1

An accused man shall render justice within 7 days, Ine 8

Of an ewe's value until 14 days after Easter, Ine 55

Of finding a blemish in a beast within 30 days of purchasing it, Ine 56

If a thief is recaptured before a night has passed, Ine 72

If a night has elapsed since the theft, Ine 73

A perjurer shall remain in prison 40 days, Alf. 1 § 2

Right of sanctuary in a church shall last for 7 days, Alf. 5

Of removing a tree which has killed a man, within 30 days, Alf. 13

If a mutilated criminal lives for 3 days, E. & G. 10

A thief shall remain in prison 40 days, II As. 1 § 3

Sorcerers etc. shall remain in prison 120 days, II As. 6 § 1, § 2

Fortresses shall be repaired by 14 days after Rogation Days, II As. 13

The meeting of the assembly shall be announced 7 days ahead, II As. 20

He who is tried by ordeal shall attend mass for 3 days, II As. 23

Nine; (ninefold) Abt. 1, 4; (ninth Indiction) Wiht. Pr.; (-parts) I As. 3; (-men of the tithing) VI As. 3

Nobleman. '*Eorl*,' '*Eorlcund*,' '*Gesiðcund*,' '*Syxhynde*,' '*Twelfhynde*,' '*Gesið*'

If a man is slain on a nobleman's premises, Abt. 13

If a man lies with a nobleman's serving maid, Abt. 14

The compensation for the violation of the *mund* of an *eorlcundre* widow, Abt. 75

If an *esne* slays a nobleman, whose wergeld is 300 shillings, H. & E. 1

If a nobleman enters into illicit union, Wiht. 5

A nobleman must pay a sum equal to his wergeld for harbouring a fugitive, Ine 30

If a nobleman is slain on a foray, Ine 34 § 1

Fine for breaking into the premises of a nobleman, Ine 45

If a nobleman comes to terms with king on behalf of his dependants, Ine 50

If nobles (*landagende* 7 *unlandagende*) neglect military service, Ine 51

If anyone is accused of homicide and wishes to deny the deed, Ine 54

If a nobleman moves his residence, Ine 63

If a nobleman is evicted, Ine 68

Of the relationship between a nobleman's wergeld and the *manbot*, Ine 70

Of a noble who plots against the life of his lord, Alf. 4 § 2

Of adultery with a nobleman's wife, Alf. 10

Of outrage against a woman of noble birth, Alf. 11 § 5

If a nobleman is slain by a band of marauders, Alf. 27, 28, § 1

Of the compensation for fighting in a nobleman's house, Alf. 39 § 2

The fine for breaking into a nobleman's premises, Alf. 40, § 1

If a nobleman belongs to too powerful a kindred to be punished, III As. 6; IV As. 3; VI As. 8 § 2

Of the respite granted to a thief by a nobleman, IV As. 6 § 2

Nose. Compensation for injuries to, Abt. 45, 48, 57; Alf. 48

Nun

If anyone takes a nun from a nunnery, Alf. 8 f.

If anyone lustfully seizes a nun, Alf. 18

Nunnery. See *Monastery*

Oath '*aþ*,' '*manað*,' '*foreað*,' '*cyreað*,' '*rimað*,' '*cyningæde*,' '*aðwyrðe*'

An accused man shall satisfy his accuser with money or an oath, H. & E. 10

A bishop or the king need not give an oath, Wiht. 16

A clerk's oath must be supported by three men of his own class, Wiht. 19

Of the oath of a stranger and a king's thegn, Wiht. 20

The oaths of a commoner and three of his own class shall be incontrovertible, Wiht. 21

Of the oath of a lord who is, or is not, a communicant, Wiht. 23

An *esne* may be cleared by his lord's oath, Wiht. 24

Of the oath when accused of belonging to a band of marauders, Ine 14

Of the oath when accused of taking part in a raid, Ine 15

Of a communicant's oath, Ine 15 § 1

A thief may not produce an oath when in the king's power, Ine 15 § 2

Of the oath of him who kills a thief, Ine 16

Of him who finds meat which has been stolen and hidden, Ine 17

Of the oath of a *cyninges geneat*, Ine 19

How a dead man may obtain an oath of exculpation, Ine 21, § 1

Of the oath when stolen property is attached in the hands of a trader, Ine 25 § 1

Of an oath to carry on no vendetta against the captor of a thief, Ine 28

Of the captor's oath when a thief escapes, Ine 28 § 1

Of an oath when a man is accused of harbouring a fugitive, Ine 30

Of an oath that a slain man was a thief trying to escape, Ine 35

The compensation for swearing a false oath (*mænan að*), Ine 35 § 1

Of the oath when one is accused of *burgbryce*, Ine 45

Of an oath when a man is charged with stealing cattle, Ine 46

Of an oath, when the accuser is an Englishman or Welshman, Ine 46 § 1

Of an oath to enforce scourging, Ine 48, 54 § 2

Of the oath when swine are found intruding in a mast-pasture, Ine 49 f.

Of an oath when accused of making an illicit compact, Ine 52

Of an oath when a stolen slave etc. is attached, Ine 53

Of an oath (*cyningæde*) when anyone is charged with homicide, Ine 54

A wife may declare, with an oath, that she has not tasted stolen meat, Ine 57

If a man, required to give an oath, confesses his guilt, Ine 71

Every man shall abide by his oath and pledge, Alf. 1, § 1, § 2

Of the oath when a man is charged with plotting against the king, Alf. 4 § 1

Of an oath, when a noble or commoner plots against his lord, Alf. 4 § 2

Of an oath when a woman is accused of fornication, Alf. 11 § 4

Of the oath of accusation (*foreað*) to be made in four churches, Alf. 33

Of the oaths given by councillors, A. & G. Pr., 5

Of the oaths of king's thanes, A. & G. 3

Rendering of oaths is forbidden during festivals and fasts, E. & G. 9

Of production of an oath instead of witnesses, I Edw. 1 § 2, § 3

Of an unselected oath (*ungecoren að*), I Edw. 1 § 3

Of a selected oath, I Edw. 1 § 4

Of an oath when an evil man brings a counter-charge, I Edw. 1 § 5

If an oath collapses in a charge of perjury, I Edw. 3

Of loss of right to produce an oath (*aðwyrðe*), I Edw. 3; II As. 26; Ine 46

If anyone breaks his oath and pledge, II Edw. 5, § 1, § 2

Of the oath when one is accused of sparing a thief, II As. 1 § 1

Of the oath when one is accused of harbouring an outlaw, II As. 2 § 2

Of recourse to the selected oath (*cyreað*) when livestock is attached, II As. 9

Of the *rimað*, II As. 9

Of the oath when demanding redress for a slain thief, II As. 11

Of the oath when accused of harbouring a fugitive, II As. 20 § 8

Before going to the ordeal, a man shall swear an oath of innocence, II As. 23

Of him who swears a false oath, II As. 26

Of the oaths and pledges given to the king and his councillors, IV As. 3 § 2

Of the punishment for violating oaths, V As. Pr. § 3

Of the 'unselected' oath (*aþ butan cyre*), V As. 1 § 5

Oath, *continued*

The trail of cattle shall serve as the oath of accusation (*forađ*), v As. 2

Of an oath with regard to stolen cattle, vi As. 8 § 8

Of the threefold oath, Append. i

Every man shall precede his accusation with an oath, ii As. 23 § 2

For the valuation of the oath in hides, see *Hide*

Oferhiernes. See *Insubordination*

Offence. See *Scyld, Lyswæs, Unoffending, Dæd, Yfel*

Ordeal '*ordal*,' '*ceac*'

If a thief is proved guilty in the ordeal (*ceac*), Ine 37; iv As. 6; vi As. 1 § 4

If anyone is accused and the ordeal is being forced upon him, Ine 62

Trials by ordeal are forbidden during festivals and fasts, E. & G. 9

Perjurers shall always be tried by ordeal, i Edw. 3

Threefold ordeal shall be forced upon those who plot against their lords, or break into churches, or practise witchcraft, etc., ii As. 4, 5, 6, § 1, § 2; Append. i

Of those proved guilty in the simple ordeal, ii As. 7

Those charged with coining base money shall go to the ordeal, ii As. 14 § 1

Of a slave found guilty in the ordeal, ii As. 19

Of one who compounds for an ordeal, ii As. 21

Of the conduct of the ordeal, ii As. 23, § 1; Append. i, ii

Ores, E. & G. 3 § 2, 7

Orgilde 'unpaid for' (by a wergeld, *q.v.*); Alf. 1 § 5; E. & G. 6 § 7

Orwige 'not liable to vendetta' (*q.v.*); Alf. 42 § 5, § 7

Outlaw '*wreccena*,' '*utlah*,' '*flyma*.' See also *Fugitive*

Of him who harbours outlaws, Alf. 4; ii As. 2 § 1, § 2

He who slays a collector of church dues shall be an outlaw, E. & G. 6 § 6

Own, Owner. See *Agan, Agend*

Ox. See *Cattle*

Pannage; Ine 49 § 3

Peace. See *Frið*

Penal Slave. See *Slave*

Penny. *Gafolhwitel* shall be worth 6 pence, Ine 44 § 1; an ox horn, 10 pence, Ine 58; a cow's horn 2 pence, an ox's tail 4 pence, a cow's 5 pence, an ox's eye 5 pence, a cow's 4 pence, Ine 59; a fleece 2 pence, Ine 69; a tree 5 pence, Alf. 12; Alf. 3, 47, 71; a shank of bacon or a ram worth 4 pence, As. Ord. 1; theft of over 8 pence, ii As. 1 § 1, 12 pence, vi As. 1 § 1, 12 § 3; attaching stock worth over 20 pence, ii As. 9; buying goods worth more than 20 pence outside a town, ii As. 12; 4 pence, the annual contribution to the guild, vi As. 2; 30 pence the fine exacted by the guild, vi As. 3, 8 § 5; a cow is worth 20 pence, a swine 10 pence, vi As. 6 § 2; of *ceap-gild* over 30 pence, vi As. 6 § 4; 12 pence for killing a thief, vi As. 7

Perjurer, Perjury '*manswara*'; vb. '*forswerian*,' '*manaþ swerian*.' See also *Oath, Witness*

If one man calls another a perjurer in another man's house, H. & E. 11

If a man in orders commits perjury, E. & G. 3

Perjurers shall be driven from the land, E. & G. 11

Of those proved guilty of perjury, i Edw. 3

Of the punishment for perjury, ii As. 26

Permission '*leaf*,' '*leafnes*,' '*unaliefed*'

Of a tonsured man wandering about without permission, Wiht. 7

If anyone moves away without permission from his lord, Ine 39

It is permissible to repudiate bail, Ine 41

If *unaliefed* swine are found in a mast-pasture, Ine 49

If permission is given to a thief to redeem his hand, Alf. 6 § 1

If one takes a nun from a nunnery without permission, Alf. 8 f.

If trees are burnt or felled without permission, Alf. 12

Of lustfully seizing a nun without her permission, Alf. 18

If property is entrusted to a monk without permission from his lord, Alf. 20

A.   16

Property, *continued*

If stolen property (*feoh*) is reclaimed by the owner, H. & E. 7

Of a man of Kent (*feoh*) who buys property in London, H. & E. 16 f.

He who fights in the king's house shall forfeit all his property (*ierfe*), Ine 6

Of him who finds meat which has been stolen and hidden, Ine 17

Of claiming the value (*angylde*) of stolen property from a surety, Ine 22

If stolen property (*ðiefefioh*) is attached in a trader's hands, Ine 25 § 1

Of vouching a dead man's grave to warranty for stolen property (*fioh*), Ine 53, § 1

Of a wife's share of the household property (*sceat*), Ine 57

Of him who must forfeit his weapons and property (*ierfe*), Alf. 1 § 4

A nun shall not inherit the property (*ierfe*) of him who abducts her, Alf. 8 f.

If property (*feoh*) is entrusted to a monk in another's service, Alf. 20

Of a priest's share of the monastic property, Alf. 21

Of him who must pay three times the value of stolen property (*ðrygylde*), A. & G. 3

The number of witnesses shall vary according to the value of the disputed property (*ceap*), I Edw. 1 § 4

Of taking security from a man's property, II Edw. 3 § 1

Of him who has no property (*æht*) or other security, II Edw. 3 § 2

Of tithes of the king's property (*god*), I As. Pr.

Of him who is liable to confiscation of all his property, IV As. 3 § 1

Powerful wrongdoers shall be banished with their property (*ærfe*) etc., v As. Pr. § 1

Of compensation for stolen property (*yrfe*) paid by the association, VI As. 2

Every one shall pay a shilling who owns property (*yrfe*) worth 30 pence, VI As. 2

Of payments from the common property (*feoh*) of the association, VI As. 7

Of making everybody's property (*þing*) secure against theft, VI As. 8 § 9

No one shall be slain for thieving property (*yrfe*) worth less than 12 pence, VI As. 12 § 3

Prostitutes. See *Adultery*

Protection. See *Borg*

Raid. See *Here*

Ram. A poor Englishman shall be given a ram worth fourpence, As. Ord. 1

Rape. See *Adultery*

Reeve '*gerefa*'

The reeve shall be a witness to the buying of property, H. & E. 16 f.; I Edw. 1; II As. 10, 12

The reeve shall exculpate an *esne* of a bishop or the king, Wiht. 22

A nobleman who moves his residence may take his reeve, Ine 63

Of coming to terms with the reeve, when a thief is allowed to escape, Ine 73

The king's reeve shall provide a kinless prisoner with food, Alf. 1 § 3

If anyone makes an accusation before the king's reeve, Alf. 22

Traders shall bring their men before the king's reeve, Alf. 34

Reeves shall fix a day for deciding each suit, I Edw. Pr.

Suits concerning 'folkland' and 'bookland' shall be decided before the reeve, I Edw. 2

Of reeves who do not exact legal fines, II Edw. 2

Every reeve shall hold a meeting every four weeks, II Edw. 8

Of the reeves' duty to distribute charities, As. Ord. 1, 2

Of the reeves' duty to pay tithes etc., I As. Pr. 1, 4, 5

Of reeves who have been accessories of thieves, II As. 3 § 2

Of reeves to act as witnesses when cattle etc. are exchanged, II As. 10, 12

Of reeves who are unwilling to carry out the king's commands, II As. 25; III As. 7 § 3; IV As. 7; v As. 1 § 2

Fines shall be exacted from reeves by the bishop, II As. 25 § 1

Of the appointment of reeves to take charge of estates, III As. 7 f.

Of a reeve who takes bribes, v As. 1 § 3

Slave, *continued*
> Of payment for a female slave stoned to death for thieving, IV As. 6 § 7
> Of the slaves owned by members of the association, VI As. 6 § 3

Slaying. See also *Death Penalty, Wergeld*
> If one man slays another on the king's premises, Abt. 5
> If a man slays a freeman, Abt. 6.
> If a man slays a king's smith or messenger, Abt. 7
> If a king's *fedesl* is slain, Abt. 12
> If one man slays another on a nobleman's premises, Abt. 13
> If a man is slain with borrowed weapons, Abt. 20
> Of the ordinary wergeld when one man slays another, Abt. 21
> 20 shillings must be paid before the grave is closed, Abt. 22
> If a man slays the dependant of a commoner, Abt. 25, 26
> If an *esne* slays an *esne*, Abt. 86
> If an *esne* slays a noble or commoner, H. & E. 1, 2, 3, 4
> If a homicide escapes, Abt. 23; H. & E. 2, 4
> If a man is slain in the act of thieving, Wiht. 25
> A stranger, leaving the road and not blowing a horn, may be slain, Wiht. 28; Ine 20
> A man may be slain for fighting in the king's house, Ine 6
> A thief shall be slain, Ine 12
> Of him who kills a thief, Ine 16, 35
> If a slain man's wergeld is claimed, Ine 20, 21
> If anyone slays a foreigner, Ine 23, § 1, § 2
> If a penal slave (an Englishman) is slain, Ine 24, § 1
> He who has been on a foray in which a man was slain, Ine 34
> If anyone is accused of homicide and wishes to deny it, Ine 54
> If a Welsh slave slays an Englishman, Ine 74
> If a godson or godfather is slain, Ine 76 f.
> If one resisting capture is slain, Alf. 1 § 5
> If a fugitive is slain during the time of asylum, Alf. 2 § 1
> If the child of a nun is slain, Alf. 8 § 3
> If anyone slays a woman with child, Alf. 9
> If one man kills another unintentionally, Alf. I3
> If a guardian is accused of causing the death of a ward, Alf. 17
> If murder is committed with borrowed weapons, Alf. 19, § 1, § 2
> If a priest slays a man, Alf. 21
> If a band of marauders slays a commoner or nobleman, Alf. 26, 27, 28
> If a man without paternal or (and) maternal relatives slays a man, Alf. 30, § 1
> If an Englishman or a Dane is slain, A. & G. 2
> Of slaying one collecting church dues, E. & G. 6 § 6
> Of one who brings about his own death, E. & G. 6 § 7
> If an attempt is made to deprive of life a man in orders, or a stranger, E. & G. 12
> If one abandoned by kinsmen is slain, II Edw. 6
> Of a thief over twelve years old, II As. 1; VI As. 1 § 1
> An outlaw may be slain, II As. 2, § 1
> No thief whatsoever shall be spared, IV As. 6, § 1, § 2
> A fugitive thief shall be slain, IV As. 6 § 3
> How a free woman who is a thief shall be slain, IV As. 6 § 4
> A male slave, guilty of theft, shall be stoned, IV As. 6 § 5
> A female slave, guilty of theft, shall be burned, IV As. 6 § 7
> Those who aid and defend thieves shall be slain, VI As. 1 § 2, § 3, § 4, § 5
> No one under fifteen years old should be slain, VI As. 12 § 1, § 2
> No one shall be slain for stealing less than twelve pence, VI As. 12 § 3

Smith
> If a smith in the king's service is slain, Abt. 7
> A nobleman may take his smith with him when he moves, Ine 63
> If a smith receives a tool to refurbish it, Alf. 19 § 3

Theft, *continued*
If an Englishman or a Welshman brings the accusation, Ine 46 § 1
A man may clear himself of harbouring stolen goods, Ine 46 § 2
If a penal slave is accused of thieving, Ine 48
If a stolen slave etc. is attached, Ine 53
If a husband steals a beast, Ine 57
He who steals on Sunday, at Christmas, etc., Alf. 5 § 5
He who steals anything from a church, Alf. 6
The fines for stealing gold, horses, bees, etc., Alf. 9 § 1, § 2, § 3
If anyone steals a cow, mare, foal, Alf. 16
Of theft by a man of a lower order than king's thegn, A. & G. 3
If a man in orders steals, E. & G. 3
Of those who have found a lord for one accused of theft, II Edw. 3
Of theft of over eight pence, by a twelve-year-old thief, II As. 1
If anyone spares such a thief, II As. 1 § 1, § 2
If a thief is put in prison he shall stay there forty days, II As. 1 § 3, § 4
If anyone defends a thief or renders him assistance, II As. 1 § 5
Of a lord etc. who is accessory to theft by one of his slaves, II As. 3 § 1, § 2
Of those who avenge a thief, II As. 6 § 2, § 3
Of trial by ordeal for those accused of theft, II As. 7
Of him who demands redress for a slain thief, II As. 11
Of him who takes bribes from a thief, II As. 17
Of the punishment for theft, II As. 20 § 3
Of those of such powerful kindred that they cannot be restrained, III As. 6; IV As. 3
A thief, man or woman, noble or commoner, whether taken in the act or not, shall have no right of appeal if proved guilty, IV As. 6
Of a thief who seeks the king, archbishop, or a church, etc., IV As. 6 § 1, § 2
If a thief escapes he shall be pursued to his death, IV As. 6 § 3
Of the payment of compensation for theft, without the fine, V As. 3 § 1
Of the punishment of thieves over twelve years old, VI As. 1 § 1; cf. VI As. 12 f.
Of the disposal of a thief's property if he is put to death, VI As. 1 § 1
Of harbouring and defending thieves, VI As. 1 § 2, § 3, § 4
Of a thief proved guilty in the ordeal, VI As. 1 § 4
Of him who wishes to avenge a thief, VI As. 1 § 5
Of the reward for killing a thief, VI As. 7
Of thieves who cannot be proved guilty on the spot, VI As. 9
Thegn
How a king's thegn shall clear himself, Wiht. 20; A. & G. 3
Of the *burgbryce* of a king's thegn, Ine 45
If anyone accuses a king's thegn of homicide, A. & G. 3
Of the oath of a king's thegn, A. & G. 3
Of the thegns of Kent, III As. Pr.
Of the respite granted to a fugitive by a thegn, IV As. 6 § 2
Of a thegn who does not obey the king's ordinances, IV As. 7
Of a thegn who takes bribes etc., V As. 1 § 4
Of thegns in possession of land who permit secret compacts etc., VI As. 11
Throat. Compensation for injury to, Alf. 51; Abt. 49(?)
Thumb
Compensation for injuries to, Abt. 54, § 1; Alf. 56, § 1
Of pannage when the bacon is a thumb thick, Ine 49 § 3
Tithe 'teoðung'
Of withholding tithes in a Danish and an English district, E. & G. 6
Æthelstan's ordinance relating to tithes, I As.; III As. 1 § 1
Tithing 'teoðung'
Of dividing the people into groups of ten, VI As. 3
Of the levy on the tithings to trace lost cattle, VI As. 4
The officials of the tithings shall meet once a month, VI As. 8 § 1
Toe. Compensation for injuries to, Abt. 70-72; Alf. 64-§ 4

252 INDEX

Tongue
Of the punishment for uttering a public slander, Alf. 32
The tongue and eye shall be valued at the same price, Alf. 52, 47

Tracing Trail. See also *Cattle*
He who traces meat which has been stolen and hidden, Ine 17
Of the men appointed to guide others in tracing cattle, II Edw. 4
The trail of lost cattle may serve for a *fore-að*, v As. 2
Of provisions for tracing lost cattle, VI As. 4, 8 § 4
Of defraying the cost of tracing cattle, VI As. 7

Trading. Traders
If a trader from over the border is entertained for three days, H. & E. 15
Of a trader who makes his way inland, Ine 25
If stolen property in the hands of a trader is attached, Ine 25 § 1
Of the men traders take with them on their journeys, Alf. 34
Of the days on which slaves may sell, Alf. 43
Of trading between Danes and English, A. & G. 5
Of trading on Sunday, E. & G. 7; II As. 24 § 1; IV As. 2; VI As. 10
No one shall trade except in a market town, I Edw. 1
The fine for trading outside a market town, I Edw. 1 § 1
No one shall exchange cattle unless he has a trustworthy witness, II As. 10
No one shall buy goods worth more than 20 pence outside a town, II As. 12
All trading shall be carried on in a town, II As 13 § 1
No man shall send a horse across the sea, II As. 18
Of permission to trade outside a town, IV As. 2

Treasurer *'hordere'*
Of royal treasurers who have been accessories of thieves, II As. 3 § 2
The treasurer etc. shall witness the exchange of cattle, II As. 10

Tree
If a stranger travels through a wood off the highway, Ine 20; cf. Wiht. 28
Of destroying trees by fire, Ine 43; Alf. 12
Of felling trees with an axe, Ine 43 § 1; Alf. 12
Of cutting down a tree that can shelter thirty swine, Ine 44
If a man is killed while felling trees in company, Alf. 13

Tun
If a man is slain in the king's *tun*, Abt. 5
If a man is slain in a nobleman's *tun*, Abt. 13
Of making forcible entry into another's *tun*, Abt. 17
Of the witnesses when anyone is charged with stealing a man, H. & E. 5
A perjurer shall be put in prison at a king's *tun*, Alf. 1 § 2
If commoners have to fence a *gærs-tun*, Ine 42
Of fines to be divided among the poor of a *tun*, As. Or. 2
A swearer of a false oath shall not be buried in a consecrated *lictun*, II As. 26

Twelfhynde 'one whose wergeld is 1200 shillings.' See also *Nobleman*. Ine 19, 70; Alf. 10, 18 § 3, 28, § 1, 39 § 2, 40; VI As. 8 § 2

Twelve. Twelvefold compensation, Abt. 1; Ine 4; of one left unransomed for twelve months, Ine 24 § 1; twelve shillings will buy off a scourging, Ine 23 § 3; of an oath in twelve churches, Alf. 33; twelve ores, E. & G. 3 § 2, 7; of the twelve men in each party at an ordeal, II As. 23 § 2; theft of goods worth twelve pence by thieves twelve years old, VI As. 1 § 1, 12 § 1, § 3

Twyhynde 'one whose wergeld is 200 shillings.' See also *Commoner*. Ine 33, 34 § 1, 70; Alf. 26; A. & G. 2; VI As. 8 § 2

Unaliefed 'without permission.' See *Permission*
Unceas 'inhostility,' Ine 35. See *Vendetta*
Underfon 'to take into service,' 'receive,' Alf. Introd. 19 § 3, 37 § 2; II Edw. 7; II As. 22; V As. 1
Ungewintred (wifmon), Alf. 29. See *Maiden*
Unlandagende, Ine 51. See *Land*
Unmaga 'helpless person,' Alf. 17. See *Child*

Unoffending '*unsynnig*'
  If one servant slays another who has committed no offence, Abt. 86
  If a band of marauders slays an unoffending man, Alf. 26–28 § 1
  Of offences against an unoffending commoner, Alf. 35–§ 6
Unriht 'unlawful,' Alf. 1 § 1. See *Riht*
Unrihthæmed, Wiht. 3. See *Adultery*
Unscyldig, Ine 2 § 1 (H); II As. 23. See *Scyldig*

Vendetta
  Vendetta against him who captures a thief is forbidden, Ine 28
  Vendetta against him who kills a thief is forbidden, Ine 35
  Of vendetta against a Welsh slave who kills an Englishman, Ine 74 § 1
  Of ransoming a slave from vendetta, Ine 74 § 2
  Of a man without relatives who commits homicide, Alf. 30 § 1
  When a man may fight without being liable to vendetta, Alf. 42 § 5–§ 7
  Of instituting an unjustifiable vendetta, II As. 20 § 7
Vengeance '*wracu*,' '*wrecan*'
  If anyone exacts redress before pleading for justice, Ine 9
  Of attempting the life of strangers and ecclesiastics, E. & G. 12
  Of those who avenge, or seek to avenge a thief, II As. 6 § 2, § 3
  If anyone tries to avenge one who has been put to death, II As. 20 § 7
  Of a thief who shall be slain *on þa þeofwrace*, VI As. 1 § 4
  Of him who wishes to avenge a thief, VI As. 1 § 5
  Of rewarding him who avenges a wrong done to us all, VI As. 7
  Of avenging wrongs done by powerful groups of kinsmen, VI As. 8 § 3
Vouching to Warranty '*team*'; vb. '(*ge*)*tieman*'
  Of vouching stolen goods to warranty at the king's residence, H. & E. 7, 16, § 1, § 2, § 3
  If a man is vouched to warranty who has previously disowned the transaction, Ine 35 § 1
  A slave may not be vouched to warranty, Ine 47; cf. II As. 24
  Of vouching to warranty a dead man's grave, Ine 53, § 1
  If a stolen chattel is attached and is vouched to warranty, Ine 75
  Every man shall have knowledge of his warrantor, A. & G. 4
  Every man shall have a warrantor to his transactions, I Edw. 1
  How far the production of warrantors shall be continued, I Edw. 1 § 1
  Of the procedure in vouching to warranty, I Edw. 1 § 2–§ 4
  Of vouching to warranty when an evil man brings a counter-charge, I Edw. 1 § 5
  If a man buys cattle and afterwards has to vouch it to warranty, II As. 24

Walls. Of sanctuary within the walls of a church, E. & G. 1
Warranty. Warrantor. See *Vouching*
Water. Of the ordeal by water, II As. 23, § 1, 2; Append. II
Weapons '*wæpen*,' '*spere*,' '*sweord*,' '*scyld*'
  Of lending weapons, Abt. 18, 19, 20
  If a man draws his weapon where men are drinking, H. & E. 13, 14
  If anyone lends a sword or spear to an *esne*, Ine 29
  Of a man who shall surrender his weapons, Alf. 1 § 2
  Of a man who shall forfeit his weapons, Alf. 1 § 4
  If a fugitive surrenders his weapons, Alf. 5 § 3
  If anyone draws his weapons in the king's hall, Alf. 7
  If anyone draws his weapon before an archbishop, *ealdorman*, etc., Alf. 15, 38, § 1, § 2, 39, § 1, § 2
  If anyone lends a weapon to another to commit murder, Alf. 19, § 1, 2
  If a sword-furbisher receives a weapon, Alf. 19 § 3
  If a man is transfixed by a spear, Alf. 36, § 1, § 2
  If an adversary surrenders his weapons, Alf. 42 § 1, § 4
  No shieldmaker shall cover a shield with sheepskin, II As. 15; III As. 8
Wedd. See *Security, Pledge*

Wergeld, *continued*
Of the payment of wergeld for fighting one collecting divine dues, E. & G. 6 § 5
When no wergeld shall be paid, E. & G. 6 § 7
Of kinsmen who have no right to the wergeld, II Edw. 6
If anyone spares a thief etc. he shall pay to the amount of his wergeld, II As.
1 § 1, § 4, § 5
A lord shall forfeit his wergeld if an accessory to theft by his slave, II As. 3
§ 1
Of the wergeld when death is due to witchcraft etc., II As. 6 § 1
Of forfeiting the wergeld for taking bribes from a thief, II As. 17
Of forfeiting the wergeld for harbouring a fugitive, II As. 20 § 8
Of paying the wergeld for a second violation of the ordinances, II As. 25 § 2
Of ransoming a thief proved guilty in the ordeal, VI As. 1 § 4
Of a thief who must remain in bondage until his wergeld is paid, VI As. 12 § 2
Widow
The compensation to be paid for violation of her *mund*, Abt. 75
If a man takes a widow who does not belong to him, Abt. 76
She shall have half the goods when her husband dies, Abt. 78
If a man dies leaving a wife and child, H. & E. 6; Ine 38
Everyone shall pay a shilling to the guild except poor widows, VI As. 2
Wife. See also *Husband, Child, Adultery*
Of providing a second wife for another man, Abt. 31
If a man dies leaving a wife and child, H. & E. 6
If a husband makes offerings to devils without his wife's knowledge, Wiht. 12
If anyone steals with, and without, the cognisance of his wife, Ine 7, § 1, 57
If anyone buys a wife and the marriage does not take place, Ine 31
If a husband has a child by his wife and dies, Ine 38
Of lying with the wife of a *twelfhynde* or *syxhynde man,* or of a commoner,
Alf. 10
If anyone finds a man lying with his wife, Alf. 42 § 7
Of the wives and children of powerful wrongdoers, IV As. 3; V As. Pr. § 1
Of the wife's share of the property when her husband is put to death, VI
As. 1 § 1
Winter; H. & E. 6; Wiht. Pr.; Ine 38, 40, 61; Alf. 29; II As. 1; VI As. 1 § 1,
12 § 1
Witches. Wizards; E. & G. 11; II As. 6
Witeþeow 'penal slave'; Ine 24, 48, 54 § 2; As. Ord. 1. See *Slave*
Wiðertihtle 'counter-charge'; I Edw. 1 § 5
Witness 'æwda,' '*gewitnes*'
(i) Of the witnesses when a homicide escapes, H. & E. 2, 4
Of the witnesses when one is charged with stealing a man, H. & E. 5
Of the witnesses when property is bought in London, H. & E. 16 f.
Of witnesses when oaths are sworn, Wiht. 19, 21, 23
If anyone bears false witness in the presence of a bishop, Ine 13
Of traders and their witnesses, Ine 25, § 1; I Edw. 1
Of the king and bishop as witnesses in land suits, Alf. 41
He who vouches another to warranty shall have witnesses, I Edw. 1 § 1, § 2
He who wishes to substantiate a plea of ownership shall have witnesses,
I Edw. 1 § 3
Of nominated witnesses, I Edw. 1 § 4; II Edw. 2; V As. 1 § 5
Of selection from nominated witnesses, II As. 9
The reeve, or mass-priest etc. shall be a witness to the exchange of cattle,
II As. 10
Of bearing false witness, II As. 10 § 1
Of buying in a town before the town-reeve etc., II As. 12; VI As. 10
Of the witnesses at a trial by ordeal, II As. 23, § 2
Of vouching to warranty cattle bought before a witness, II As. 24
Of him who claims an indemnity for a horse, VI As. 6 § 1
A man should call his neighbours to witness when he has lost his cattle,
VI As. 8 § 7

PRINTED IN ENGLAND BY J. B. PEACE, M.A.
AT THE CAMBRIDGE UNIVERSITY PRESS